URBAN MAPS

Urban Maps
Instruments of Narrative and Interpretation in the City

RICHARD BROOK AND NICK DUNN

Manchester School of Architecture, UK

ASHGATE

Published by
Ashgate Publishing Limited
Wey Court East
Union Road
Farnham
Surrey GU9 7PT
England

Ashgate Publishing Company
Suite 420
101 Cherry Street
Burlington,
VT 05401-4405
USA

www.ashgate.com

British Library Cataloguing in Publication Data
Brook, Richard.
Urban maps : instruments of narrative and interpretation in the city.
1. Cities and towns--Interpretive programs. 2. City planning.
I. Title II. Dunn, Nick, 1974-
307.7'6-dc22

Library of Congress Cataloging-in-Publication Data
Brook, Richard.
Urban maps : instruments of narrative and interpretation in the city / Richard Brook and Nick Dunn.
p. cm.
Includes bibliographical references and index.
ISBN 978-0-7546-7657-7 (hardback) 1. Cities and towns--Maps. 2. Urbanization--Maps. 3. Urban geography. I. Dunn, Nick. II. Title.

G140.B76 2011
526.09173'2--dc22

2010053201

ISBN 9780754676577 (hbk)

MIX
Paper from responsible sources
FSC
www.fsc.org   FSC® C018575

Printed and bound in Great Britain by the MPG Books Group, UK

Contents

List of Figures

About the Authors

Richard Brook is a Senior Lecturer in Architecture and a qualified Architect. He is head of the 3rd year undergraduate course at the Manchester School of Architecture and co-director of [Re_Map], an MArch level 'research by design/design by research' unit. He has had a long association with electronic arts, through rave culture, electronic music and post-graffiti generative environments. His assertion that architecture is made of more than built objects directs most of his enquiry into the contemporary city.

Nick Dunn is a Principal Lecturer and Director of Studies for the MArch Master of Architecture programme at the Manchester School of Architecture. He is co-director of the [Re_Map] unit, whose research is concerned with the mapping and representation of urban networks, data and conditions. His PhD thesis, *The Ecology of the Architectural Model* proposed a new methodology to study and map the design behaviour of architecture students and further understand the complex process of design. It was awarded in 2005 and has since been published as a book (Peter Lang, 2007). His primary research interests are in the fields of visualization, modelling, mapping, representation in architecture, infrastructure, post-industrial landscapes and urbanism. His position on the contemporary city, as a series of systems, flows and processes, is explored through experimentation and discourse addressing the nature of urban space: its perception, demarcation and appropriation.

Preface

We use the term 'map' loosely to describe any form of representation that reveals unseen space, latent conditions or narratives in and of the city. Maps, by their characteristics, show us interpretations of context and can be singularly focused to expose particular essences of space and place, whether experientially or thematically driven. As both the physical and social make-up of our cities is increasingly complex, the tools with which we view the urban environment too become diverse in media and application. Maps can be made inside films and within networks; objects and marks yield their own discourse and narratives about space and brand has consumed, demarcated and achieved cognitive presence in our vision of the city. All of these entities will be discussed in respect of their meaning and interpretation in the context of urban critique, using case studies to explore particular practice or themes of each. Certain practitioners or practices cross the classifications formed here and the interrelationship of the chapters is inevitable, the collective texts describe a breadth of works, conditions and objects that have been explored in the studio teaching of architecture and urban design in our work at the Manchester School of Architecture.

The association between the arts and architecture is rarely called into question, the proximities are considered explicit and there persists an assumption that these relationships are easily read and ideologies transposed between disciplines.[1] As the study of architecture moves steadily towards concerns of urban space and the life between buildings, there can be value ascribed to the repositioning of a critique of the practice of the arts associated with the urban environment. Discourse around 'the urban' has superseded 'the city' as the generic 'environment' that crosses academic disciplines and the sheer proportion of the global population that live in urban conditions has made this territory essential to a contemporary critique of intervention.

Intervention is a far-reaching term that has been used to describe any number of acts, marks, forms, dispositions, transformations and records that are constructed of more than their formal content to expose, examine and question the nature of space and environment. It is unsurprising that the act of intervention whether exploratory, on paper, or realized has become part of the mode of inquiry within contemporary architecture. The evolution of practice concerned with the latent condition of the urban environment took place as critique of the city found a place in academia through the emergence of map-based models used in sociological analyses of city form, dispersal and zoning. The application of abstract ideas and geometries concerned with the manufacture of space grew from the post-modern tradition in architecture and gained notoriety in the critical cul-de-sac of the Deconstructivist movement. The leap made by Hadid and Koolhaas to depart this imposed stylistic affliction[2] did not leave behind the techniques of map-based intervention as design code and generator, and these practices become paramount as we are forced to engage with a fast burgeoning datascape that is somehow connected to our physical landscape.

Endnotes

1   For a good account of these relationships see Rendell, J. (2006), *Art & Architecture: A Place Between* (London: I.B. Tauris).
2   Papadakis, A.C. [ed.] (1988), *Deconstruction in Architecture* (London: Architectural Design Profile, Wiley Academy). Hadid and Koolhaas were both included in the AD publication that questionably pre-empted and imposed subjective definitions and associations upon the Deconstructivist movement in 1988.

Acknowledgements

This book would not have been written without the fertile studio landscape at the Manchester School of Architecture and the gritty city in which to explore and expand thoughts, conceptions and inventions. We are therefore indebted to colleagues and students alike who have encouraged, activated, participated and critiqued our sideways vision to examine architecture without necessarily looking at buildings. Our work took us away from Manchester and for that we should thank John Hyatt from the Manchester Institute for Research and Innovation in Art and Design (MIRIAD) for supporting our research both enthusiastically and financially.

Whilst in New York Momo gifted Richard the birthday treat of a tour of 'art you might never see', on bicycles with limited capacity for braking, and introduced us to the best Japanese café in Williamsburg where we were entertained with stories of his exploits in pursuit of making marks on the city. Back on Manhattan and Christina Ray of Glowlab was gracious in her accommodation of two post-birthday punks who probably weren't at their most articulate or effervescent. Joseph Heathcott of the New School sorted us out with high-grade caffeine and cake, affording an extended chat about urbanity, its ills and the opportunities of chance. We'd like to thank Steve Powers (ESPO) for his evasive tactics and ultimately coming through with some solid answers to our abstract inquiries and positivity concerning our approach. Madrid was another level of hospitality and thanks in no small amount to Rafael Schacter, Eltono and *Equipo Plastico* for showing 'Dos Mancunios' nothing short of the funniest evening with the coolest bunch of international hipsters we've ever had. The *tortilla español* was to die for, not to mention the 3.00am call of, "follow me, I've got me plus 15 on the guest list" and "we never pay to get in anywhere"! Thanks also to Eltono for the cover image; it's a pleasure and a privilege. We should have met Javier Abarca in Madrid and we wish we had. His contribution, as the world's leading academic expert on graffiti and street art, has been hugely encouraging and invaluable. Massive respect to Space Invader and Truth who were swift and positive in their responses to questions that they didn't need to answer. We thank Doug Aitken, Jan De Cock, Lisa Jevbratt and Stanza for being so engaging and encouraging in the contribution and discussion of their work for this book. Similarly, Gwen Chanzit, Daniel Hopkinson and Onek NM TDT went beyond the call of duty to provide specific images or information on how to find them.

Our colleagues Rick Dargavel, Isabelle Doucet and Ray Lucas from the Manchester School of Architecture and Steven Gartside from Manchester Metropolitan University for their valuable feedback on our writing along the way. Craig Martin for admirably sharing the pressure cooker of our working office with melancholic grace and refreshing tired minds with his second-wind anecdotes.

Bhatti and Engy for their constant berating and challenging of suppositions and conceptions. Ben Stringer and Lorraine Farrelly for giving us considerable encouragement in this venture. The students in our [Re_Map] unit for absorbing our tangential outbursts and relentless sarcasm in the humour it was intended, in particular Peter Millar for the production of several diagrams.

Valerie Rose made a leap of faith in the original commission and subsequently Carolyn Court, Aimée Feenan and Sarah Horsley from Ashgate ably advised and assisted in the production. We are indebted to Jane Rendell and Pedro Gadanho for their very kind words and feedback on the finished result. On a more general note, we wish to extend our gratitude to the many creative people and organizations who enabled us to illustrate this book so thoroughly with their projects and images and who were always helpful and typically generous in our dialogue with them. Finally, and perhaps most critically, Jen and Nina, along with both our families, for their patience and support throughout the entire process and allowing two incorrigible, overly enthusiastic academics to wind each other up.

Introduction

The City

Prior to any discussion concerning the relevance of mapping and the divergent creative practices featured in this book, it is useful to establish the context within which we are now operating. In order to provide the reader with a clear definition and understanding of this context it is necessary to define, a critical position that accounts for a particular view of the contemporary urban environment, its global development and emergent characteristics. This definition has a dual function; firstly it is presented to guide readers through the rest of the book and secondly it is intended to provoke thought about the current urban condition and the role of architecture in an order that has witnessed the recession of tradition and convention. The latter point is particularly pertinent for designers who face the twenty-first century city as a mediated landscape of networks, nodes and fluctuating systems of density, programme, and urban space.

Specifically here, we are concerned with the forces or conditions of urbanism that are intrinsic to the supermodern conurbation. We view the city as a process driven landscape[1] that reveals more about itself by that which is 'un-designed' as opposed to that which is designed. The capitalist driven contrast between a polarized peripheral urban condition and a formally indistinct core is intriguing for its ability to subsume planning ideals. The slow but steady destruction of context as a materially and formally constrained condition can be accounted for with two distinct events that have occurred by accretion during the twentieth century: 'the erosion of place' and the 'confusion of space'.

'Erosion of place' is a wide-ranging term that encompasses the (socio-physical) forces of modernity that have diluted, compressed, devolved and dissolved the traditional notion of a focal point for community, the physical landmark that envelops realities of community, exchange and contemplation.

> A sense of place in itself enhances every human activity that occurs there and encourages the deposit of a memory trace.[2]

By supposing that erosion of place is a typical feature of the late twentieth century it is also suggested that the memory traces of the inhabitants of this time are somehow dissolved or diluted, perhaps more accurately, dis-apparent. The cause of displacement of memory is inherent to the erosion of place. These two events are concurrent: 'Abstract market forces that detach people from social institutions have overpowered specific forces of attachment identified with place.'[3]

Place has been defined as a notion ascribed to familiar objects or scenarios that provide reference for orientation and recollection. In *The Image of the City*,

Lynch describes the contents of city images, with reference to physical form. His classification reveals five elements: paths, edges, districts, nodes and landmarks.[4] It is essentially these elements, or a combination of, that define physical place, or delineate space. Whilst Lynch's elements were considered in the text in terms of their use as cognitive navigational aids, their compound presence may be perceived as 'of place'. The notion of place is also a result of a social consciousness or the mental association of certain properties to a particular location by a section of the population. The 'market' as a physical entity perhaps best embodies Lynch's five elements, as each of the five is intrinsic to the model of a medieval market. The historic notions of market and place are interdependent. In its original form, a market was both a literal place and a socially constructed space. Markets were inextricably connected with local communities and the church, the event predominantly occurred in the same place at the same time. The incidence of interaction and exchange provided the means for community, both materially and culturally.[5] The market was a fixed event in space and time, wherein the nuances of a locality could be confined, and described within the matrix of small-scale commodity production. 'The social institutions of market and place supported each other.' Indeed, the relationship between not only market and place, but also market and urbanism is made by Henri Lefebvre. He observes:

> The city in Vitruvius is conspicuous by its absence/presence; though he is speaking of nothing else, he never addresses it directly. It is as though it were merely an aggregation of "public" monuments and "private" house ... Only in the sixteenth century, after the rise of the medieval town (founded on commerce, and no longer agrarian in character), and after the establishment of "urban systems" in Italy, Flanders, England, Spanish America and elsewhere did the town emerge as a unified entity-and as a subject.[6]

This statement preserved its integrity into the eighteenth century as larger towns developed, markets defined streets and districts. It was the industrial age that slowly separated market and place.[7] The shift of production, from a home or shop based activity to factories, ultimately led to the development of factory towns. The factory town was a method of permanently attaching skilled workers to their place of work through the provision of a highly ordered social infrastructure; Port Sunlight, Bourneville and Saltaire in Britain are all examples of this approach (see Figure 1.1). The paternalistic nature of the entrepreneurial directors of these grand schemes intended, through the provision of public buildings, private housing and modern utilities, to create a tempered version of urbanism without the social promiscuity of the city. Market no longer internalized place, place began to internalize market.[8]

In contrast to the pre-eminence of markets, modern culture dilutes the idea of place. The language of modernism expresses a universal experience of movement away from place and aspires to submerge the concept into a larger whole.[9] In the same way that the train and the camera began to alter concepts of distance, technology reinforces the notion that geographically localized communities are

Figure 1.1 Port Sunlight, built by Lord Lever between 1889 and 1914 in the garden suburb style
Source: Author's own, 1999.

archaic. Electronic information exchange connects even the furthest and most uninhabitable locations, but erodes the social distance that made experiencing them so distinctive.[10] As markets have globalized, place has diminished. We are conditioned to perceive place as a geographical location, we are almost equally comfortable with the idea of specific places as concentrations of a 'type' (person, economic activity, landscape). Place, in a wider context, is a cultural artifact of social conflict and cohesion, it expresses how a spatially connected group of people can mediate the demands of cultural identity, local authority and economic gain. Place as a descriptive for a whole city is no longer applicable. In European culture a city was once something defined by walls and gates. The gates of our modern city are the passport control of the airport or the platform of the station or the modem attached to the computer. Regulated, configured cities no longer exist; the city is a composite of invisible networks devoid of landmarks and overrun by nodes.

> *Speed expands time by contracting space: it negates the notion of the physical dimension.*[11]

The built environment of the city obviously still exists but its apparent permanence disguises the facts of transience and temporality. Architecture once governed proportion, and buildings were a symbol of meaning. Today when a church can become a design studio, a warehouse, a penthouse, the permanence of meaning becomes obsolete. The grand narratives of our society, progress and the liberation of humanity are only precursors to the crisis of themselves. The boundaries of progress and liberation have no limits; there is no homogenous goal. In cyberspace and in real time we inhabit a fractured, disconfigured, deregulated world.

The morphological and physical changes that have occurred during the late twentieth century are often complex and difficult to define, the precise nature and form of these changes, even more so. Locally, variations in topography, climate, culture, economy and politics all have a bearing on the wider implications of global societal shifts. The 'confusion of space' is a wide-ranging term that aims to define spatial characteristics that represent and are symptomatic of the most basic ways in which the urban landscape has been transformed. The spatial fragmentation of the urban landscape is directly correlated to the social shifts associated with the erosion of place. These characteristics have confused the categorization of space in several ways: (1) by the simultaneous, paradoxical policies of decentralization and concentration, which has given rise to (2) a fragmented urban landscape full of voids. (3) By the high definition of peripheral developments, which contrast against the (4) neutrality of the spatial envelopes they contain. (5) By the chaotic mix of functions within a chaotic palette of forms, rendering the task of the urbanist, one of establishing significance and event that will justify the ostensibly indescribable urban matrix. Symptomatic of the same condition is (6) the blurring of the distinction between categories of space. Spaces that once defined themselves, expressing purism (natural/cultural), now combine social and commercial functions, sponsors and symbols. Time, that was perceived as distinctive due to the finite nature of the social experience, is now compressed; social functions and experiences have become closely combined both physically and by mental association.

It would be too simple a definition to suggest that the 'erosion of place' is simply correlated to any one of the conditions described above, or that the 'erosion of place' is the only spatial symptom of hyper-cities. Info-media communications technology, indeed technology at large, can though, be held accountable. Essentially the advances in speed of communication have altered the way we work, eat, holiday, talk, be entertained, travel; the way we are. The common factor amongst these is speed; everything is faster, thus more efficient, with far tighter margins, higher expectations and demand for profit, thus less occasion for flexibility and adaptability. This sequence not only defines the way we work but the buildings we work within. The speed and ease of movement that has spawned drive-through restaurants, conveyor-type visits to the controlled environment of the supermarket, robot-like transitions through airports, has interfered with the experiential, accidental event, landmark, district or path that once defined place. The nature of the urban environment as one of flux, is not a new or unique state, as illustrated, but one that has accelerated through time and ultimately manifested itself in a generic form, indistinguishable from its neighbour or even its distant cousin. As actual places decline in significance and particularity, the space between them increases in prominence and quality. 'Roads no longer merely lead to places: they

Fortes, M.6 Motorway, Charnock Richard.   ET.406

Figure 1.2 Postcard showing Charnock Richard Services on the M6
Source: © Valentine of Dundee Ltd.

are places'[12] (see Figure 1.2). Whilst Brinckerhoff-Jackson's statement here implies a violent shift, it is used in this context to reinforce an idea. It *has* been shown that the association between roads and place does in fact have some historical precedence.[13]

The erosion of place is symptomatic of both the confusion and the polarization of space, the contrast between intensely defined space and functionally bereft space that are subservient to one another. Capitalism and the economic need for development inextricably link place and space in this context where there is no necessity for development in the first instance. The evidence of zoning and rigid programmatic demarcation manifests itself most at the periphery, the remaining bastion of open space around a city that was unoccupied and thus controllable through planning. The language of the periphery is the 'decorated shed',[14] occasionally these sheds emerge as icons of the 'supermodern',[15] predominantly however they nullify the urban periphery, sentencing it to a corrugated box patchwork of motorized enclosure. The strongly defined and heavily demarcated territories of the shopping centre, modern business/media/science park or industrial estate leave little room for the occasion of 'place'. Road, kerb, verge, footpath, cycle path, verge, fence, planting, kerb, road, car park, kerb, planting, kerb, car park, kerb, planting, kerb, car park would be a typically notated section through some such environment. This level of definition leaves little space for the occasion of temporary occupation

Figure 1.3 Neutral façadism in the parcelled and demarcated blank-box landscape of the periphery
Source: Author's own, 1999.

or natural intervention, indeed any direct physical experience beyond the confines of the car is positively excluded or controlled to such a degree that it is impractical to use, the tarmac of the footpaths and cycle-ways of this territory gathers dust on its surface. Yet this level of security and controlled movement is in stark contrast to the actual intense neutrality of the spatial envelopes they serve (see Figure 1.3).

Whilst the periphery has achieved high-resolution polarization of space, the urban centre has rapidly transformed warehouses to penthouses, churches to media-labs, banks to bars and bars to banks. No single idea or image can represent the urban landscape in its current agglomeration, as supposed by Martin Heidegger in the 1950s; the post-modern condition is a series of unbounded spaces where mass production and mass consumption reproduce a standardized quasi-global culture. The perception of any legible spatial order has been rendered impossible by the accelerated flux of urban development and the constant temporal layering of infrastructural devices, upon and within existing territories.

The Map

One of the key issues when attempting to engage with the city is the sheer enormity of the subject and the complexity of its emergence as a fluid superorganism; the myriad elements of which ebb and flow, often without any apparent underlying logic. In response to the increasing complexity of cities, various conceptual models have been developed through history to assist in our understanding and afford design strategies and tactics to be conceived and implemented. Indeed, urban theorists have sought to define various normative patterns for cities as both analytical and design tools for architects and urban designers, proposing notions of what urban developments should seek to encourage, whilst addressing the more negative aspects of large urban systems. Given the variety of different cities globally, an important feature of these models is that they are usually simple organizational frameworks that promote effective assimilation across a range of contexts. It is not the intention to recount the history of urban modelling here, rather to provide a sufficient platform from which the contemporary city may be understood.

Of particular importance in this regard is the work of Robert E. Park and Ernest W. Burgess, who during the 1920s initiated a groundbreaking programme of research on the nature of the urban environment whilst working in the sociology department at the University of Chicago. Throughout various research projects concerned with the city of Chicago, Park and Burgess evolved their theory of urban ecology, which in essence drew direct analogies between the natural and built environment, especially the notion of evolution in Darwinian terms and the intrinsic elements of competition and survival. Transposed to an urban context, Park and Burgess proposed that scarce urban resources led to competition between communities, thereby resulting in the subdivision of cities into demarcated ecological niches that offered appropriate resources for people who shared similar social values and behaviour, since they were subject to the same environmental forces. The differentiation of urban space that occurred as a result of this competitive process initially produced areas of high desirability in city centres but this was subsequently followed by a cycle through which people gradually moved away from the centre as their personal wealth increased. Park and Burgess referred to this process as 'succession', a term borrowed from plant ecology, and it was a key feature in their urban model of 'concentric zone theory' first published in their book, *The City*, in 1925. Concentric zone theory was one of the earliest examples of a conceptual model produced to assist in the understanding of urban organization and proposed that cities would adopt the form of five concentric rings with prosperity increasing as areas moved outwards and urban decay becoming more prominent near the centre (see Figure 1.4).

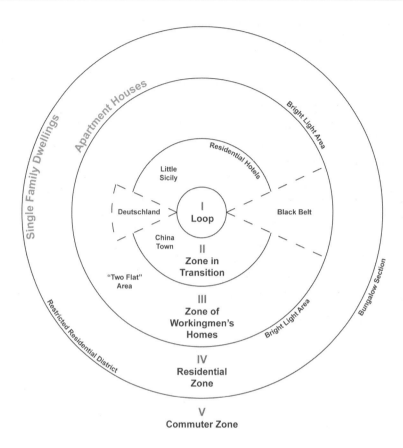

Figure 1.4 Concentric zoning diagram based on Park and Burgess' models produced at the Chicago School of Economics as published in *The City*, 1925
Source: Author's own, 2010.

With this in mind it is useful to move forward a few decades and refer to the highly influential theorist of urban form, Kevin Lynch, who viewed such models as a representation of theory. Whilst his classic book *The Image of the City* published in 1960 contained a wealth of innovative ideas and techniques for analysing and explaining urban conditions, it is his later work that is of interest here. Lynch's position evolved in relation to a critical development in city planning during the 1970s that favoured a process of analysis of fluid urban characteristics and patterns over the production of 'finished' plans which offered little flexibility or provision for contingency.[16] An emergent trend from this development, given further gravitas by recent computational software developments, in particular parametric modelling, is the description of the city as a complex, self-organizing system. The root of this approach to urbanism is widely acknowledged to be found in Jane

Jacobs' synthesis of behaviour in urban neighbourhoods and how such complexity may first be examined:

> *Thinking has its strategies and tactics too, much as other forms of action have. Merely to think about cities and get somewhere, one of the main things to know is what kind of problem cities pose, for all problems cannot be thought about in the same way. Which avenues of thinking are apt to be useful and to help yield the truth depends not on how we might prefer to think about a subject, but rather on the inherent nature of the subject itself.*[17]

Whilst contemporary discourse on cities as complex systems continues to flourish as a considerable number of designers and theorists explore the interface between complexity theory and design variables, it is important to highlight that this is only one avenue being pursued.[18] A primary factor that sets the work of Lynch apart from many other urban theorists is the inclusive approach he adopted. Whilst his work drew upon the traditional, rational and even scientific methodologies and data of geographers, city planners and economists, to provide a quantitative framework, it also afforded qualitative approaches and information to be integrated. This position of the city as not simply being an object for analysis but also a subject from which feedback could be gathered and synthesized to provide a loop system for further design strategies was developed further by Hall et al. in their 1969 article 'Non-Plan: An Experiment in Freedom'[19] which argued passionately in favour of adaptable and flexible local systems over potential huge city-region master plans that were widely advocated at the time. From this catalyst, Cedric Price sought to integrate feedback systems into his own designs, enabling users to adapt and revise their environment in response to the flows and variables of the city, an approach taken even further as a polemic by Archigram (see Figure 1.5).

In his engaging history and manifesto of urban modelling methodologies, David Grahame Shane summarizes the relevance of such work to the manner in which we approach the city as both subject and object of narrative and interpretation:

> *Lynch, in the spirit of Italo Calvino – whose fictional Invisible Cities (1972) he praised in A Theory of Good City Form for its description of a series of fantastic cities, each housing a 'society that exaggerates the essence of some human question' – believed that each city model corresponds roughly to a specific city theory. Values, in other words, shape cities. And because values can only be understood imaginatively and sympathetically, Lynch stressed the role of imagination in the understanding of cities. This makes his city theory one of the few recent attempts to construct a pluralist city in our imagination, emphasizing the possibilities of multiple interpretations.*[20]

The three normative city models proposed by Lynch in *A Theory of Good City Form* were the *City of Faith*, the *City as a Machine* and the *City as an Organism*. These types were in some ways preceded by Reyner Banham's 'The City as Scrambled Egg'[21] and visualized, in typical comic style, by Cedric Price who compared three different varieties of cooked egg; boiled, fried and scrambled, to three corresponding types of city; the pre-modern with its centre and distinct enclosure, the increasingly amorphous city with defined centre but sprawling suburbs, and the network city which is entirely mixed without differentiation between the centre and the periphery (see Figure 1.6).[22] Current debate on the high degree of connectivity prevalent in cities through digital technologies and the emergent attempts to close the gap between this and the comparatively fragmented physical context of cities may have a tendency to view the city as a non-hierarchical metropolis, favouring a polycentric model but this has yet to be adopted on a wide scale beyond the pages of theory and conceptual designs. In reality, whilst the contemporary city is unquestionably emerging as a mediated landscape or, to use Manuel Castells' term, 'space of flows', the nature of what we may consider to be urban has not altered radically. What can be identified, however, is a gradual and residual process of the 'city' ceding to the 'urban'. In his classic analysis on the dialogue between

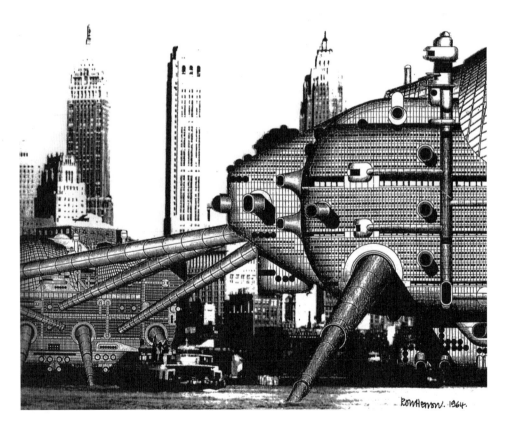

Figure 1.5 *The Walking City in New York*, **drawing by Ron Herron of Archigram, 1964**
Source: © Archigram/Simon Herron.

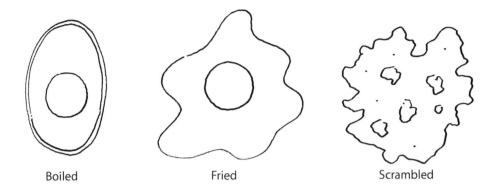

Boiled   Fried   Scrambled

Figure 1.6 Diagrams based on Cedric Price's originals for *The city as an egg*
Source: Author's own, 2010.

urban space and form, *Ladders*, Albert Pope writes about the disorganization of contemporary space:

> *To state it most simply, beyond the point where traditional categories break down, there exists the possibility of alternatives. New conceptions of urban space or new conceptions of the natural, for example, are not invented out of nothing, but emerge out of the transformation or in this case 'slurring' of traditional structures of form and thought.*[23]

The resulting fragmentation of the urban landscape has led to a proliferation of discontinuities and voids, partially influenced by the hybridization of centre and periphery and also by various processes of decentralization and concentration.[24] Despite earlier attempts to address this phenomenon such as Rowe and Koetter's influential *Collage City* which described the city as a multi-scalar system comprised of various components and proposed a number of strategies for dealing with the fragmentary urban landscape, there still remains a significant knowledge gap in architecture and urban design in this regard. This therefore highlights the need for us to consider ways in which we can make sense of the urban situation, not only to aid our understanding of it but also so that we may be able to develop meaningful design strategies and tactics.

The use of maps in relation to cities and our experience of them is both a familiar one and historically extensive. Our engagement with an unknown city is nearly always translated through the map whether illustrating streets, tourist destinations or transportation systems. Indeed, urban experience in an unfamiliar context is typically an exchange between cartographic spaces and the materials of the built environment. Considered in this manner it is evident that urban and cartographic spaces are entwined and continue to exist in a mutual relationship with each other, surviving temporal shifts and developments. The various

11

transformations of urban environments may often be revealed and reconstructed through studying the progressive layers of the city as a palimpsest. This returns us not only to its physical layout and order but discloses social, religious, political and commercial characteristics and behaviour, i.e. the city as a 'lived experience'. In cities with complex underground rail systems considerable time may pass before the strata of the subway map is comprehensively integrated with the above surface experience of the user, particularly when the graphic content of the former posits significant discrepancies in relation to distance and proximity in the latter. The mutuality between the map and the city has been drawn throughout history wherein the map has been used to plan and regulate the city's development or, conversely, the existence of the city has been preceded by it. Maps are not, as raised earlier, simply limited to the construction and changes of the physical fabric of the urban environment, with many used to document data beyond the city's material presence. It is here that it is possible to understand mapmaking as a highly creative process which intervenes in urban space in a bi-fold manner; on the one hand it records the physical structure of the city and the lived experience of it, whilst on the other hand it informs and subsequently transforms these by virtue of its production, i.e. cartography is performative and intrinsic to urban life. Current thinking on the role of mapping acknowledges it as a confluence of practices that facilitates emergent characteristics to reveal themselves to both the producer and user. Kitchin et al. summarize thus: 'As such, the map does not represent the world or make the world: it is a co-constitutive production between inscription, individual and world; a production that is constantly in motion, always seeking to appear ontologically secure. To conceive maps in this way reveals that they are never fully formed but emerge in process and are mutable (they are re-made as opposed to mis-made, mis-used or mis-read).'[25] This process and its inherent duality of recording and creativity has led to widespread appeal beyond traditional disciplines connected to cartography towards artists and other creative practitioners.

For example, the concentric zone theory developed by Park and Burgess to describe areas of social degradation across Chicago evolved through extensive use of mapping the spatial distribution of issues such as crime and unemployment to afford analysis. Burgess in particular was a keen advocate of mapping and required his students to attain proficiency in mapmaking. His devotion to the process led to scouring the city of Chicago for information that could be incorporated into various maps, making more extensive use of census data than any other social scientist of the time.[26] The subsequent system of concentric rings transcended the original research, becoming one of the most recognized and influential models in urban sociology and studies. An indication of its sustained legacy is its reformulation in Mike Davis' *Ecology of Fear*, published in 1998, in which the author used concentric rings to illustrate the deterioration of Los Angeles and its inner core of 'urban decay metastasizing in the heart of suburbia' (see Figure 1.7).[27] Perhaps of even greater consequence than the model itself was the legacy of the urban ecology research that resulted in mapmaking becoming an integral methodology within the disciplines of sociology, criminology and public policy.

As this chapter will reveal, the activities of the Situationists in the mid-twentieth century, to move across the city and experience everyday life unconstrained by regulatory urban bodies and recognized conventions, was a total rejection of what they perceived as the legacy of modernity. By refusing all hierarchy of urban places, the group favoured arbitrary discontinuities by revelling in the walking and view of the streets as performance art, more in tune with the jump-cuts and reframing, suggested in the assemblage of Phyllis Pearsall's original *London A–Z* of 1935, than the city as a cohesive whole. Subsequent champions of this method of intervention with urban conditions such as Michel de Certeau and Rosalyn Deutsche have served to add considerable influence to the adoption and sustained

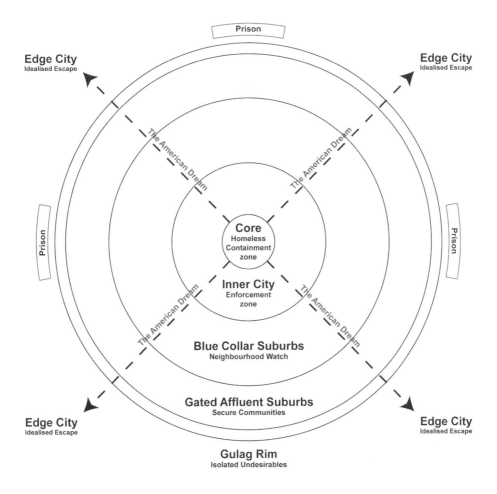

Figure 1.7 Zoning diagram based on Mike Davis' reworking of Park and Burgess' original

Source: Author's own, 2010.

growth of mapping within cities by artists in the last three decades. Such mappings may appear to utilize the quantitative and analytical techniques of cartography but the creative capacity of mapmaking should not be underestimated, with digital technologies affording an ever-expanding set of tools to engage with the process. Key to this activity is the dominant desire to provide legibility not necessarily in a conventional or material capacity but as a medium through which the lived experience of urban spaces is communicated. Of course this approach is not simply the preserve of artists, with architects and urban theorists deploying these methodologies as exemplified by Kevin Lynch's *The Image of the City*, an integral element of which were the psychological interviews and mapping exercises he engaged inhabitants of the city in as part of his research.

If, as Paul Virilio has suggested, 'the representation of the contemporary city is no longer determined by a ceremonial opening of gates, by a ritual of processions and parades, nor by a succession of streets and avenues' and that, 'from here on, urban architecture has to deal with the opening of a new "technological space-time"'[28] then where does this leave us in relation to urban conditions? The complex challenges combined with the myriad of opportunities that mapping both represents and affords when applied in the contemporary city is argued favourably by Denis Cosgrove:

> *Indeed, the map may be the only medium through which contemporary urbanism can achieve visual coherence. There remains a strong, if unrecognised, celebratory dimension to urban mapping, not merely in the banal sense of cities' self-promotion through advertising or tourist maps and plans, but in the choice of scale, content, design and colour of the myriad cartographic devices (many today interactive), developed by public agencies and private bodies to communicate and regulate contemporary urban systems and processes. The goal of rendering legible the complex, dynamic and living entity that is a city remains an urgent one. But today's acute awareness that cartographic images can never be innocent vehicles of information dissolves neat distinctions between celebratory and regulatory urban maps. Urban space and cartographic space remain inseparable; as each is transformed their relationship alters.*[29]

The recent expansion of digital technologies and computational software has considerably extended the spectrum of tools and techniques for mapping the urban domain both in terms of what types of data can be recorded and how, subsequently, it can be visualized. With the increasing growth of potential opportunities and creative practice for urban mapping it is important to remember that the critical discourse surrounding public space and notions of privacy and place must continue in order to parallel such developments and frame them in an intelligible manner. One of the most prevalent capacities of the information age is the accessibility and exchange of data, rendering the previously latent visible. Our encounters with the Internet can often be mixed as we balance the advantages of the seemingly limitless datastream with the ability to navigate our way through it and identify relevant material; just because it is there doesn't mean you are anywhere. As the global markets and community have reconfigured and evolved in response to emergent networks, mapping has become an essential method of orientation and comprehension in these new digital infrastructures. This book therefore asserts that mapping is an increasingly important activity, transcending disciplines and professions and, perhaps of particular relevance in this context, negotiating the apparent gap between physical urban conditions and digital landscapes. Considered in this way, mapping is a central, albeit often subconscious or tacit, element of design behaviour. By designing things we develop techniques for the communication of our ideas to facilitate expression and stimulate discourse. This raises issues regarding representation that will be discussed later in this chapter with specific reference to architecture and urban design.

Before we immerse ourselves in the world of mapping it is worth examining why it is such a significant activity and explain some of the key developments that have led us to this position. The first issue is one of abstraction, which as J.B. Harley has stated, has fundamental implications for the information concerned as they become social constructions, 'Far from holding up a simple mirror of nature that is true or false, maps redescribe the world – like any other document – in terms of power and of cultural practices, preferences, and priorities'.[30] The second and perhaps less immediate issue is the activity or process that is inherent to mapping. As the landscape architect James Corner has explained, 'mapping is particularly instrumental in the construing and constructing of lived space', as it 'unfolds potential; it re-makes territory over and over again, each time with new and diverse consequence'.[31] The explicit action of this description of mapping, which, unlike a map that infers a finished artifact, infers an ongoing process, adaptable and indeterminate. The recent widespread growth in mapping is evident as a cross-disciplinary and cultural phenomenon, both as a data-gathering exercise, i.e. what to record and why, and as explorative activity in visualization, i.e. how best to represent such information. John Noble Wilford asserts that digital technology has enabled a revolution in the manner in which maps are both produced and used that has not occurred since the Renaissance and identifies two primary strands that are pertinent with respect to this book.[32] In the first instance, the democratization of Geographic Information Systems (GIS) has afforded a new generation of mapmakers who typically operate within groups and often without any background in cartography. Secondly, whereas physical maps had a dual function providing both a visualization and database in one object, computational software has separated the database from the interface by enabling easy customization of content that may be endlessly reconfigured via its connection to massive digital storage capacities. This recent shift and bifurcation in the nature of mapping is summarized by Janet Abrams and Peter Hall: 'Before the advent of aerial photography, satellite tracking and computerized data-gathering, a map was expected to represent its territory with comprehensive accuracy. Freed of that responsibility, cartographers can manipulate their data into any number of visual representations – an act so potent it has attracted the attention of other disciplines.'[33]

However, whilst the use of digital technologies and novel computational techniques to date may indicate exciting new territory for mapping and be the catalyst for some sophisticated debate across various disciplines and practices, the full potential of these emergent modes of inquiry and their implications can only be speculated so let us return, quite literally, to earth for a moment. Topographical maps still retain considerable value as communication tools for describing spatial relationships between regions, people and goods but are very limited, if not altogether redundant, for an entire range of relationships that are in flux (whether cultural, economic or technological) and are topological in nature. This latter category has become embedded in society and requires a total rethink in the way in which mapping may contribute to our understanding of them. It is here that we may enter the world of design, with architecture and urban design possibly holding the key as suggested by Stan Allen:

> *Architects seem condemned to work on the surface of the city and not its structure. This is a situation that is historically determined and unlikely to change significantly as a result of anything the architectural profession does. But it can also be argued that architects have yet to examine the consequences of this shift. If architecture has lost its historic capacity to fix and determine the limits of urban space and territory, are architects left to work exclusively with images? Or is it possible to accept the reality of this new condition, and to creatively reinvent the tools of the discipline in order to meet these new challenges?*[34]

If the role of architecture and urban design is one of location and orientation of people in the world then it is able to embrace dynamic situations as part of this transformation. Architects have already attempted to develop 'techniques that engage time and change, shifting scales, mobile points of view, and multiple programmes' that 'suggest new ways of working with the complex dynamics of the contemporary city'.[35] An influential precedent in this regard was the unbuilt, yet widely published, *Parc de la Villette* master plan by OMA that utilized exploded views to offer a total reconceptualization of space. More recently, the visualization of detailed system flows and patterns has been an integral element of communication and design development in the work of UNStudio whilst MVRDV have investigated the datascapes of urban conditions to navigate extant and speculative territories in relation to the capacity and density of urban growth (see Figure 1.8).[36] Such dynamics are not confined to the proposal of design ideas but are also evident in the material and technological fabric of buildings themselves. This locomotive aspect of data flows and networks has developed a parallel need for mapping to be able to accommodate this flux and adaptability.

Maps that depict movement and overlap could also be called animations; they animate reality. The data furnished by GIS systems, statistics, search engines and visualization software serve less to situate things in relation to one another than to reveal their mutual force fields. They are not about fixed positions, but rather a

Figure 1.8 *Datatown, Sector Waste*, **MVRDV, 1999**
Source: © MVRDV.

matter of visualizing tensions of various kinds. As increasing amounts of data and many more parameters are processed, recalculated and visualized by computers, a dynamic reality becomes visible. This very dynamism causes us to lose our way and fuels the demand for new maps – smarter maps – that may not really help us find our way, but allow us to retain a hold on the thin thread of understanding that ties us to the complex reality of our world. We don't need direction as much as orientation. One of the most urgent questions of our time is how to move from movements to trajectories, from strict singular targets to shared vectors. Whilst it is immediately obvious that buildings cannot yet make this shift, there is no question that maps have this ability. If, as Stan Allen and others have hinted, architects make the shift to this new kind of practice, it will be because they are unwilling to concede their role as providers of cultural context. Consequently, mapping continues to do two separate things at once. As an act of understanding the world, it helps separate main issues from a multitude of side issues, and allows us to discern what really matters. On the other hand, the opportunities for manipulation are inexhaustible. For example, instead of merely suggesting an order, modern maps also present processes, in all their inexorability. Sometimes it seems that maps do not help us understand the world, they also actively prevent us from doing anything with this knowledge. With today's dynamic maps, you can end up thinking you understand

17

everything without being able to change anything. You can stand above reality and simultaneously be overwhelmed by it.

Designers who aspire to remain actively influential in the formation of the city (as they once were, as master builders) simply cannot ignore the new representations of reality. They need to engage with mapping in order to understand the big issues and dilemmas. Only then will their designs go beyond solving practical problems, and acquire cultural relevance. Despite this, there is a growing gap between the fantastic studies in which hidden forces are revealed and interconnected, and the master plans and scenarios that are supposed to change the appearance of those maps. There is a sense in which every design – whether it is called a master plan, a blueprint or a floor plan – is a map, because it organizes people in relation to material. Now that this type of organization has evolved beyond buildings into the movement of patterns of information, knowledge and capital, architects must change their maps to conform to the new reality. Until now they have done so very cautiously; it is quite something for a progressive insight to be discovered during a design's research and conceptual phase. Such discoveries at least make for improved orientation. But they don't help one to find the way. That is only possible when making a map is the same as making a road. In a society of flows, the need is above all for road maps and these are not discovered but created.

The Motion

Whilst the abstract visual cartography of the urban was not emergent until the 1920s, the literary exploration of the sensation of the city began with the work of Thomas de Quincey, English author and intellectual. In *The Confessions of an English Opium Eater* he discusses his experiences with the 'oriental drug' (opium) and his explorations as an East End flâneur in almost identical terms; the dreams of the opiate are delivered with similar prose to that of his meanderings through London's streets.

De Quincey was a Mancunian, incredibly intelligent and orphaned at the age of seven. He was put into the care of four guardians and attended Manchester Grammar School. At the age of 15 he was able to speak fluently in classical Greek and also compose poetry in the same. De Quincey was fond of his second guardian, a scholar and Head of Manchester Grammar School, Mr Lawson, but not necessarily a lover of Manchester due to his unfortunate childhood circumstance.

The descriptions of his opiate-fuelled half-existence in the dark streets of London's East End are tales haunted by gargantuan tropical plant life and exotic immigrant populations from the Far East. The exploratory narrative is delirious and confused, but somehow more accurately descriptive by virtue of its arrangement and tone, the street described as an experience where one 'must be the first discoverer of some of these *terræ icognitæ*, and doubted, whether they had all been laid down in the modern charts of London'.[37] De Quincey likens the East End to Asia itself and whilst his explorations are shrouded in a haze, the conscious mind of the Victorian reader was all too well aware of a widening fissure between the cosmopolitan character of West London and the apparent unfettered 'barberesque' East.

De Quincey is at once fearful and fascinated by the urban maelstrom that he exists within and observes. He interprets conversation and gestures as subversive and manufactures an imaginary geography wherein the mysterious world he creates, by expanding fact through his opium filtered version of the streets, is the antithesis of the purportedly civilized Victorian life. This creation of De Quincey's has been referred to as an 'Internal Orient' and menacing to the hub of the Empire.[38] The potential for social contagion and combination is perceived as dangerous as it is uncontrolled by the wider context that normally binds communities.

Despite his apparent dislike of Manchester, De Quincey was again drawn north, possibly to purge his life of the associations of opium and addiction. He wrote *Confessions* when he was finally recovered and had kicked the habit, following personal crisis and self-reflection. De Quincey is known as one of the English Romantics and was associated with Wordsworth, for whom he held an admiring disdain. He twice set off to introduce himself to the Lakeland poet before turning back, only quelling his nervous admiration on his third attempt, yet he scorns Wordsworth for his physical frailty and alludes to him as being a rural romantic in a derogatory sense. Nonetheless, he contentedly moved into Dove Cottage as the Wordsworths left in 1809, though this is accredited to the isolated location as discouraging his debtors from travelling to recover their monies. De Quincey's prose is full of sweeping exaggerations counterbalanced by unnaturally accurate descriptive text to imply a greater truth than is actually written. The accuracy of his descriptions here is unimportant; it is the act of exploration by drifting and its subsequent description that sets De Quincey apart from his peers.

The Parisian Tradition

De Quincey's drifting, strolling around London with no aim other than to see what was around the next corner, albeit fuelled by certain addictions and desires, emerged as a tangible mode of artistic expression in Europe through the twentieth century. The Surrealists in the 1930s, the Lettrists in the 1950s and the Situationists through the 1950s and 1960s developed the practice by placing definition on some or all of the activity; planning it and mapping it. The idea of simply moving through the city and the record of these meanderings through texts or photographic essays was the secondary product of actions by the Surrealists which revolved around Breton's notion of automatism. It was the burgeoning scale and tract of the urban, its unpredictability and the occasion of chance events that was understandably attractive and alluring to Breton:

> *The means were simple enough; merely buy a Sunday ticket at a suburban railway station and shunt for hours and hours on all the tracks of a landscape of dislocation, on a journey whose end is never fixed in advance.*[39]

Sadie Plant, in her book about the Situationist movement, discusses the value of this characteristic allure to Breton: 'It was Breton who had described the street, "with its disturbances and its glances" as "my one true element. There I partook, as nowhere else, of the wind of circumstance". Surrealism had invoked a world of floating encounters through which the hunter of marvels drifts according to whims and desire.'[40]

As well as being a confirmed fan of drifting, Andre Breton wrote one of a trio of books by Surrealist authors that contained first-person narratives of wandering in Paris: *Nadja* by Breton, *Paysan de Paris* by Aragon and *Last Nights of Paris* by Soupault. Breton and Soupault sexualized the city, using it as the backdrop for tales of pursuit and anti-heroines embroiled in prostitution. Contrastingly and perhaps more aligned to subjects of Surrealist thought, *Paysan de Paris* has no narrative, it is instead organized around geography. Aragon made the city and its objects themselves the subject, and imbued the city with romantic connotations. At a time when Modernist thought was concerned with light and air, Aragon conceived an architecture of darkness and enclosure.[41] Whilst Aragon was not an architect, he created architectural space in words, describing thresholds, doors, the spaces between and the dereliction of the city. Whilst these interstices posed events that satisfied a Surrealist curiosity, the nature of the examination perpetuates Parisian critical thought as the spectacle of the everyday.

Walter Benjamin was fascinated by Aragon's book, it was his first introduction to the culture of the arcades with which he became obsessed. Given Benjamin's acknowledged romanticism, it is not unusual that it is Aragon's work, out of the three, that he cites as influential. There are similarities between *Paysan de Paris* and Benjamin's work *One-Way Street*. *One-Way Street* (*Einbahnstrasse*) was Walter Benjamin's first effort to break out of the narrow confines of the academy and apply the techniques of literary studies to life as it is currently lived. For Benjamin criticism encompasses the ordinary objects of life, the literary texts of the time, films in current release, and the fleeting concerns of the public sphere.

Benjamin first visited Paris in 1913 and stayed for longer and longer periods until he moved there at the end of the 1920s. Benjamin was a great walker of the streets and he wrote of the same. Even when in his home city of Berlin he wrote of Paris and was held fascinated by its labyrinthian qualities. Paris fulfilled his romantic notions of a city that could only truly be experienced by meandering and wandering, a spatial order that contrasted with the emergent linear methodologies of the machine age. Benjamin also studied the work of Charles Baudelaire as a basis for his unfinished life work, *The Arcades Project*,[42] a collection of writings on the city life of Paris in the nineteenth century, especially concerned with the iron-and-glass covered 'arcades' (known in French as *passages couverts de Paris*). These arcades came into being as a result of Haussmann's plans for Paris, which fostered the city's emerging and distinctive street life and provided a backdrop for the practice of flânerie.

Baron Georges-Eugène Haussmann was hired by Napoleon III in 1852 to modernize Paris. His work destroyed much of the medieval city, it is estimated that he transformed 60 per cent of Paris' buildings. Where once the streets had been narrow and crowded, the new arcades afforded the gentry the occasion to parade their opulent wealth and their capacity to be at leisure. Benjamin writes that it was the fashion of the 1840s to walk at the pace of the turtle that was walked on a lead through the arcades.[43] The term flâneur is of uncertain origin but whether used to refer to a slacker or a heady self-awareness it was constant in its ascription to the Parisian gentleman. The nineteenth-century encyclopaedia Larousse cites that the flâneur may only exist in the great metropolis since provincial towns would provide too restricted a stage for flânerie. The flaw in the idea of flânerie comes when one considers historical accuracy, there are no first-hand accounts of people actually walking turtles; it is Benjamin who constructs this concept. He may though have been influenced by an account from Huysmans.[44]

The most celebrated of Huysmans' novels broke decisively from the Naturalist fashion of the day via the introduction of a single exuberant character, de Esseintes, whose explicitly homosexual encounters were a benchmark for other authors, including Oscar Wilde. In À Rebours[45] Huysmans' eccentric protagonist buys a turtle and, to match it with an opulent carpet, he has its shell glazed over with gold and encrusted with gemstones in the shape of a flower (see Figure 1.9). Breton, in one of his multitude of lists in which he constantly restructures the surrealist trajectory, refers to Huysmans as a 'surrealist avant-la-lettre' (a proto-surrealist).[46]

There is undoubtedly the extrovert in all of us, but not one flâneur of quite the extreme described by Benjamin; again this configures with the image of Benjamin as a romantic, his character created as a highly embellished version of the truth. Perhaps the most telling phrase employed in this regard by Benjamin is his reference to the city as a 'virgin forest' explored by 'naturalists … botanising on the asphalt'. The work was not completed due to his death in uncertain circumstances during the Second World War. Written between 1927 and 1940, *The Arcades Project* has been posthumously edited and published in many languages as a collection of unfinished reflections. This has, unsurprisingly, caused scholarly dispute, but raised interest in the flâneur in the late twentieth century. The 1989 Beauborg and ICA retrospectives of the Situationists, and the death of Guy Debord in 1994, brought the Situationist International to prominence and the two revived ideas of walking, whether promenading as the flâneur or drifting as the artist, were instrumental in a re-envisioned art practice of movement.[47] This was distinct from the walks of the Land Art movement, which were concerned with the idea of limitless space. These walks were concerned with experiential sensation, matter and new urban narratives. Artists have conveniently appropriated the term psychogeography to lend precedent and context to the work.

Psychogeography, a Situationist neologism, remains a pleasantly ill-defined term that tries to somehow encompass and describe the indeterminate meandering and uncontrolled experience of the city. Debord described the word as 'retaining a rather pleasing vagueness'. It is now claimed by various arts and sciences and is embroiled in a well-mannered scramble to align it definitively with one of the '-ologies'. Social psychology is probably the most pertinent area of research; it has the ability to apply methodological approaches with results and conclusions

Figure 1.9 Figure and jewel encrusted turtle by Arthur Zaidenberg from the 1931 illustrated edition of *À Rebours*

to the area of psychogeographical research. Somehow, though, the formalization of psychogeography detracts from its allure and romance as an un-prescribed activity. In architecture, however, it is the material, the prescription, the reading or the cartography that is of paramount concern and it is the tangible products of writing or mapping the city that may be transposed into an architectural discourse.

It is a reaction against modern architecture that informed Ivan Chtcheglov's *Formulary for a New Urbanism*.[48] He writes about a random exploration of Paris and evokes a sense of his boredom with the status quo; he is frustrated that the modern mode of architectural production serves to numb the senses, to nullify the dream. He contrasts this with the fabled ease of 'the hacienda', an image of aristocratic leisure. In reference to the idea that the continued process of mechanized urbanization will only induce less imaginative visions he writes the phrase adopted universally by artistic subcultures, 'Now that's finished. You won't see the hacienda. It doesn't exist. The hacienda must be built'.

In 1933 the Surrealists had called for the irrational embellishment of Paris, including a proposal to replace the towers of Notre Dame with a giant glass cruet filled with blood and sperm and other such anti-societal questioning propositions.[49] This was countered by the Lettrist demands for the 'Rational Embellishment of Paris', which called for proposition of an equally challenging level of intervention but with an uncannily socialist agenda. The opening of the Metro at night, the abolition of museums, the connection through minimal intervention of promenades across roofscapes were all contained therein.[50] Each of these proposals increases the chance for unusual circumstance and seeks to intensify the urban experience through unexpectedness or shifted aspect.

Chtcheglov continues to make the assertion that 'all cities are geological', implying that social behaviour is directly conditioned by an architectural environment composed of fragments of the past. He considers that this exemplifies a domination of the past over the present and proposes an inversion of this process to define the architecture of tomorrow as 'a means of investigation and a means of action'. His imagined city is a responsive environment that is full of modifiable elements that bend to the will of their inhabitants, pre-empting and probably informing Constant's later work, *New Babylon* (see Figure 1.10). Chtcheglov's is a city that could be reconstructed or built from nothing and feelings would characterize the various districts, he supposes that a Bizarre Quarter, Happy Quarter and a Sinister Quarter, amongst others, might exist; 'Everyone will live in their own personal "Cathedral"'. It is within this imagined antithesis to the boredom of the city that Chtcheglov defines the principal activity of the inhabitants as the 'continuous dérive'. Here, then, is the association between a reactionary negation of the present as lacklustre and the need for aimless meandering to question this reality.

This text was widely adopted by the Lettrist International (LI), formed in 1952 by Guy Debord, Gil J. Wolman, Jean-Louis Brau and Serge Berna. The LI emerged from a rapidly shifting avant-garde landscape in Paris during the 1940s and 1950s founded on earlier Surrealist and Dadaist ideas. The Romanian born Isidore Isou pioneered Lettrism, which was concerned with the deconstruction of language and art and focused on the letter as a singular compositional unit in creative texts. Isou and his contemporaries sought to reinvigorate poetry and painting by replacing the central construct of verse with clusters of images and sounds freed of semantic constraints. The continued dissatisfaction with conventional modes of representation is evident in the Lettrist construct, as is the elemental reordering of the component parts of a particular landscape. These modes of inquiry were to persist and developed as the Lettrist International fused with the London Psychogeographical Association (LPA) and the International Movement for an Imaginist Bauhaus in 1957 to create the Situationist International (SI).

The LPA was first referenced in 1957 by the British artist Ralph Rumney, in his role as one of the curators of the First Exhibition of Psychogeography in Brussels, in which his work was included.[51] It is uncertain as to whether the group actually had any other members at this point and it has been variously referred to as the

Figure 1.10 Constant Nieuwenhuis, *New Babylon*, 1959–1974
Source: © Gemeentemuseum.

London Psychogeographical Institute, Committee or Society. In any case, the LPA was short-lived, given its absolution into the SI within its first year of being. Rumney's association with the SI was equally curtailed following his expulsion at the hand of Debord for allegedly failing to submit a psychogeographic report on Venice on time.[52] The formation of the SI, despite Debord's notoriously unstable and contradictory nature, proved to be the longest serving of the post-war avant-garde organizations and between 1957 and 1968 used the construction of situations to form a Marxist commentary on media, art, language and politics commonly bound by their discourse with the urban environment.

> *Of all the affairs we participate in, with or without interest, the groping search for a new way of life is the only aspect still impassioning. Aesthetic and other disciplines have proved blatantly inadequate in this regard and merit the greatest detachment. We should therefore delineate some provisional terrains of observation, including the observation of certain processes of chance and predictability in the streets.[53]*

Debord developed the psychogeographic mantra through his continued association with the practice of drifting and his widely accepted definition of 1955; 'the study of the precise laws and specific effects of the geographical environment, consciously organized, or not, on the emotions and behaviours of individuals'.[54]

Debord wasn't a fan of the car, he felt that it took away from the everyday subtleties of the shift in mood, atmosphere or perceived safety one could experience when turning the corner of one street into another. Debord has been described as having believed himself to have 'invented' the notion of the dérives or drifting. His authoritarian prescriptions for subversion were somewhat borne out by the use of slogans from the SI by students in the 1968 uprising of Paris (see Figure 1.11).[55]

Whilst feigning ignorance of the artistic tradition that had been a precursor to his dérives, Debord was willing to acknowledge the influence of earlier cartographers in the fields of ethnography and sociology. Two researchers, employed by urban anthropologist Paul-Henry Chombart de Lauwe, created a map that depicted the routes taken by a young woman over the course of one year, in and around the sixteenth arrondissement of Paris. This map was published in 1952 as part of the wider and influential study, *Paris et l'agglomeration Parisienne*, and criticized by Debord in his *Theory of the Dérive*. It is not the process or production of the map that provokes Debord's criticism, it is her limited exploration of the city that the subject reveals by her triangulated pattern of movement around her residence and two places of study (see Figure 1.12). Debord expresses his 'outrage at the fact that anyone's life can be so pathetically limited'. He also describes the map itself as an example of 'a

Figure 1.11 Slogans and posters from the SI magazine: *The enemy revealed* **and** *Back to normal,* **1968**

modern poetry capable of provoking sharp emotional response', which it clearly elicits in him. Whilst Chombart de Lauwe is not known to have referenced the earlier studies of Park and Burgess, there is a certain graphic and aesthetic debt to the work. Debord himself is familiar with the Chicago School and in the same essay refers to 'ecological science, despite the narrow social space to which it limits itself, provides ... abundant data' and that 'such data ... will undoubtedly prove useful in developing dérives'. In this sense the proximities and overlaps between art, networks, urbanism, sociology and the power of the abstracted and representational map in this discourse were recognized. The mapping of socio-morphology and latent infrastructural networks, that are represented in contemporary urban geography and planning settings, was both acknowledged and challenged here, as Debord perceives the use of this data to his trajectory, thus exposing its limits as non-sensory. The very ideologies of the psychogeographer and the ethnographer too, collide; the SI remained interested

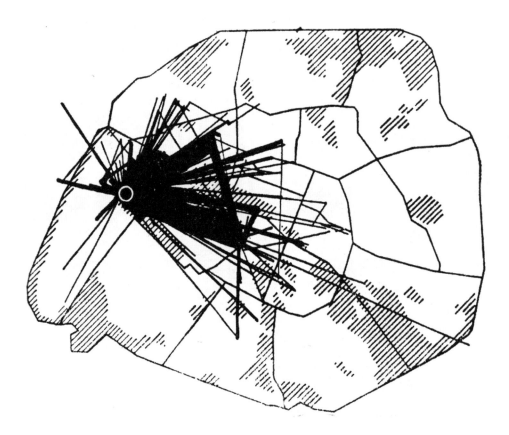

Figure 1.12 All of the movements made in the space of one year by a student living in the sixteenth arrondissement, Paul-Henry Chombart de Lauwe, 1952
Source: © Chombart de Lauwe, P-H. from *Paris et L'agglomeration parisienne*, Volume I, 1952.

in the destabilization of their own reality and the production of knowledge was incidental to this pursuit, whereas it was the explicit aim of the ethnographer.

The production of the French Situationists was largely controlled by Debord's assertion that their art was not concerned with the act of making. He is known to have expelled Constant for his mere association with a German architect who had built a church.[56] Nonetheless, and perhaps as a product of our consumptive and image-laden society, the series of maps produced in Paris in the late 1950s became icons of the movement. Of these, the most reproduced and discussed is the map of the Naked City (see Figure 1.13). The production of this particular map was informed by Debord's pyschogeographic studies and made using the process of détournment, wherein pieces of existing works are reformatted in new fragments or dispositions with the intent of revealing new readings. Other experiments of a directly physical nature and concretely bound to the idea of creating new situations were practised in Holland during the 1950s, known as Unitary Urbanism. Unitary Urbanism consisted of making different parts of the city communicate with one another, sometimes with the use of walkie-talkies,[57] it presupposed, the now accepted notion, that a series of fragmented or niche events are typical of the contemporary urban experience and that parts of the city are connected by means other than their physical relationship. Further

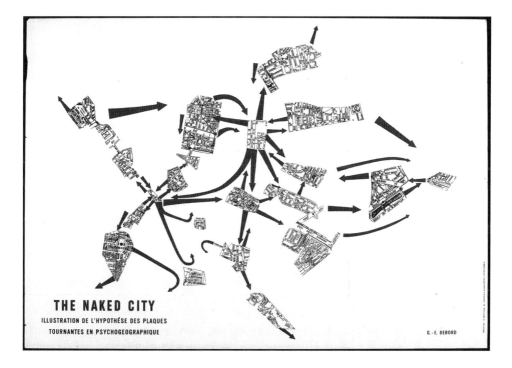

Figure 1.13 *The Naked City*, **Guy Debord, 1957**
Source: © Guy Debord.

maps included *Discours sur les passions de l'amour*; Pinder (1996) discusses the production of these maps and argues that they represented an 'attempt to disrupt existing representations and convey different visions of the city. Rather than being entirely new products, his psychogeographic maps were thus modified or "improved" versions of ordinary maps'.[58]

Whilst a conventional map may communicate a specific, yet abstract, geometric version of the truth about the environment it represents, the maps produced by the SI were intended to convey an experiential, societal or existential truth. The nature of the maps as discontinuous yet networked sequences of space is simultaneously representative of the emotive connectivity experienced by the participant and the actual fragmented physical city. Paris was changing as Debord navigated it, the gentrification projects in Le Marais and the Ile St. Louis combined with Pierre Sudreau's 1958 *ravalement des façades* were fast freezing central Paris into the mummified historic centre it has become.[59] The maps do reveal the prevalent but incongruous event of a sensational or character shift that may occur simply by crossing to the other side of a street and in this deconstruction of conventional cartographic space provide a graphic representation of this apparently unquantifiable experience. The practice of the dérive by the SI all but ceased around 1960 as the concept of the 'spectacle' emerged.[60]

Many of the physical locations explored and mapped by the Situationists were sanitized and even demolished not long after the publication of the map of the Naked City, the latent nostalgic inference here parallels Benjamin's concern about the destruction of his manufactured romanticized vision of the city. It is somehow contradictory that Benjamin, as a preservationist, chose to romanticize the city rather than be accepting of the dirt and grime that existed in the Paris he described. In paradox, Debord, who revelled in the gritty city, can be seen as a romantic, as evidenced by his attraction to older dying parts of the city. He is also known to have contradicted himself concerning the maintenance or removal of buildings and institutions, particularly those of the church. It is ultimately this inconsistency, an unrelenting mode of rejection and a wilful manipulation of theory to his own end that calls to question Debord and the Situationist International. Henri Lefebvre in interview describes Debord and his own reluctance to be part of this or any group, 'I knew (his) character and his manner, and the way he had of imitating Andre Breton, by expelling everyone in order to get at a pure and hard little core'.[61] Despite this ego-driven context, the SI magazine challenged perception of normality and compliance by the use of provocative statements that exposed the truths of the apparent freedom of democracy. Debord could observe the loss of choice long before it became of major public debate, as evidenced by the provocative montage images adopted by the student revolutionaries of 1968.

Jean-Francois Lyotard, philosopher and literary theorist, effectively removed ego from his critique of the dérive. In his 1973 work Lyotard transposes the idea of the urban act into the realm of theory and in so doing manages to transcend Debord's subjectively imposed constraints. Plant (1992) describes this transposition as the use of the 'aimless playfulness locomotion without a goal'[62] to parallel drifting thought, wherein an imposed dialectical order can be abandoned and negate the arrogance of the theorist who forms judgement and subsequent subjective representations of thought.

> *Where do you criticize from? Don't you see that criticizing is still knowing, knowing better? That the critical relation still falls within the sphere of knowledge, of realization and thus of the assumption of power? Critique must be drifted out of. Better still: Drifting is in itself the end of all critique.*[63]

Lyotard was the first person to begin to intellectualize the dérive. Essentially Lyotard agreed with Foucault concerning dialectical thought; that the dialectic set up an opposition between two systems that pre-existed within a social power base and was subsequently impossibly objective and bound by the limits of the subjective.

De Certeau continued to use the act of walking as a basis with which to conceive the nature of the contemporary city, most particularly the concept of its space. He was a much gentler character than Debord, a French Jesuit and scholar whose work combined psychoanalysis, philosophy and the social sciences. His most cited work is *The Practice of Everyday Life*, where he picks up the surrealist notion applied by Aragon of the description and study of the unconscious navigation of normality. It is the chapter 'Walking in the City' that is considered the most influential and the most relevant to this narrative, not least for its critical exploration of the urban experience, but also the description of the city. As he defines his three-point synopsis of preceding urban and utopian discourse and proposes the city as a 'concept', he writes of the datascape of the city and understanding it as a series of matrices based on legislative and administrative processes interrupted by schisms, whether within the market or socially driven. The unrelenting power of urbanization and that progress is linguistically embedded with constructing the 'urban' rather than the 'city' is perceived to give way to spacelessness and afford opportunity and canvas for 'contradictory movements that counterbalance and combine themselves outside the reach of panoptic power'. This condition is largely apparent in the contemporary city, though the panopticon strives to control by processes of surveillance not necessarily considered by de Certeau.

Using the act of walking as a basic example of spatial practice as a mechanism to explore the 'contradiction between the collective mode of administration and an individual mode of reappropriation', de Certeau describes movement at street level. In contrast to the manifestly unified representations of the organizing bodies, maps, plans and grids, the pedestrian is tactical, meanders, avoids and takes shortcuts and cannot be determined. This conception of the city supports the proposition that everyday life is composed of layers of convergence, the appropriation of the territory of others and the juxtaposition of rules, processes and products that pre-exist, but cannot be calculated with respect to their influence on a given moment. It is perhaps within this order that certain contemporary spatial practice can be considered. This is not however the point at which the text departs to assess walking in contemporary art. The revived interest in this particular practice is largely technologically, rather than ideologically, driven. The advent of electronic GIS and global positioning systems (GPS) has had some impact and this will be afforded further investigation in later chapters. However, there is not a prevalent exposition of new theory that accompanies new art practice, much is referential to the material discussed here. It may be argued that both the practice and the critique were effectively concluded in Paris by 1984, though the idea of the body as a mediator of space persists, most notably in Sennett's *Flesh and Stone*.[64]

New York – New Depression – New Art

The theory of art action within the streets faded from discourse in the latter part of the twentieth century, but the act of art within the streets began to grow at an unprecedented rate. Unhindered by critical thought, and seemingly without motive, graffiti began to consume the surfaces of Western cities. The history of modern graffiti related to urban subculture is unclear, some think it started in Philadelphia, others New York. Taki 183, a delivery boy in New York, was the first to be acknowledged by the mainstream press as being 'All City', a phrase adopted later and modified to 'All City King', referring to the individual whose name was most prevalent across all the districts of the city. Taki had been operating since 1969; in 1971 a *New York Times* article entitled 'Taki 183 Spawns Pen Pals' exploded the activity and its hypertrophic growth the world over was initiated.[65] Jean Baudrillard was sufficiently interested to comment on the movement in 1976[66] and draws it into his discourse on signs, which may also be viewed as unpredictable elements within de Certeau's regulated urbanism. His analysis at that particular time is important as it is contemporary to the birth of graffiti and precedes most photographic or sociological publications on the subject. His assertion that 'this movement has stopped' has not really been borne out by the passage of time, yet his description of the city at this juncture calls to mind Park and Burgess' ideas of zoning and those of the 'urban' overwhelming the 'city'.

> The urban city is also a neutralised, homogenised space, a space where indifference, the segregation of urban ghettos, and the downgrading of districts. Races and certain age groups are on the increase. In short, it is the cut up space of distinctive signs.[67]

Graffiti is described as an assault, in the manner of earlier riots, but one concerned with the altering of content and terrain, 'a new type of intervention in the city' as a reaction to the terrorist power of the corporatized media and the dominant culture of signs. It is this reactionist approach most often cited as the reason that graffiti exists and the same that perpetuates the negative perception of the practice. Practitioners themselves will actively promote an anti position and revel in the contrived notion that this upsets the art world in their constant need to commodify.

Self-appointed, but undisputed, Style Master General, Michael 'Dondi' White, was one of the early New York graffiti writers. The tales of Dondi, his crew and his influence in the structure and organization of a host of urban assaults only really came to light at the turn of this century upon the publication of his book, co-authored by Zephyr.

> *When the CIA (Crazy Insides Artists) boys were at work in the train yards, everyone was delegated a responsibility. While Dondi was filling in on one end of the car, DURO was working on the background. Dondi conducted the orchestra and outlined most of the work. Within the workings of CIA, every detail was attended to. Eric 7000 was even appointed CIA photographer.[68]*

Illegal entry to train yards and subways was all part of the 'game'[69] and remains so to this day (see Figure 1.14). These organized acts of infiltration and painting involve significant exploration, reconnaissance and research, the nature of the spaces in which they operate demand such, so great are the risks. In New York, as graffiti gestated, the primary territories were the subway trains and yards, ultimately the entire lines and the city itself became canvases. Accessing hidden parts of the city, moving underground and climbing are all secondary to the act of making a mark

Figure 1.14 Rust One and friends, train yard, Manchester, 1989
Source: © Zach Turner, 1989.

and it is the pursuit of the act that determines paths and routes thus, unknowingly, inverting the practice of the dérive. The strategy of crews in doing serious 'hits' on full cars has become more and more extreme. The practice of scaling buildings and locating rooftop spots visible from the lines was commonplace and this mode of practice has now been appropriated and bastardized by artists who span the boundary between gallery and street and provide a new urban discourse around their works and their placement. They make readings of and utilize public space, much in the manner of a skateboarder, that their action leaves a semi-permanent mark maintains a discourse with the site and the street, and even its eradication has a relationship with urban space (see Figure 1.15).[70] The availability of a surface and the approach required to paint that surface are key to the execution. Method and placement are as important as the act of painting and as the result itself.

> Consequently, the particular serial effect which characterizes this pictorial genre is turned into a game of hunting down the images in the series. Signs are repeated at different points of town; this repetition, tracing out a circuit, triggers the perception of a network: various series form a narrative network, and each image is at once a fragment and an echo of it.[71]

Here, Bailly adopts Baudrillard's term, sign, to describe the repetitive motif of the artist who inscribes the street from the position of the viewer. He makes himself a participant in an imagined game that concerns the perception of the city. He suggests that there is an established resonance between the images and thus the place in which those images exist, they call to mind a memory of one location in their imposition at another. By virtue of its own illegality, the artist seeks placement where there is less visible security (of course the opposite is true and often celebrated), thus marking out a trace of dereliction and back street sequential motion. These motifs are never the same and the mutation of form, according to context, seeks its own discourse that is as significant as that which considers the whole 'narrative network'. This is true of both traditional graffiti forms and more recent 'post-graffiti'[72] expression.

The idea of a perceived network in the serial production of images mirrors the cognitive association of sign with product that many successful brands trade upon and is used by Bailly in the context of one city, but even practitioners of graffiti can now consider themselves 'all-world'.[73] This at once mirrors the networked globalized condition into which we have manoeuvred ourselves. Such a position has altered conceptions of space but has yet to yield any manifest physical order, other than the erosion of place that commenced with the birth of mobility. Unfortunately we do not exist within Constant's *New Babylon*, Debord's habitable labyrinths for dérives or Chtcheglov's bespoke cathedrals. Physical and communicative mobility can be seen to have contributed to the death of the city, alongside the mechanisms of exchange upon which it was built, yet the datascape has still informed the landscape only by processes of superseding and dereliction. Neither material technology, communication, nor the capacity to process data driven landscapes has significantly altered our perception of self within our environment, layers

Figure 1.15 Gray Ghost, Fred Radtke, and his multiple markings made in the eradication of graffiti in his home town of New Orleans
Source: © Paul Counts, 2008.

of administration only constitute denser regulated networks; the desire to order perpetuates disorder.

The Internet can, though, be seen to have had its own impact on the ways in which the urban is observed and recorded. The bottom-up model of forums and peer-to-peer exchange has created numerous specialist interest groups that criticize, examine and explore aspects and spaces of the city with a host of motivations and results. The top-down model of mega-domains has provided more information about cities, space, place and environment than one can possibly process in a lifetime. Google Maps and its associated interfaces and plug-ins provides one such mega-domain, powerful both by virtue of the data it has collected and its capacity to process and embed others' content into its own environment. The 'Street View' function provides an image of a host of cities, and one can imagine eventually the whole world, street by street, at approximately the level of a pedestrian's eye (see Figure 1.16). Arguments rage over the unsolicited photographs and articles of human rights, websites have emerged with classified typologies of 'Street View' incident, the topless, the vomiting, the crash, and yet these snapshots are neither totalitarian nor utopian, they are symptomatic of a reality deficit. The entire urban

Figure 1.16 Screengrab of Google Street View function showing the entrance to the Manchester School of Architecture
Source: Google, accessed 30 May 2010.

environment is mapped, recorded, indexed and classified to a saturation point at which discovery is bound to a monitor and reality yields little new experience. This condition has been described as the 'anti-dérive'.[74] The creation of alternative virtual realities has had comparatively less success than the representation of the real world, the most prominent, Secondlife, depopulating with a collective rapidity as the novelty wore off.

It is without surprise then, that the act of exploring space that is untouched, unknown or forgotten is growing internationally; everything is mapped, recorded and visualized in the electronic world therefore the desire to touch a lost past or a grimy underbelly grows within those of inquisitive nature; man is nought if not an explorer. Urban Exploration (UE), in the contemporarily coined phrase, is a direct reaction to networked and surveyed space. It is both a product of and the antithesis of the Internet, clearly indicated by an alternative phrase used within the community of 'reality hacking'. As ascertained here, the act of exploring marginal urban space is not new; indeed the community make reference to Philibert Albairt, a Parisian lost in the city's catacombs in the 1780s, his body undiscovered for 11 years. The reportage attached to the activity is that which is intrinsically bound to the web and without forums and social networking sites, the practice may have remained largely 'underground'.

Protagonists are without classification and act with a multitude of motives, UE typically encompasses a breadth of specialist interest groups, industrial archaeologists, drain explorers and thrill seekers all participate. Its public presence

Figure 1.17 Urban explorer photographed taking photographs
Source: © Michael England, 2009.

revolves largely around the production of the image and the practice of photography and its online publication is perhaps overtly definitive of the act (see Figure 1.17). This medium of account and recollection is somewhat blunt unless in the hands of a talented writer. Explorers will assert that the sensations attached to the act are hyper-real, an exaggerated form of reality attained by isolation and endeavour beyond the everyday, as with graffiti, the attitude prevails that unless you are active, you cannot understand. It is unnecessarily wrought with contrived ethics in an attempt to legitimize its practice. Its recent published history revolves around Toronto and one individual using the moniker Ninjalicious.[75] His *Infiltration* 'zine, printed between 1996 until his death in 2005, was the definitive guide to UE and gained notoriety and acknowledgement from other fringe activities.[76] Web forums, most notably 28dayslater in the UK, subsequently provided practitioners with space to share, view, compare and exchange information and reports.

UE is essentially adults playing in the city, the small element of risk attached to all but the most extreme ventures perhaps provide sufficient doses of endorphins and adrenalin to satisfy otherwise neutralized existences. That isn't to say it is without worth, merely to acknowledge that an element of the attraction is clearly the urge to challenge convention in a fairly passive manner; there is not really a victim in trespass. Critique of the practice[77] revolves around issues of nostalgia, the aesthetic of ruin,[78] disenchantment and escapism and these are all definitely bound within. Outwardly it would appear as if there is no embedded, politically driven ideology. Perhaps though, this in itself is symptomatic of a neutered consumerist landscape; participants know that they wish to act against the grain, but the homogenized environment of political space is absent of contrast. The notion of image over content is prescient here in a political context, that of the soundbite, and will be discussed in more detail in later chapters. It is, however, worth considering that this practice takes place at the margins, and discernibly within the remnant spaces,[79] of capitalist production, and that it is consumerist models of global reach that have diluted the political landscape to a neutralized centre-right position in the West. The association between physical site and social context can be construed as tangible a response to environment as the areas of the city ceding to modernism were to the Surrealists.

Exploration is one of the cultural acts that define us, whether recorded or unrecorded, conscious or deliberately unconscious, the process of familiarization and the subsequent unrelenting need to supersede and upset familiarity via layer upon layer of new experience is innate. It parallels the ways in which we learn as we grow and reinforces the idea of progress by the mechanism of play. Relevant at this juncture is as much the act of seeing as the act of recording, the identifiable products of this loose history have their place in architecture, and the influence and impositions of these traditions in art and architectural practice will be discussed further in the proceeding chapters. The idea of making a reading of the normal, the everyday, requires that the observer or participant sets aside any preconceived notions of what a thing might be or how it may behave and simply look, with an aim to see. The seemingly repetitive can reveal nuance and individuality and the mundane an opulence to behold. These traditions have found a place in architecture and in the education of architecture in the UK, particularly through the teaching and practice of the Smithsons and onward by Sergison Bates et al.

This particular history of urban exploration is one that is formed not for the acts necessarily contained within, nor their products, it is an attempt to illustrate a genesis of practice and theory that are interrelated in the emergent analysis of the city, and subsequently the urban, through the course of the twentieth century. It can be seen that there is a convergence between the arts and sciences and that the ideas informing each are interchangeable and whilst not consistently overt in the texts of the critics discussed, the thematic ideas of looking at the city with different eyes (whether this examination is analytical or experiential), is valuable in reading and negotiating space in the contemporary environment. It is with this set of ideals that the works of various artists in assorted media may be referenced in the context of urban design. Objects and marks that are within the streets, brands which consume the streets, films about the streets and networks of the city all look at the urban with different sets of eyes and it is through these fresh lenses that a new version of the city can be seen, interpreted and represented.

The following chapters seek to make a critique of the contemporary urban environment, its perception and representation by using a series of terms, which may be seen to imply form or narrative, but are not necessarily within the realm of architecture. These chapters can be seen as independent, but are bound by a contingent narrative that revolves around the ceding of architectural discourse from the 'city' to the 'urban' during the latter part of the twentieth century. It will be argued that the analysis of the city using devices that are not conventional within the architectural canon may actually reveal more about the nature of an accelerated, shifting urbanism, which is principally in opposition to the stasis of architecture.

Chapter 2 will reinforce the idea of the spatially confused city as overrun by a flickering kaleidoscope of imagery that is produced by desires rather than need and that the meta-physical presence of certain pervasive brands further complicates a reading of the city, yet perversely affords context in a generic physical landscape devoid of such. The role and position of brands and their subsequent re-reading and cultural dissolution and hacking will be used to expand ideas about the operability of signs and symbols within the urban landscape.

Chapter 3 seeks to explore the ideas of the unseen elements of our cities. Typically now viewed as ethereal virtual connections it will be illustrated that the network as the organizing grid of modern settlement was founded on the streets themselves and physical infrastructures buried beneath. The subsequent evolution of telecommunication and its apparently exponential expansion can be seen as unnavigable territory. Chapter 3 will use the work of contemporary artists and architects to describe how these territories, both physical and virtual, can provide the context for new descriptions of the city and its form.

Architecture, whilst perhaps engaged with the 'idea' of interstitial space, residual space and non-space, has not outwardly engaged with the social contexts of marginal space in the way that certain contemporary films have chosen to represent these niche environments. The lived experience of the city is almost negligible in the idealized and unoccupied depictions of architecture that surround the discipline and as such Chapter 4 will demonstrate the capacity of audio-visual media as maps of inhabitation that afford a wider discourse on the urban landscape.

Chapter 5 begins to elucidate the ceding of architecture from 'of the city' to 'of the urban' and thus establishes a position wherein artist practitioners in the city can reveal more about the fabric of our urban environment, its composition and condition, than a traditional formal and material architectural discourse is now able to yield. Using case studies and interviews, a history of irreverent and challenging practice will be shown to be complementary to the branded and networked society framed in the preceding chapters.

Chapter 6 builds upon the narratives established within Chapter 5 to demonstrate the operational characteristics of particular interventions in the urban environment and how their context and location is exploitative of the types of space and typologies created by the forces of urbanism. The role of architecture in the order of a sign-object dialectic, within a branded and networked environment, will be argued as one that has simultaneously homogenized by force and polarized by contingency. The introduction of ideas concerning emergence and regulation will be discussed in these terms and in the production of cities.

Endnotes

1   Jefferies, T. and Swanson, N. (1999), *The Landscape Channel*. A BArch Unit at the Manchester School of Architecture.

2   Lynch, K. (1960), *The Image of the City* (Cambridge, MA: The MIT Press) p. 119.

3   Zukin, S. (1991), *Landscapes of Power: From Detroit to Disneyworld* (Berkeley: University of California Press) p. 4.

4   Lynch (1960) pp. 46–48.

5   Polanyi, K. (1957), *The Great Transformation* (Boston: Beacon Press) pp. 178–191.

6   Lefebvre, H. (1991), *The Production of Space* (Oxford: Blackwell) p. 271. Translated by Donald Nicholson Smith from Lefebvre, H. (1974), *La production de l'espace* (Paris: Editions Anthropos).

7   Zukin (1991) p. 7.

8   Ibid. p. 9.

9   Burgin, V. (1996), *In/Different Spaces* (Berkeley: University of California Press) pp. 143–148.

10   Meyerowitz, J. (1985), *No Sense of Place: The Impact of Electronic Media on Social Behaviour* (Oxford: Oxford University Press) pp. 115–125.

11   Tschumi, B. (1996), *Architecture and Disjunction* (Cambridge, MA: The MIT Press) pp. 154–168.

12   Brinckerhoff Jackson, J. (1994), *A Sense of Time, a Sense of Place* (New Haven: Yale University Press) p. 190.

13   See Ingold, T. and Vergunst, J.L. [eds] (2008), *Ways of Walking: Ethnography and Practice on Foot* (Aldershot: Ashgate).

14   Venturi, R., Scott-Brown, D. and Izenour, S. (1972), *Learning from Las Vegas: The Forgotten Symbolism of Architectural Form* (Cambridge, MA: The MIT Press). Venturi and Scott-Brown first defined and used the term 'decorated shed' to describe the commercial vernacular emergent in the desert city of Las Vegas during the post-war years. The city as a pure product of capitally driven development was a precursor to the sprawl and peripheral growth that characterized the latter part of the twentieth century.

15   Ibelings, H. (1998), *Supermodernism. Architecture in the Age of Globalization* (Rotterdam: NAi Publishers). Ibelings describes the emergence of superficiality and neutrality in architecture as having achieved 'special significance'.

16 For an authoritative account of the 'systems revolution' that occurred during this period and the developments that led to it please refer to Hall, P. (1988), *Cities of Tomorrow: An Intellectual History of Urban Planning and Design in the Twentieth Century* (Oxford: Basil Blackwell).

17 Jacobs, J. (1961), *The Death and Life of Great American Cities* (New York: Random House) p. 428.

18 For example, the work of the Centre of Advanced Spatial Analysis at the University College London has developed a number of research projects that engage emerging computational technologies in response to issues related to geography, space, location and the built environment. This approach is discussed further in Batty, M. (2005), *Cities and Complexity* (Cambridge, MA: The MIT Press).

19 Banham, R., Barker, P., Hall, P. and Price, C. (1969), 'Non-Plan: An Experiment in Freedom', *New Society*, 20 March, No. 338, pp. 435-443.

20 Shane, D.G. (2005), *Recombinant Urbanism: Conceptual Modeling in Architecture, Urban Design, and City Theory* (Chichester: John Wiley & Sons Ltd.) p. 31.

21 Banham, R. (1959) 'City as Scrambled Egg', in *Cambridge Opinion*, no. 17.

22 This latter analogy was picked up nearly two decades later by the International Society of City and Regional Planners at their 2001 conference, Young Planners, in which they extended these descriptions to three models of the 'informational city'; *Archi Città, Cine Città* and *Tele Città*.

23 Pope, A. (1996), *Ladders* (New York: Princeton Architectural Press) p. 205.

24 This argument is convincingly presented in 'Chapter 2 – The Complexities of Posturban Space' by Ghent Urban Studies Team (1999), *The Urban Condition: Space, Community, and Self in the Contemporary Metropolis* (Rotterdam: 010 Publishers) pp. 26–45.

25 'Thinking about Maps', in: Kitchin, R., Perkins, C. and Dodge, M. [eds] (2009) *Rethinking Maps: New Frontiers in Cartographic Theory* (Oxford: Routledge) p. 21.

26 Bulmer, M. (1984), *The Chicago School of Sociology: Institutionalization, Diversity, and the Rise of Sociological Research* (Chicago: University of Chicago Press).

27 Davis, M. (1998), *The Ecology of Fear* (New York: Metropolitan Books) p. 363.

28 Virilio, P. (1991), 'The Overexposed City', in *Lost Dimension*. Translated by Daniel Moshenberg (New York: Semiotext(e)), pp. 9–27.

29 Cosgrove, D. (2006), 'Carto-City', in: Abrams, J. and Hall, P. [eds] *Else/where: Mapping New Cartographies of Networks and Territories* (Minneapolis: University of Minnesota Design Institute) p. 157.

30 Harley, J.B. (2001), 'Texts and Contexts in the Interpretation of Early Maps', in: Laxton, P. [ed.] *The New Nature of Maps: Essays in the History of Cartography* (Baltimore and London: Johns Hopkins University Press) p. 35.

31 Corner, J. (1999), 'The Agency of Mapping: Speculation, Critique and Invention', in: Cosgrove, D. [ed.] *Mappings* (London: Reaktion) pp. 213–252.

32 See Wilford, J.N. (2002), 'Chapter Twenty-three: Dynamic Maps: A New Geography', in *The Mapmakers: The Story of the Great Pioneers in Cartography – From Antiquity to the Space Age*. Revised edn (London: Pimlico) pp. 409–425.

33 Abrams, J. and Hall, P. (2006), 'Where/Abouts', in: Abrams, J. and Hall, P. [eds] *Else/where: Mapping New Cartographies of Networks and Territories* (Minneapolis: University of Minnesota Design Institute) p. 12.

34   Allen, S. (2000), 'Mapping the Unmappable: On Notation', in: Allen, S. and Agrest, D., *Practice: Architecture, Technique and Representation* (Amsterdam: G+B Arts International) p. 38.

35   Ibid. p. 40.

36   See MVRDV (1998), *FARMAX. Excursions on Density* (Rotterdam: 010 Publishers); MVRDV (1999), *Metacity/Datatown* (Rotterdam: 010 Publishers); MVRDV (2005), *KM3. Excursions on Capacities* (Barcelona: Actar).

37   De Quincey, T. (1821), *Confessions of an English Opium Eater*, originally published as a series in *London Magazine*, September to October 1821 (New York: Dover Publications Inc.) p. 42.

38   Cohen, P. (2005), 'A New Orientalism? The Anglo-Gothic Imagination in East London', in *Rising East Online* (London: UEL), available from: www.uel.ac.uk/risingeast/ archive02/features/neworientalism.htm [accessed 12 November 2007]

39   Breton quote is cited in Plant, S. (1992), *The Most Radical Gesture: The Situationist International in a Postmodern Age* (London: Routledge) p. 59. Nadeau, M. (1965), *The History of Surrealism* (London: Macmillan) pp. 106–107.

40   Plant (1992) p. 59.

41   Read, G. (2003), *Louis Aragon's Armoire.* Paper delivered at the *Intersense Symposium on Synæsthesia as Madness and Method,* Penn State University, 22–24 October 2003. Available from: http://art3idea.psu.edu/synesthesia/papers/grayread2.html [accessed 8 October 2009].

42   Benjamin, W. (ed. Rolf Tiedemann, trans. Howard Eiland and Kevin McLaughlin) (2000), *The Arcades Project* (New York: Belknap Press).

43   Benjamin, W. (1973), *Charles Baudelaire: A Lyric Poet in the Era of High Capitalism.* Translated by Harry Zohn (London: New Left Books). This reference only occurs as a footnote to Benjamin's text, but has been widely adopted as the definitive descriptive passage for the flâneur. It is unusual that a footnote buried in this piece has become one of the most often cited of Benjamin's narratives. One could speculate that it is the incredibly visceral image of a flamboyant gent with the turtle on the lead that has perpetuated this citation.

44   Charles-Marie-Georges Huysmans (1848–1907) was a French novelist who published his works as Joris-Karl Huysmans.

45   Huysmans, J.-K. (1884), *À Rebours.* Translated by R. Baldick as *Against Nature* (London: Penguin Classics, 1956, revised edn) pp. 40–41.

46   From: www.artandpopularculture.com/What_is_Surrealism%3F [accessed 21 April 2010]. *Qu'est-ce que le surréalisme?* is a lecture by André Breton given in Brussels on 12 May or 1 June 1934 at a public meeting organized by the Belgian Surrealists at the Musée des Beaux-Arts in Brussels, and issued as a pamphlet immediately afterwards by René Henriquez. At least one edition has Magritte's *Le Viol* as cover art. It includes a list of those who Breton considered as Surrealists before the birth of the movement.

47   Hart, J. (2004), 'A New Way of Walking', in *Utne Reader*, July/August 2004, p. 2. Article and interview with Christina Ray, convenor of *Conflux* psychogeographic festival in New York. Available from: www.utne.com/2004-07-01/a-new-way-of-walking. aspx?page=2 [accessed 27 October 2009].

48 Chtcheglov wrote *Formulary* under the pseudonym Gilles Ivain in 1953 and circulated it as a report, not published until June 1958 in the first edition of the journal *Internationale Situationniste*. The text was appended to in its first full publication and translations to English are from a number of sources.

49 Breton, A. (1933), 'Sur certaines possibilités d'embellissement irrationnel d'une ville', in *Le surréalisme au service de la révolution*, no. 6, May 1933, Paris, p. 18, cited in Marcus, G. (1989) *Lipstick Traces: A Secret History of the Twentieth Century* (London: Secker and Warburg) p. 410.

50 Anon. (1955), '*Projet d'embellissements rationnels de la ville de Paris*', in *Potlatch*, no. 23, Paris, October 1955 and in Marcus (1989) pp. 410–411.

51 *Situationist International Online*. Available from: www.cddc.vt.edu/sionline/chron ology/1957.html [accessed 21 April 2010]. 'February 2 to 26: First Exhibition of Psychogeography, presented by the International Movement for an Imaginist Bauhaus, the Lettrist International and the London Psychogeographical Committee at Taptoe Gallery in Brussels. The catalogue lists paintings and ceramics by G.-E. Debord, Asger Jorn, Yves Klein, Ralph Rumney, Michèle Bernstein, Mohamed Dahou and a "mad psychogeographer", but only Jorn, Klein and Rumney participate.'

52 The *Telegraph* obituary cites an elaborate ill-fated series of events as having impacted upon Rumney's submission deadline, whilst the *Guardian* claims he was wrongly accused of having not completed the project. The piece concerns the pursuit of Alan Ansen around the streets of Venice and recording his mood and the subsequent representation of the footage as a montage comic strip. Imrie, M. 'Ralph Rumney', *Guardian*, 8 March 2002. Available from: www.guardian.co.uk/news/2002/mar/08/ guardianobituaries.arts1 [accessed 29 December 2009]; 'Ralph Rumney', *Telegraph*, 9 March 2002. Available from: www.telegraph.co.uk/news/obituaries/1387176/Ralph-Rumney.html [accessed 29 December 2009].

53 Debord, G. (1955), *Introduction to a Critique of Urban Geography*. Originally published in French as *Introduction à une critique de la géographie urbaine* in Belgian journal, *Les Lèvres Nues*, no.6, September 1955. Translation available in Knabb, K. (2006), *Situationist International Anthology*. Revised and expanded edn (Berkeley: Bureau of Public Secrets). Also available from: www.bopsecrets.org/SI/urbgeog.htm [accessed 21 April 2010].

54 Ibid.

55 Solnit, R. (2000), *Wanderlust: A History of Walking* (London: Penguin Books) p. 213.

56 *Henri Lefebvre on the Situationist International*. Interview conducted and translated 1983 by Kristin Ross. Printed in *October 79*, Winter 1997.

57 Ibid.

58 Pinder, D. (1996), 'Subverting Cartography: The Situationists and Maps of the City', *Environment and Planning A*, 28(3), pp. 405–427.

59 McDonough, T. (1996), 'The Derive and Situationist Paris', in: Andreotti, L. and Costa, X. [eds] *Situationists. Art, Politics, Urbanism* (Barcelona: Actar) p. 57.

60 Hussey, A. and Edwards, P. (1999–2001), *Abolish Everything! A Correspondence*. A series of letters published concerning the accuracy of Hussey's review of Sadler's *The Situationist City*, Hussey and Edwards manage to agree that the psychogeographic wanderings and the idea of 'unitary urbanism' were both instrumental in the creation

of notions concerning the Society of the Spectacle. Available from: www.users.zetnet. co.uk/amroth/scritti/debord6.htm [accessed 12 December 2009].

61   *Henri Lefebvre on the Situationist International.* Interview conducted and translated 1983 by Kristin Ross. Printed in *October 79*, Winter 1997.

62   Plant (1992) p. 121.

63   Lyotard, J.-F. (1973), *Dérives à Partir de Marx et Freud* (Paris: Union Générale d'Editions). The English translation appears as 'Adrift', in Lyotard, J.-F. (1984), *Driftworks* (ed. Roger McKeon) (New York: Semiotext(e)) p. 13.

64   Sennett, R. (1994), *Flesh and Stone: The Body and the City in Western Civilization* (London: Faber & Faber).

65   Cooper, M. (2008), *Tag Town* (Arsta, Sweden: Dokument Forlag + Distribution). For the best account of early tagging practice, Martha Cooper's 2008 book, *Tag Town*, provides as accurate a record as any written to date.

66   Gane, M. (trans.) (1993), *Symbolic Exchange and Death* (London: Sage) p. 76. From Baudrillard, J. (1976) *L'échange symbolique et la mort* (Paris: Gallimard).

67   Ibid.

68   Witten, A. and White, M. (2001), *Dondi White: Style Master General, The Life of Graffiti Artist Dondi White* (New York: Regan Books) p. 19.

69   A term used in hip-hop culture to refer to any life circumstance that involves negotiation; business.

70   These ideas will be discussed in more detail in Chapter 5.

71   Bailly, J.-C. (1986), 'Traces', introduction to *Paris Graffiti*, photographs by Joerg Huber (New York: Thames and Hudson) pp. 8–9. This book is not about graffiti inspired by hip-hop culture, more the precedent markings and inscriptions found across Paris. This short introduction effectively assumes the position of the viewer as a participant. Jean-Christophe Bailly is a contemporary French theorist who now teaches the History of Landscape at the National School.

72   Abarca, J. (2008), *Urbanario* blog is the home for writings on art in the environment by Javier Abarca, he was the first author to use the term 'post-graffiti' to refer to work that is of the street, but not necessarily within the established conventions of graffiti. It does not automatically imply a chronological lineage, as much of the work to which he refers occurred as parallel practice to the evolution of graffiti. See www.urbanario.es.

73   Powers, S. (2009), Interview conducted by the authors by e-mail. 15 December 2009.

74   http://onewaystreet.typepad.com/one_way_street/walter_benjamin/index.html [accessed 21 October 2007].

75   'Jeff (Ninjalicious) passed away on Tuesday, August 23, 2005 at age 31, he had been battling a failing liver and an incurable cancer. In his early twenties he spent long periods of time in the hospital battling various diseases. Often bored, he and his IV pole would go exploring the hospital, investigating the basement, peeking behind doors, looking for interesting rooms and equipment. It was here his love for the under explored side of buildings developed, and upon returning to health he created Infiltration – the zine about going places you're not supposed to go. Ninjalicious had a strong code of ethics which he promoted, including no stealing or vandalizing while exploring. In life Jeff shunned fame, and would often turn down media requests in order to prevent over-exposure to his favourite hobby. When he did do interviews, it was to promote a more

societal acceptance of urban exploration.' Edited extract from obituary online at http://torontoist.com/2005/08/death_of_a_ninj.php [accesssed 23 October 2007].

76 Respected UK graffiti magazine, *Hold no Hostage*, asserted to contain '98.8% graf' featured *Infiltration* in 1998, providing contact details for mail order subscriptions.

77 See Edensor, T. (2005), *Industrial Ruins: Space, Aesthetic and Materiality* (Oxford and New York: Berg).

78 See Trigg, D. (2006), *The Aesthetics of Decay: Nothingness, Nostalgia and the Absence of Reason* (Oxford: Peter Lang).

79 Typical sites for exploration are post-industrial, institutional and infrastructural, the types of dystopian spaces seen in science fiction films such as *Blade Runner* and *Robocop*.

2

Brand, Image and Identity

This chapter will examine the role of 'brand' in an attempt to understand how the nature of a consumptive society has impacted upon our urban experiences and narratives. The spatial orders of the contemporary city and their illegibility, defined in Chapter 1, are negotiated by brand led identities in an effort to supersede one another and establish their own clarity and networks. To begin to understand that which is defined as 'brand' in a modern urban context it is essential that the value of the 'image' and 'sign' are explored from both a historical and contemporary perspective. It will be shown how the beginnings of a Western visual culture transformed our perception of self and of environment, and how rapidly the sense of sight or vision found its primary role in modernity. The traditional definitions of aesthetic and the relationship of aesthetic to the exploded cultural catalogue of abstraction, will identify the role of architecture in this order, as an art that was both hindered and slightly contradictory during the early part of the twentieth century. The notion of aesthetic, when considered now, without architectural order or classical geometry, is so subjective that it is almost obsolete; Klingmann (2007) refers to this as the shift from the 'functional' to the 'experiential'. The latter part of this chapter will illustrate the ways in which image, as an entity, now has a greater cultural impact than aesthetic; a higher value. Image value is distinctly a condition of modernity. The value of the image, the power of the image and the proliferation of the image, as proposed by Baudrillard and Lefebvre,[1] exist within a context of placeless and spatially confused urbanism. Image can be seen to have supplanted reality; the sheer volume of visual media bears a direct comparison with globalized economic networks. The 'predatory colonisation of open space'[2] demanded by a global market is a metaphor for the all consuming sprawl of the image. Image value is sign value is brand value.

The notion of brand has become so pernicious that it is present as a discourse in even the smallest of enterprises, which may only require advertising as opposed to brand development. Brand competes with brand and thus the consumptive nature of the sign, the predominant physical manifestation of brand, is relentlessly applied across our urban landscape. This self-fed, self-replicating industry of proclamation demands a steady increase in scale and luminosity, until close to a perceived saturation. At this point, tactical and strategic devices are employed to usurp, attract and impose their 'unique selling point' in more 'subtle' or 'clever' ways. It is useless to argue with the order of this imposition on our landscape and essential to engage with formal devices that are fundamentally outside of the realm of an urban master plan and, with few exceptions, conventionally viewed in architectural expression as an 'application', carrying all the negative connotations of the term.

The use of the term 'brand' has become prevalent, its permeation, from a consumer context, simply acting as an indicator of where to make a purchase, into a socio-spatial domain, that can define, streets, districts and cities, is one indicator that Western cities have ultimately arrived at a consumptive juncture. The term is applied without being hindered by scale; a city may have a brand or be branded as successfully as a neighbourhood, a shop or a consumable object. The notion of brand that is critical here rests within an ostensibly objectified condition, that of the 'sign', though it is acknowledged that branding does not always assume physical properties. Branding is the antithesis to many of the events or practice described in the proceeding chapters. Whereas many of the examples to come are responsive to the city, brand is part of the city's super-organism and the strength of a brand can allow subtle gestures to imply its presence. In this context branding now serves as the identifier, as the cursor, or as Kevin Lynch would phrase it, the 'landmark'. It is characteristic of the age that from the 'building, sign, store or mountain'[3] which were the objects to which Lynch ascribed the descriptor 'landmark', that the 'sign' and 'store' should homogenize to become the definitive urban 'landmark'; 'It is two doors down from Starbucks'. The element of landmark that Lynch excluded from his definition was that of repetition. Landmarks, to Lynch, were unique, brands necessitate repetitive episodes for their message. However, the repeat application of a motif, moniker or branded identity[4] can be seen to form a network, it is this powerful characteristic that makes it impossible to exclude the notion of brand from any urban discourse concerning place, space, navigation and narrative.

As a means of demonstrating the interrelationship of these texts it will be shown that an overt, networked object may operate as a latent 'landmark'. Critical to understanding the role of art in the environment, which will be discussed in the following chapters, the built history of brand (brand as object) and the recognition of the value of brand in the context of urban navigation and as a global construct (brand as network) will also be explored. By using a case study history of brand and its development in relationship to architectural theory, the ideas of clarity, non-physical brand and proliferation will be discussed with regard to their impact on urban form and urban experience, through active and reactive processes.

Visual Culture, the Consumption of Form

It is the Renaissance period that is widely understood as the beginning of modernity, when the perception of self began to change, as highlighted by both historians and art theorists. Sennett[5] uses the writings of nineteenth-century historian Jacob Burckhardt to describe the Renaissance idea of living in the present tense:

> *Man was conscious of himself only as a member of a race, people party, family or corporation – only through some general category. In Italy this veil first melted into air; an objective treatment and consideration of the State and of all things of this world became possible. The subjective side at the same*

time asserted itself with corresponding emphasis; man became a spiritual
individual and recognised himself as such.[6]

Burgin (1996) illustrates the birth of visual 'culture' from a Western perspective;
he observes the rapid move from the Renaissance revival of Vitruvian humanist
geometry to the values of visual perception that proceeds.[7] He quotes Francoise
Choay's article from the *Nouvelle revue de psychanalyse*,[8] which describes the
way in which Vitruvian doctrine was written into the works of Alberti and
other architectural theorists of the Italian Renaissance. Humanist authorities
wrote that men first derived their unit of measurement from hands, arms and
feet. Renaissance descriptions and drawings of anthropomorphic cities make
it apparent that the human body was perceived as the origin of the entire built
environment. Alberti in his text on painting, *De pictura*, provides the first written
description of the representational technique of perspective, the perspective grid
based on the common unit of measurement, the *braccio*, equivalent to one-third
the height of a standing man. Perspective allowed the interface of corporeal space
and architectural space, with the erect male body at its origin.[9] This quickly ceded
its place to what Lefebvre describes as 'the spiriting away or scotomization of the
body',[10] the disembodied, metonymic representative, the eye.

The beginnings of modernity saw the convergence of previously disassociated
geometric and mathematical practices and their domination of many forms of
visual representation, from painting to architecture. The same order was applied
to navigational charts, maps and city plans in an attempt to enhance their
instrumentality.

In conformity to the exigencies of an expansive capitalist mode of production,
the image of the convergence of parallel lines toward a vanishing point
on the horizon became the very figure of European global economic and
political ambition. The optical-geometric device was synonymous with the
advancing ideology of colonialist capitalism and governed Western European
representations for three centuries.[11]

In this way, image and form closely mimicked the ideology of the time and were as
legible as the class-driven society they served.

As a form of representation, the panoptical-instrumental space was blown apart
at the start of the twentieth century, which witnessed the birth of analytical cubism
and twelve-tone scale jazz, both alternate representations of space within their genre.
Lefebvre proposes that the existing orders of Euclidean space and perspectivist
space did not vanish from cultural knowledge or educational techniques, but were
part of a layer of spatial representation that became 'porous' and allowed the new
layer to show through.[12] This explosion of space and form in music, poetry and the
arts was not generally mirrored in architectural production, the modern movement
had its confluence with the machine age and the standardization idiom swept
abstraction in architecture under the carpet, only for it to emerge in the late 1980s
as Deconstructivism.

Burgin uses the words of Mao Tse-Tung when he states that 'the relationship between the existing instrumental space of political modernity and the emergent space of aesthetic modernism was one of "non-antagonistic" contradiction.' The term *'aesthetic modernism'* may seem contrary to the notion of modernism as a functional expression of technology and material. In respect of this it is useful to examine Mies van der Rohe's Pavilion, 1929. The pavilion was built solely for the signature of the King of Spain in a golden book, to commemorate Germany's participation in the Barcelona Exposition and its return to international good standing, a decade after the First World War. There was no programme, and due to the significance of the event, no budget restrictions;[13] Mies was commissioned to create a pure architectural abstraction.[14] The building, free of function, was gifted by Mies its archetypal inhabitant, and like the architects of the great cathedrals of Europe, Mies engineered a sequential journey, at the epicentre of which was the humanistic Kolbe sculpture (see Figure 2.1). The sculpture, a last minute replacement for a Lehmbruck, could equally have been any humanoid figure, this is testament to the way in which Mies had set the stage, but is also revealing, in that a 'stage' or 'frame' was ultimately what he had built.

Marshall McLuhan and Quentin Fiore in their 1967 book *The Medium is the Massage*[15] express the view that societies have always been shaped more by the nature of the media by which men communicate than by the content of the communication.[16] Applied to the Pavilion, this view can further the understanding of the term *'aesthetic modernism'*. The nature of the media (material) in the pavilion is more overtly explicit of its contrast to the typically dense brick or stone buildings that preceded it, than any recognition of the wilful application of expensive cladding materials or ambiguous spaces. Thus, the aesthetic of modernism was camouflaged behind the expression of the material as synonymous with the factory age, smooth and machined; Venturi describes the Pavilion as a monumental 'duck'.[17] The widely held assertion amongst early modern architects that 'form follows function' and 'less is more' can thus be challenged and the term *aesthetic modernism* seen to expose the paradoxes within the production of modernist buildings considered as 'pure' reflections of their functional requirements. The notion of ornament as crime *became* an aesthetic and an escape from decoration became a stylized and aestheticized commodity before 1930.

Aesthetic though, as a term and a definable quality, has expanded as much as the notion of space. No longer bound by quantifiable rules or order, as within classicism and all of its idioms, and used to define landscapes, narratives and systems, aesthetic may be subject to shifting definitions from uncontrolled external forces driven by consumption. Towards the end of the twentieth century Baudrillard describes his reading of aesthetic. He argues that the terms beauty and aesthetic have become confused, aesthetic has overridden beauty in the same way that the semiological order has succeeded the symbolic order. Whilst it is clearly accepted that aesthetic can be a subjective emotional state, the theory of aesthetics, once concerned with the forms of beauty, has become the theory of a generalized compatibility of signs, of their internal coherence and of their syntax. 'Aesthetic value connotes the internal functionality of an ensemble, it qualifies the

Figure 2.1 Kolbe sculpture at the midst of Mies' sequential journey around the pavilion
Source: Author's own, 2002.

(eventually mobile) equilibrium of a system of signs. It simply communicates the fact that its elements *communicate* amongst themselves according to the economy of the model with maximal integration and minimal loss of information'.[18] The text draws contemporary aesthetics into the realm of fashion, and as such, the market economy, wherein lies a cyclical capitalist driven need for new product. The tone of Baudrillard's writing in respect of this definition of aesthetic is one of negativity; that aesthetic should be so inconsequential as to be influenced by fashion seems to irritate the author. The use of the term aesthetic as a descriptive mechanism with which to define visual experience is perhaps now more obsolete than confused, only those high arts that retain an historical order, classical ballet for example, find a practical application of aesthetic. Aesthetic value has been superseded by sign value, the meaning, the contrast, the distinctiveness, are all qualities that are used to measure contemporary visual culture – an image culture.

The power of the image as a force of modernity has only been critically acknowledged in the last 50 years. Where Baudelaire, Benjamin and their contemporaries may have predicted the extent to which we would experience image as part of a modern society, they did not care to speculate on the results. The power and nature of image first came under critical scrutiny in the 1960s when academics and professionals began to consider the codes of new media and advertising. It is unsurprising that an expanding and colourful visual media should be the first to provoke analysis of its meaning, particularly when the image is a component of a proactive process designed to influence behaviour. Architecture was again chasing the critical leanings of other arts. Following McLuhan's seminal work concerning the power of the image in the field of design,[19] in *Learning from Las Vegas*, Venturi began to examine the association between image and form in architecture, but more often than not, his analysis tends towards maintaining a clear distinction between that which is sign and that which is building. The now immortalized 'Long Island Duckling' (see Figure 2.2) from Peter Blake's *God's Own Junkyard*,[20] is the extreme symbolic realization of the building as sign. Within his text Venturi fails to commit to a true acceptance that this duck is the ultimate resolution of strip architecture, as if he feels he has pushed the limits of critical acceptance far enough, he neatly sidelines the further analysis of the duck by questioning its modern relevance. The fact that this roadside sculpture has both embodied and amplified all the

Figure 2.2 *Long Island Duckling,* **as immortalized by Peter Blake**
Originally built in 1931 by duck farmer Martin Maurer in nearby Riverhead, and used as a shop to sell ducks and duck eggs. It was added to the US National Register of Historic Places in 1997.
Source: © Robert F. Walter Jr., 2009.

components that remain distinctly separate in the 'decorated shed', that it *is* the conclusion, is not acknowledged. The text, despite its unique and experimental nature, is critically confined by the era and concerned with using the duck and the shed as a mechanism for analysis. Venturi uses terms that almost make the leap; 'the purest decorated shed'[21] is a contradiction, the decorated shed only reaches architectural purity when the decoration is the shed; the duck. It is easy to understand why Venturi fails to read the duck in this way; his concern is with not just image or sign, but with process and linear hierarchy. The comic, autonomous, simplicity of the duck and its completely anti-contextual expression is at odds with even Venturi's analysis, which contextualizes by referring form to the influence of the motorcar and by exploring elements common to the strip that may be used as metaphors to bring historical references into the work. Venturi accepts the point at which the sign *becomes* the building, when the form of the Golden Nugget Casino is completely overwhelmed by the adornment, the next evolutionary step in his schematic should be when the sign *is* the building. It is not a case of shed *versus* duck, but shed *becomes* duck. This order is eventually acknowledged by Venturi in his 1996 publication, *Iconography and Electronics upon a Generic Architecture*, under the sub-heading *From Las Vegas to Las Vegas*, where he simply states 'from: the decorated shed to the duck'.[22]

Subsequently architecture has witnessed a rapid blurring of these typological definitions due to a combination of ingenuity and advancing material technology, there are many more 'ducks' in existence. Entire structures that fulfil their function as shop, stadium, swimming pool are now performing a dual task, as a sign (see Figure 2.3). The age of façadism is consigned to dazzling memorial, where the luminescent appendages are now as superficial to the order of Las Vegas as the gloss, washed over the entire city in the desert. Klingmann[23] describes the 'inverted shed' and the 'inverted duck' and their emergence and unification as a single hybridized entity, this is the confluence of architecture, advertising and technology in pursuit of experience and often governed by brand. Where the American industrial model led the twentieth-century commercial vernacular, the global power and presence of the image is adding a new layer to the process, the *advertising* vernacular. The term 'layer' is here applied because the advertising vernacular does not ignore the commercial, indeed the two are obviously bound, but where the commercial traditionally pursued efficiency and rapid turnover, the advertising vernacular operates at a polarized luxury position. The irony here is that the brands commissioning buildings as adverts, also maintain a commercial position. This is truly both the arrival of architecture as advertisement and the reinforcement of architecture as collectable commodity.

Brand and identity are as much architectural forces as they are economic. Brand was not new or unique to the late twentieth century, when its presence warranted discourse within the architectural community, though the vivid global presence of a small number of companies was a distinctively new condition. The Russian Constructivists and members of the Bauhaus were content to positively engage with the realm of advertising, building and technology; the potential presented

Figure 2.3 Allianz Arena, Munich, Herzog and De Meuron, 2005
The ETFE-foil cushions are internally illuminated by LEDs to allow the entire stadium to assume the signifying colour of the teams that play there.
Source: Author's own, 2006.

therein was as much of an opportunity to design, as a limit on such. The distinction between high-art and popular culture that would impose implied critical boundaries, albeit eventually exploited by the Pop artists, was not of concern to these early protagonists. The mechanization of production was not yet sufficiently virulent to begin to restrict designers, more, designers were viewed as providing solutions or indeed seeking opportunity in developing material technology and production techniques. The fantasy far outweighed the reality and the dizzying cocktail of coloured electric light, recorded and projected sound and image and the possibilities contained therein proved to be as seductive to the avant-garde as the realization was to the populous. Of particular note in this field and of this era is the speculative work of Herbert Bayer (see Figure 2.4) and the seminal designs for Leningrad Pravda by the Vesnins (see Figure 2.5), both of which proposed a multimedia catalogue of sound and light scaled as a billboard might be, but embedded within the fabric of the building, the branded building as a sign.

A student of the Bauhaus, Bayer clearly adopted the modernist style and, like J.J.P. Oud, was influenced by the city grids of Mondrian. Attached to this was a yearning for future technologies to be applied and enhance the experiential characteristics of his designs. Although not exclusively graphically orientated, there is a level of graphic coherence amongst a certain portion of his work that

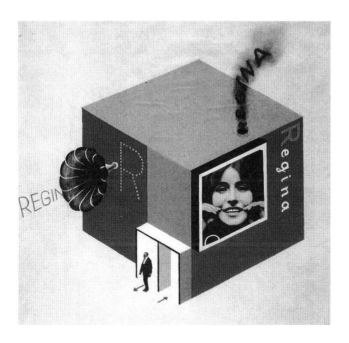

Figure 2.4 Design for multimedia kiosk for fictional brand of toothpaste, 'Regina' by Herbert Bayer, 1924
Source: © DACS.

serves to celebrate the value of visual communication. His project for an exhibition pavilion for a toothpaste manufacturer included rear projected film, flashing electric sign, loudspeaker and letters that were formed by smoke. The integrity of this particular project as a symbol or sign is severely challenged, when the all-singing, all-dancing components are discounted it simply becomes an un-'*decorated shed*'. The tram stop on the other hand has the potential to be a successful signifier today. The juxtaposition of scales and colours provide clear annunciation of the event, this coupled with a dual functionality and the availability of commercially exploitable surface would undoubtedly stand in its favour as an economically viable product. The compositional device that Bayer uses to generate his form would attain metamorphic qualities on approach from different directions,[24] thus enabling the structure to be both distinctive and distinguishable, yet discernibly sculptural in its undoubtedly urban context.

If not a clear intention in the design of the tram stop, Bayer's interest in visual perception is clearly demonstrated in his design for the 'Deutscher Werkbund' exhibition in Paris of 1930. The exhibition directed by Walter Gropius in collaboration with Marcel Breuer and Moholy-Nagy, used photo panels suspended on wires at various angles. In his 1967 book on his work, Bayer recognizes the role of image in the dissolution of form. 'The traditional three-dimensional "room" is dissolved by detaching the display from the static wall surface and creating

Figure 2.5 Design for Pravda Soviet newspaper by Leonid, Viktor and Aleksandr Vesnin, 1924
Source: Author's own, 2008.

new relationships through divisions, angles and directions'[25] (see Figure 2.6). The diagram from the exhibition catalogue clearly omits the 'room' from the image, this introduces the suspended planes as the main structural element and, as an image, is not unlike developmental sketches by Zaha Hadid or Steven Holl. The intrigue that Bayer held for sensual perception combined with the graphically orientated representation of his devices produced projects and aspirations that were engaging with urban issues that are now contemporary, and concerned with experiential space over form.

The Depression of the 1930s and the outbreak of the Second World War in 1939 signalled a halt in style in many ways, particularly in Europe. The art-deco period was brought to a glorious halt and the 1940s are known for their utilitarian and functional design solutions. In Britain, the post-war recovery saw buildings of the late 1940s and early 1950s displaying minor deco flourishes in architectural detailing, albeit pared down versions. Advertising and branding

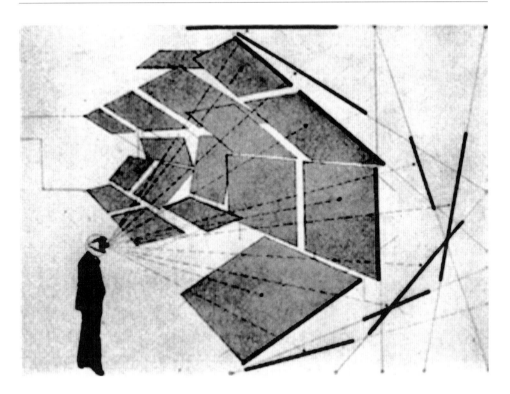

Figure 2.6 Design for the 'Deutscher Werkbund' exhibition in Paris of 1930, Herbert Bayer
Source: © DACS.

took a back seat as the economy stuttered to even advance style, the language of brand identity grew in the nationalized industries of the UK and in the burgeoning multi-nationals of computing and oil in the United States. This was, perceptibly, a golden age of branding and design acting in tandem, when the value of design was truly celebrated in the context of advertising, when brand was still identity, and identity mattered. From global corporations to municipal departments, the development of new, but legible and concise, fonts and logos, throughout the post-war era, was remarkable. The timely and fortuitous collision of mass production and the advanced art of typography, just prior to the advent of the computer as a design tool, saw the mass implementation of quality fonts with perfect kerning and character spacing. It was this early work that laid the visual foundations upon which many brands were to ultimately found their cognitive presence.

The work of Jock Kinneir and Margaret Calvert for the Department of Transport's (DoT) Anderson and Worboys committees is perhaps exemplar of the quality of output during this period. Their now ubiquitous 'Transport' font was developed for the rapidly expanding British motorway network from a German sans serif font, the ironically named, *Aksidenz Grotesk*.[26] The demand for legibility imposed by the

Figure 2.7 M60 motorway sign
Source: Author's own, 1999.

anticipated speed of travel meant that the engineer-specified, uppercase, directional signs of the pre-war era would not suffice. Kinneir and Calvert developed a system based on clarity and the geometries of the letters, it was the spacing between the characters that ultimately determined the size of the sign, the content driving the form. The signs were tested in London before being installed along the country's first motorway, the Preston bypass (M6) in 1958, generally hailed as a success, this initial foray into traffic applications led ultimately to the pair being commissioned for the wider development of an integrated national highway signage scheme.[27] The systematic and coded approach that seems so familiar, almost unquestionable, in its expression and application, was at once both pioneering and classical; it remains virtually unchanged to this day (see Figure 2.7). This type of visual communication emerged as a response to speed and shifting spatial envelopes and experience, that it was concomitant with post-war production meant that its conclusion would be a translation to commodity. This is manifest typologically as two formal devices that may be applied to building or sign alike; the *silhouette*, the icon and the *billboard*, the sign.

Whilst sign is not the embodiment of most brands, the sign was the most common method of physical communication in a commercial context, whereas livery had perhaps been the preserve of identifiably 'national' organizations. As companies and corporations became global in their presence, the convention of inscribing buildings, vehicles and anything else associated with the brand was increasingly commonplace, yet still, the retention of designers of repute and of testifiable calibre was recognized for the qualitative associated value. In a relationship that spanned over a decade, Eliot Noyes' work for petroleum giant Mobil anticipated the design of everything, from forecourt to fleet, all governed by a comprehensive design manual. It is this scale and depth of commercial visual communication practice that is akin to the national programmes undertaken and executed earlier in Britain. Noyes had worked in the office of émigré Walter Gropius, immediately following his graduation, and the impact of a pseudo-Bauhaus education and the intrinsic attitude towards the holistic nature of design practice and the German tradition of *Gesamtkunstwerk* was evident in his practice. Paul Rand for IBM and Dieter Rams at Braun can perhaps be seen to have similar, if not total, impact on the brands for whom they designed. The brand though, if truly successful, becomes bigger than the designer and is governed by rules established and so immutable that they are applied unquestioningly and thus demonstrate their conscious acceptance. The growth of image value and sign value over formal value as the true emergence of visual branding collided with production and asserted the strength of the image. In architecture, post-modernism and its formal appendages are exemplar as the aesthetic resolution of consumption; the decorated boxes of modernity.

Brand Value

The modern recognition of brand and the strength and malleability contained therein was not truly apparent until the defining moment in 1988 when Phillip Morris paid $12.6 million for Kraft; six times the value of the company. Wall Street was of course aware of the value that a company name gathers above and beyond its controlling assets during its time trading. This purchase, however, put a monetary value on something that was previously abstract and unquantifiable, the brand name.[28] It was 'Marlboro Friday' that was responsible for the over-hyped 'death of the brand'. A surprise 20 per cent cut in the price of Morris-owned Marlboro cigarettes, previously regarded as the strongest brand in American history, led to a crash in the share price of both Marlboro and subsequently a host of other brand-led companies in April 1993.[29] What the stock-market analysts had failed to recognize was that this was truly the birth of the brand. Waiting in the sidelines were Nike, Tommy Hilfiger, Disney and the Body Shop, all with a new idea of the brand. The product-led brand was not the new industry these companies had in mind, these were not manufacturers, 'the ostensible product was mere filler for the real production, the brand'.[30] Branding was integrated into the entire working practice of these companies and when this crash sent out waves of after-shocks, these particular firms were barely unbalanced. The resultant fallout of this crash made explicit the two primary marketing and consumerism events of the 1990s, left standing strong were the large-scale commodity providers (Wal-Mart et al.) and the lifestyle companies (Nike et al.). Image manipulation, control, resampling and strategic deployment are all governing tactics adopted by advertisers in the marketing of product, but the most tuned in of agencies realize that presence alone is not enough to sell your wares.

> We live in twenty-four hour market world where less and less terrain remains unregulated. Less terrain falls outside of the regime of the logo and its image. Today, events, styles, cultures, technologies, memes – as well as rumours, scares and insults – pass through and are incorporated into the global image economy, reverberating with and distorting one another, all with the capacity to produce – and to erase – wealth, value and meaning.[31]

Bruce Mau describes a preliminary inventory of the territory of his practice's work in his 2000 book *Lifestyle*. In defining this territory, he demonstrates why the image is so valuable and draws together a broad canvas of event that often has a modern critical reference to reinforce his definition. His introduction proposes a society where image is embedded to an almost oppressive state, the influence of image, no longer a matter of choice. Victor Burgin[32] alludes to the same condition, his conclusion mirrors the category defined by Mau as *Camouflage Industries* which proposes image as more than simply a two-dimensional proposition but as a projected version of reality; the alteration of appearances, the value of the soundbite over the extended political debate, the shifting of the debate from one of content to form; not what she said but how she said it. The end of the week summary of political wrangling in the run-up to an election, concerned with the comparative success of the execution of respective parties' media interfa[r]ces, not policy or manifesto.

> From a world in which images were once limited in number, circumscribed in meaning, and contemplated at length, we have today arrived at a society inundated with images consumed 'on the fly'. Images from magazines, newspapers, snapshots, videos, films, broadcast and cable television and so on. The image as an object of contemplation has been blasted into so many synechdochic representatives: 'bites' and 'clips'. The fragmented universe of images today is the expanding consequence of an explosion that took place at the inception of metropolitan modernity, when Baudelaire characterised the inhabitant of the newly emerged metropolis as 'a kaleidoscope equipped with consciousness'.[33]

The inundation of space with image invests qualities to the two-dimensional surface as the enunciator for the image. Mau uses the term *surfaces of inscription* to define this ascription of value. He describes the value of the surface, and that is every imaginable surface, as a potential space for the global imaging economy. He highlights the massive scalar range of the surface as a communicative interface, and the imperative nature of inscribable surfaces. The image of a logo-printed raw egg from McLuhan and Fiore's *The Medium is the Massage*, which at the time was a theoretical project, is compared with the actual contemporary printing of bananas.

The extremes of scale at the start of the twenty-first century in the context of image and logo have reached the reductive level of atomic engineering: IBM have managed to move atoms with a tungsten electron microscope to spell out the initials of their company.[34] At the opposite end of the scale buildings and landscapes are currently the highest form of billboard, but are used in two distinct forms of advertising: the corporate, clinical digital imaging of Wieden and Kennedy[35] against the terrorist tactics of Cunning Communications who famously projected an image of a naked Gail Porter onto the Houses of Parliament for *FHM* magazine in 1999.

In respect of consumption and the consumptive nature of the image, Baudrillard may push his analyses to the extreme, rendering them more a representation than a reality, however, his use of sign value, above traditional measures such as use-value, to define and understand a commodity-based culture provides a perspective that, whilst acknowledged, has not been widely drawn into the contemporary critique of the banal, the capitalist and the resampled. Neil Leach broadly compresses Baudrillard's views of modernity as 'a world saturated by images and communication … Culture is now dominated by simulation. Objects and discourses no longer have any firm referent or grounding. Instead the real has been bypassed, the image has supplanted reality', inducing what Baudrillard has termed a condition of hyper-reality, a world of 'self-referential signs'.[36] In this wide-ranging definition of Baudrillard's philosophy, Leach actually touches on several distinctly identifiable mechanisms or conditions that qualify for reiteration, not least for the presence of similarities to those defined by Mau in 2000,[37] but also because it is these characteristics of visual culture that are inescapably embedded within the market and cannot be hindered by critical history, thus providing a true reflection of the value of the image. If we accept the consumption of form by image and sign value over use-value then the statements below are critical to a contemporary architectural agenda.

- The culture of the post(super)modern state is the image culture.
- The image culture, indeed *culture*, is a resampling culture, albeit accelerated to nano-second reproduction.
- The concept of '*contextual-less*' is a reality.
- Perception is experienced based and to control the visual experience is to lead perception (the prolific becomes the identifiable).

One of the reactions to the demand for images to be reproduced, prior to the advent of online resources, was the stock image bank.[38] The rigorous abstraction and recombination of images during the pursuit of the commodity sign and a new sign value had upped the currency value of the image, the logical conclusion was the creation of image banks, from where designers of advertisements could plunder images of anything that may enter their mind. Image banks are an institutionally rationalized system of managing a marketplace of images, that whilst making the sourcing of a high quality image fast, simple and cost efficient, also further remove the signifier from its relationship with the signified. The same or similar image may appear in multiple and diverse narratives for various companies.[39] A newspaper advert created by BBDO for Apple Computers proved embarrassing when the stock photo they had used of a corporate headquarters was revealed as that of competitor IBM in Atlanta.[40] It may be argued that the advent of Flickr and other photo hosting and sharing websites have subsequently devalued image currency by sheer volume of availability and accessibility under Creative Commons licensing and in some respects have reaffirmed the connections between image and place by the use of descriptions, tags, titles, groups and other tools which form associations and internal networked narratives that can be simultaneously local and global without tension between the two. That isn't to suggest that stock images were not ascribed network qualities or that the market in traditional stock images has completely collapsed.

Super brand systems, credit systems, incentive clubs, were all a part of a new image infrastructure that consisted of systems, agreements and alliances. The mechanisms that power these systems can be read as a metaphor for describing the role of image and sign and their relationship with value, through advertising. Judith Williamson in her 1978 book *Decoding Advertisements* broke the boundaries with her analysis of the advert and its wider relation to brand cognition. Williamson describes the advertising framework as a *'metastructure'*, 'where meaning is not just decoded within one structure, but transferred to create another'.[41] The metastructure allows tacit rules to guide the transfer; the metastructure is the framework within which sign values and currencies are assembled; the network. Within the matrices of this framework the role of the advertiser is to manipulate the transfer of meaning and value to generate *commodity signs*. A commodity sign is the symbol, psychology, brand and pervading *image* of a company, all tied together in a narrative that may only last seconds but infers all the above. Goldman and Papson elicit the example of the closing shot of a Kellogg's Special K ad wherein the calf of the model's leg is merged with half of the symbol to create the 'K': 'The product sign now stands for the object of desire that supposedly comes with the purchase of the product.' 'The commodity sign is formed at the intersection between a brand name and a meaning system summarized in an image.'[42]

It is this sense of a controlled and networked image that can be applied at a range of scales and with various tactical methods and aims that has a resonance with the theory of architectural production. The question of 'What is it?' as an absolute can be levelled at design solutions from micro, macro and meso scales; the notion of an overriding idea as having the capacity to mediate function and assist in the determination of material and form is a core reductive discourse in the production of things. The idea of brand when levelled at a building solution becomes a discourse that concerns all of the structure of that brand; is it to be mass consumed or elitist, efficient or luxurious, ethical, ecological, technological, cultural and a multitude of other values that define? These are undoubtedly embedded in the development of any number of built projects, but usually are bound within the ideology of the commissioning company at a particular point in time and thus can be rapidly exposed as unable to align with shifting ideals in a rapidly moving society. In order to explore this territory it is necessary to consider brand as a device, within architecture and within the exploded territory of the urban realm.

Brand as a Device

The best recorded instance of an early built branding can be found in a publication by Venturi collaborator Stephen Izenour and partner Paul Hirshorn. *White Towers* is a book about McDonalds, before McDonalds existed.[43] Hirshorn and Izenour recognized the cultural value of this commercial icon and, fortunately, recorded a compelling history of the architecture of these small hamburger bars before they vanished completely. White Tower buildings could be regarded as something of an anomaly themselves, presuming an architectural premise that has only latterly become apparent: the *building as sign*. Whilst the authors have been criticized for the objectified nature of the piece, they make explicit the classic characteristics of symbolic repetition. The White Tower restaurants were a chain, the first of its kind,

Figure 2.8 'Camden No. 3 (1938)', White Tower restaurant
Source: © MIT Press, 1979.

that never strayed from the original identifying formula of the very first unit in Milwaukee in 1926: 'white', with a 'tower' (see Figure 2.8). Hirshorn and Izenour developed a fascination with this brand during work for *Las Vegas* with Venturi and Scott-Brown. It was not until a chance meeting with the firm's architect and subsequent access to the company's photographic archive that the development of a book began. The capital success of the chain in its respective social context is as clear as the symbolic elements of the buildings, ultimately reduced to 'cheap and clean'. The White Tower form is as clear a sign as any referenced in this work, as the authors recognize:

> *In more than fifty years of development the White Towers have formed a particularly complete and sophisticated set of stylistic variations on one symbolic theme – a white building with a tower over its entrance – for one strict functional purpose: selling hamburgers.*[44]

These buildings are shown to be limited architecturally and to have varied little in size or form during their 50-year history. The actual design is inextricably bound to the operating system of the company, and as such begins to demonstrate characteristics that bind modern business to a particular locale. Comparable in many ways to White Tower is IKEA, the similarities that run between the businesses may be limited, but the correlation between movement, symbol and legibility in the manifested form of these companies' enclosures is obvious. The stripped version of a medieval fortress was not out of place in a 1920s America where new businesses began to distinguish themselves by adopting Moorish or Mayan styles, predominantly the new cinemas. Selling hamburgers was not the same fantasy as the exotic worlds portrayed in film hence the minimal application of stylized décor to the bold form of the White Towers. The white glazed brick had an aggressively bright impact and carried with it connotations of cleanliness and wholesomeness. In 1935 White Tower employed their first architect; for the 11 years prior, the construction had been executed by various contractors under the guidance of the company chairman. Increasing variance in sites and conditions in the rapidly expanding business made necessary the position of staff architect, one Charles J. Johnson. Johnson was responsible for over two-thirds of the built White Tower restaurants, and as such charted the changing stylistic and economic climate of the United States through the Depression and the Second World War.

The chronological stylistic shifts of the White Tower are accurately chartered by Hirshorn and Izenour, and need no further iteration within the context of this piece, the importance of the model as a tangible, legible and undiluted example of *'building as sign'* is the factor to be acknowledged here. As a sign and a symbol for its company, the White Tower form, material, scale, contextual relationships and repetition of the module all spoke volumes. The ethos and working practices of the company shone through the glazed ceramic façades: clean, cheap, friendly and efficient are all words that could equally describe the company as the building type.

Slowly, but surely, the term brand and the demonstrable physical manifestations of such began to consume our urban landscape. It is revealing that it is now possible to view Venturi's version of Las Vegas as fundamentally quaint, even for a viewer not born in the United States, the twinkling image of the Golden Nugget Casino has an air of nostalgia, its bulbs a mere speck in the luminescent carpet that has unfurled across the globe. Las Vegas was an accelerated and magnified version of the contemporary city and its existence to the service of money meant that its commerciality was exaggerated and the manifest symbols, designed for attraction and extraction, amplified to, apparently, obscene scales of brashness and vulgarity. Whilst not explicitly concerned with brand, *Learning From Las Vegas* did begin to extrapolate the role of sign, and thus brand, in the architectural order of the late twentieth century. As with Baudrillard, Venturi did not explicitly speculate on the formal responses that would evolve as a reaction to this condition. Subsequently the pernicious nature of brands and their global accretion can be seen to have conquered physical, digital and cognitive space; no one more successfully than Nike.

Nike provides an intriguing case study, for not only do they embrace and toy with an image culture, but in their pursuit of credibility through slick and stylized campaigns, have created the economy of the iconic sign. Nike is not a sportswear manufacturer, indeed the company has no manufacturing base; work is franchised to whichever Far-Eastern country can provide the cheapest labour.[45] In a commodity and sign-based environment Nike has found a seemingly spiritual niche: everybody owns footwear: everybody knows Nike: trainers are culturally valuable:[46] thus, Nike naturally assumes the status of cultural icon. The integral part of Nike's elevation to such a status lies in, 'everybody knows Nike'. The simple fact that everyone is aware of Nike's presence in the market is not alone enough to have propelled the *swoosh* to cultural icon. Many multi-national companies feel the moral backlash from pressure groups opposed to the methods employed to achieve such success. Whilst Nike is not devoid of such attention, it has not transposed to a general shift in attitude towards their product. Additionally, Nike has achieved global success with a product that carries a relative expense, accordingly, with that expense comes kudos; but the way in which Nike has maintained the balance between a global product and an individual shoe, and inspired a disproportionate expenditure on footwear amongst a generation, epitomizes the discourse of a sign-based culture. So adored by the youth, Nike has even gained its own place in the slang of British teenagers. The 'Nike one-ten' was the benchmark £110 for the most expensive shoe within each new range of Nike trainers released every three months into this country in 2001.[47] Nike both parodies and feeds on the sign economy and, in an often reciprocal relationship, has carved out a reputation as part of a street culture, not culturally confined, but an educated, perceptive and self-aware audience, who don't need telling that the shoe excels, but can be drawn into a lifestyle philosophy by cleverly self-referential and intertextual adverts. Whilst stylized adverts of this kind may now seem commonplace and open to cultural analyses themselves, Wieden and Kennedy were amongst the first to pioneer this slick approach with Michael Jordan claiming the role as the first focal point for the new global sports nexus.

The image of Michael Jordan leaping for a basket is more acknowledged than the man himself, the logo and products to which it is attached could not be more

**Figure 2.9 Michael Jordan silhouette on tongue of Nike Air Jordan
basketball boot**
Source: Author's own, 2010.

abstracted from the reality of the man as a basketball player. Such strength has the
Jordan icon held for Nike, since the first Air Jordan shoe in 1988, that the name
Nike, nor the 'swoosh', no longer appears on his signature shoe (see Figure 2.9).
The Michael Jordan icon is the print equivalent of the 'Kellogg's calf', the brand
name and its meaning are simultaneously iterated by the leaping logo. Jordan,
however, represents a further distinct condition; that of the branded human, the
celebrity. The branded human is so abstracted from the real person that they are
akin to mythological characters, particularly in the case of the branded sportsman.
Jordan is not the first to have his identity so completely consumed by product:
Chuck Taylor had a Converse shoe named after him in the 1960s, and Stan Smith
had an Adidas signature shoe. The Stan Smith shoe now carries more cultural
recognition than the achievements of the tennis player himself, particularly with
redevelopment of the Stan Smith Millennium, 38 years after the star was at his
peak both in terms of performance and media exposure. The abstraction from the
character to the product, and specifically to the logo, is no more amplified than
the case of Nike and Jordan, and the signature shoe is now a common marketing
strategy amongst sportswear manufacturers.

In respect of experiential architecture and the realization of brand, Nike Towns across the globe have been the source of much speculation and debate about what this type of retail-led experience means to architecture and to the shape of our cities. It is easy to hold up this example, but also easy to forget that it is principally just an interior environment and not a new building typology, despite all of the bells and whistles. Nike's own headquarters building is a typical peripheral development made of boundaries, manicured gardens, managed parking and curtain wall glazing, distinctly at odds with its global image as challenging your limits, under the 30-year-old banner of 'Just Do It'. Using its culturally aware advertising Nike manages to project an image of anti-establishment, which is hugely contradictory to its market presence as a multi-national lifestyle company. The facts surrounding Nike's questionable ethical practices and this very tension between brand and actuality does not seem to halt Nike's consumption of our urban space. In their marketing on the street they have perhaps gone further than other brands, releasing stickers into the hands of Berlin shoppers and inviting their participation in the branding of space by the illegal application of said stickers around the city in a cynical, yet perceptive, grasp of subversive and protest practices.[48]

The concepts of 'brandalism' and intertextuality can also be drawn into the current generated by image circulation. The logos subverted by designers are a component of image circulation, but circulation is not a phenomenon isolated in the printed image. Wieden and Kennedy successfully translated this into an audio-visual context with their TV adverts for Nike, specifically the 1990 commercial featuring Spike Lee and Michael Jordan. The advert featured Jordan talking 'trash' with Spike Lee. Lee however was in the role of Mars Blackmon, the shoe fixated character, from his own movie *She's Gotta Have It*, who refused to have sex with his girlfriend unless he was wearing his Air Jordans.[49] The advert was clever and culturally on the pulse for those who understood the cross-reference, passé, even amusing in its own right for those who did not.

It is not the astute strategy employed by Nike that allows its success in the branded environment, it is the networked nature of its presence. Those brands that are truly global supersede the city and promote business models that are adaptive and reactive. In this context it is possible to perceive the signature building that exists as part of a wider network, the Guggenheim or Prada for example, as more likely to be judged and to operate, 'successfully', in terms of their function and their critical acceptance. The architect has to be able to invest in the brand themselves in a form of symbiotic relationship wherein the aims of each party are aligned towards parallel, but complementary, objectives. Prada and Rem Koolhaas/OMA have extruded this relationship to new heights by publishing the design development process as a work in its own right, *Projects For Prada Part 1*.[50] The 'epicentre' stores are described by Klingmann for the way in which they evidence a blurring between commerce and culture and invite event and occupation as an extension, or alternative, to the public realm. More important than the designers involved, the condition of which will be discussed later in this chapter, is the identification of the opportunity for brand development through methods of architectural inquiry. The programmatic approach to design as practised and published widely by AMO/OMA is transposed to Prada's global operations, customer experience and business models and laid out as a series of fact-based graphics that appear to determinately illustrate the need for new signature stores in strategic global locations. In an altruistic act Koolhaas does 'allow' other architects to have a bite of his conditioned cherry. Before the arrival of OMA, Prada were aware of the opportunities presented as patrons of culture and Andreas Gursky's famous series of photographs are evidence of this.[51] These brands employ subtle and complex methods alongside overt advertising to control and exploit the visual content of our cities *and* culture.

Brand as the Walls of the City

Brand is brash, brand is pop, brand is consumption of every available surface, brand is coverage, brand is insipid, brand is planned, brand is all-pervading. The impact of the term 'brand' and the associated 'arts' of advertising and retail-psychology cannot be underestimated with regard to its effect on our built environment. There are certain spaces in major cities the world over where the billboard and its electronic siblings have subsumed the built surface to such an extent that they become the walls, in some senses literally (see Figure 2.10). The age of applied

Figure 2.10 Times Square, New York, 2001
Source: Author's own, 2001.

advertising remains, but technological development has transformed the role of the advert from applied surface to embedded element. Walls that change colour and can stream and screen moving images are no longer literal 'boards', they are 'walls', they are the external envelope and fabric of our global cities, not bound to our whims as the utopian visions of the Situationists imagined, but controlled by the mechanisms over which we have none.

Whilst Naomi Klein might argue that the financial value of brand was realized with the sale of Kraft, the notion of a constant 'image' and its associated qualities has been played out since the advent of the printed word. The nuance that defines 'brand' as different to 'advert' is concerned with the value implicit in the brand; that with or without sustained advertising the brand strength will continue to guarantee a share of the market. The brand of a particular product can be more important than the product itself, typically we now see two emergent models of brands, those which gestate and garner strength and those which are launched into the world amidst great fanfare with a significant focus on outlay and return. The subtleties of the consumer market cannot be sufficiently understood to necessarily ascribe either of these models with more success than the other, nor necessarily is that of concern here. The visual content of our urban environments

Figure 2.11 Times Square, 'public' realm forged from the street, 2009
Source: Author's own, 2009.

is composed almost entirely of signs; if these are not regulatory articles such as traffic lights or directional indicators then they are almost certainly imbued with brand at one level or another.

There is a situation or indeed, a tipping point, at which the sheer prevalence of brand related signage, and its application, may be said to actually ascribe place. Times Square is perhaps the most obvious example. Few places globally have quite the intensity seen in New York. Recent reconfiguration of the area in and around Times Square has produced incongruous markings within the highway to demarcate an almost indiscernible public realm (see Figure 2.11), but also gifted a terrace of seats to the visiting public from where to absorb and be consumed by the flashing, flickering and folding sequences of digitized display.

> Openings of every sort – in schedules, in urban space, on clothes, in events,
> on objects, in sightlines, in democracy, in philanthropy, in cultures, on bodies
> – are all inscribed with the logic of the market.[52]

Here Jameson touches on the nature of the image, its capitalist mechanisms, the all-consuming and confusing application and its power to transcend, and even distort, perception of time. Written in 1984 he defines a century of 'remarkable ... intensification of an addiction to the photographic image' which had crumbled into 'a rubble of distinct and unrelated signifiers'. With the image in mind, he writes, 'The retrospective dimension indispensable to any vital reorientation of our collective future [has] become a vast collection of images ... a series of pure and unrelated presents in time'. This definition is a precursor to the condition wherein event and the record of that event are both descriptive and disruptive to a reading of the time/place dialectic.

The distortion of the perception of time supposed by Jameson, is a relatively abstract concept, but the correlation between market, image and inscription is exposed when considering the modern typography. The history of typography is one of advancing techniques, from hand-drawn manuscript to the press and typesetting, each in turn has had but one result, the further expansion of printed media. The most influential component of modern image expansion is undoubtedly the computer, which has altered the traditional graphic relationship between image and text. The condition wherein through software, the first piece of which was Postscript from Adobe systems, a surface is described in one language, text becomes image, the digitized text can be stretched, merged, copied, pasted, around, within, behind or above the image. The premier exponent of early advancing graphic techniques was David Carson, who through a series of works, predominantly magazine based, exploded the catalogue of printed design. His work for the magazines *Beach Culture* and *Ray Gun* has been critically acclaimed and widely copied, but his original style and the apparent effortless understanding of the type of role text can visually afford itself, rarely surpassed. The stylistic content of his work carries a certain coherence, but there is no strong theoretical string that necessarily influences or imposes on his graphic interpretations. Beyond the obvious and banal criticism of the illegibility of pages in *Ray Gun*, designers willing to accept his style find it appropriate to search for a clear contextual relationship between the textual content and the formal resolution of the type. Carson perhaps earlier than most designers, at a time when 'meaning' was integral to many arts based discourses, made his occasional wilfulness and willingness to succumb to personal whim part of his work, partially reflective of the 'fuck context' mentality of a surfing and skating generation. Therein lies a small truth about the nature of design and the curious mechanism of post-rationalization. Carson finds a non-context, best-fit approach acceptable, and is willing to express this rather than hide behind a manufactured ideal of what other people think his work should be.

There is a paradox between technological imaging advances and the loss of credibility of the original. Forms become only momentarily stable, image culture is in a state of perpetual transformation. The highest form of flattery is imitation and the redefinition or transformation of a commercially successful image is rife, though predominant in subculture. Perhaps the most tangible commodity to have exploited this device is the T-shirt. The T-shirt is a universal item and since 1965 the territory of the commercial.[53] The punk movement and subsequently American labels like that of Sean Stussy, led the way in, if not popularizing, then maintaining the profile of the T-shirt. In between, every self-respecting laundrette owner, car dealership, ornithologists' club, anti-pigeon society and hip church choir had their own T-shirts to identify, advertise and campaign. Between 1989 and 1993 the rave culture in the UK thrived on the value of the T-shirt as not only the uniform of the raver, but also their form of expression. As rave was marginalized by media frenzy so the subculture was fed, and the humorous, but slightly 'subversive', appropriation of commercial branding for T-shirt prints became a craze. Hoover (Groover), Fairy Liquid (Fairly Hip Kid), Coca-Cola (Coke) and Johnson's Baby Powder (Junkie's Baddy Powder) (see Figure 2.12) all suffered at the hands of cheeky entrepreneurs. Other symbols have political intent in their new guises, animal rights activists stole the golden arches of McDonalds in the late 1980s and the Murder Burger T-shirt was born. In an advancing digital age, the notion of origin has also become susceptible to the power of the image and its record and reproduction, and it is with increasing frequency that versions of designs by European and American architects are being reproduced in the Far East with no input from the original designer and intensely complicated international copyright law compounding any legal action. This is exemplar of the reduction of architecture to an image, even a building as critically and technologically acclaimed as the GSW by Sauerbruch Hutton can be copied,[54] it is not just the commercial that has ceded to the power of the image and brand, a building so intrinsically linked to the history and position of its site can be reproduced without context and seemingly without irony. Both brandalism and commercialism share characteristics that alter the value of the original and thus change perceptions of our physical environment.

The idea of brandalism has, literally, moved onto the streets and the ideology of this form of activism has moved, from using a subversion of a branded identity or message with another political aim, to explicitly objecting to the presence of branding and advertising; the content of the cause is the form. Other practices, most often art in the environment, will be discussed as reactionary to a branded

Figure 2.12 Junkie's Baddy Powder T-shirt
Originally bastardized by Hysteric Glamour (1994), but then ironically replicated by bootleggers and sold for considerably less than the £45 that Hysteric Glamour were charging
Source: Author's own, 1996.

landscape and the privatization of public space, but here the networked physical assault on the city as a positive rejection of the uncontrolled expansion of commercial iconography is most relevant. A number of organizations are concerned with taking back the street from private hands, be it the visual intrusion or the limits imposed on behaviour and access, and these activists no longer simply use the urban environment to promote their message, the urban environment is their battleground. The Anti Advertising Agency, Public Ad Campaign and Illegal Billboards, amongst others, all share contempt for the unchecked and often

Figure 2.13 Anti Advertising Agency, poster disruption, New York, 2009
Source: Author's own, 2009.

unregulated application of adverts and signs and actively campaign to disrupt the companies' messages and spaces inhabited by their brands (see Figure 2.13). Most publicized is the New York Street Advertising Takeover (NYSAT) project that twice painted out over 120 illegal billboards in Manhattan and replaced them with art. This collective action involved over 100 individuals and the use of prepared maps, method and equipment, and whilst many of the billboards were reclaimed by the operating company within 24 hours, the subsequent echo of images of the blank spaces, in the online environment, was one that could not be ignored; as of March 2010, the prevention of illegal adverts has been actively enforced by the NYC authorities. The remarkably refreshing, but alien, images of billboard frames with only white in their centres brings the neutralized acceptance of this intrusion into urban space sharply into focus. Perhaps more meaningful than the subsequent art or statements applied to them, the whiteout of the boards elicits a striking and clear message as well as, in the short-term, altering the physical landscape. The use of social networks and Internet mapping tools is critical, not only in the execution of the work, but in its distribution. This type of action only ever has temporary local effects, but its record and publication can be seen to carry much more weight.

Unregulated brand application can and does result in a visual cacophony, this is perhaps most evident in the developing world, wherein well-financed agencies can operate almost unchecked by authority. The resultant landscape is one of confused scales, luminosity and a lack of discernible hierarchy in both the objects

Figure 2.14 São Paulo. Blank billboards after ban on advertising
Source: © 2007, Tony de Marco, www.nada.com.br

themselves and the city beneath. This is not judged here as a situation that has bias, the conventional view would be to judge an unregulated commercial landscape as negative, but as much as the ad hoc nature of the favelas has a particular appeal to a Western viewer, so the collision of scales and styles of brand and signs may be described as a positive example of opportunistic urbanism. So exacerbated was this situation in São Paulo that, in January 2007, the mayor announced a populist policy designed to regulate without discrimination; the removal of all advertising (see Figure 2.14). The reaction of the people of São Paulo has been slow, it is usual for Brazilians to bide their time at the implementation of a new law, to see if the authorities will actually enforce the legislation. The resultant cityscape is one of ghost hoardings, not removed, but without their applied advertising, even the shops have been limited with respect to the ratio of sign size to street frontage. This spooky but apparently serene condition has been captured by self-proclaimed 'typographer, photographer and pornographer'[55] Tony de Marco and published on website Flickr,[56] to much international attention.[57] The citywide billboard graveyard is a prescient reminder of the consumptive nature of the marketing image within a landscape of consumption, the billboard as consumer of space and diluter of place.

Branded Architecture

Whether regulated or unregulated, the formal manifestation of brand, the sign, is all-consuming. At its extremes this is seen to define landscape and place, in the middle ground it is sufficiently virulent, yet dispersed, to be conceived as pollution. This considers the physical impact of objects that are not buildings and within a set of conventions that define the branded image as a negative within an unfair system. The ways in which brand has affected the production of architecture has been discussed with respect to its giving way to image over form and the subsequent weakening by replication. When we consider the role of building as sign in respect of brand, image value *is* sign value, the formal intervention, the landmark, the built signify has had the image grafted to it, as part of the package. No more is this true than in the world of branding and advertising, but then brand is so integral to a capitalist modality that it becomes difficult to distinguish between brand and image, between that which is franchise, and that which is design. In buildings that have brand at their core, there are four distinct formal typologies, though most branded buildings adopt hybrid mixes of these types within larger metastructures or networks.

1. *The cardboard box*: the huge steel framed, clad box that alludes to its purpose with the application of distinctive colour and huge text/imaging, IKEA, B&Q, Wal-Mart, and a host of other warehouse retailers are reflective of this condition. White Tower was as demonstrative a (psychological) brand

Figure 2.15 IKEA, Warrington, seen from the M62 motorway
Source: Author's own, 1999.

as the buildings were a (physical) symbol, and it is the achievements of the brand that reinforce the positive impact of the building on the street. Today, IKEA perhaps best embody this philosophy. Where White Tower found convenient junctions for the new car-borne traveller, IKEA have found sites next to motorways beneficial to their mode of business (see Figure 2.15). Not only does the proximity to a junction provide access for customers, but the façades of the building become huge adverts for themselves. IKEA's overall strategy of reducing costs, thus always delivering a lower priced product than its competitor,[58] is reflected in the quality of their buildings, and it is ironic that a company delivering 'design' to the world successfully trades in a warehouse. Warehouse retail can be distinctive from (characteristically) and synonymous with (identifiably) branding, and the two marketing phenomena share, chronologically, their modern roots. Although IKEA characterizes the cardboard box occasion it is inevitably dependent on the strong marketing strategy it has employed across a broad media base. Similarly to Nike, IKEA are in the business of lifestyle, the brand is a philosophy. Television advertising campaigns have featured an over-animated IKEA manager expounding the latent virtues, with extraordinary visual metaphors, that bind the company and the people. This series of adverts parodies the recognition that the company is selling a lifestyle by inverting any slick subtle delivery and making an extreme version of a direct sell. This again, is the attempt to both complement and subvert the viewers' appreciation, and subsequent impact, of the advert.

2. *The graphic building*: those relatively few instances wherein the graphic nature of the facade supersedes or is intrinsic to the formal resolution of the whole. The formal characteristic that places a building within this category is primarily the manipulation of the two-dimensional elevational planes as signs in their entirety. The role of graphics in architecture is a history that finds its most palpable precedent during the twentieth century. The early protagonists of the Bauhaus and de Stijl movements recognized and executed some of the first and most successful graphic buildings around the turn of the last century. In the closing decade of the twentieth century, Veenman Printers and Maastricht Fire Station by Neutelings-Riedijk, the Ricola storage depot by Herzog and de Meuron, and Fuksas' Spar can be defined as having characteristics that place them in this category.

In Café de Unie (see Figure 2.16) J.J.P. Oud brought to the fore the contrasting role of graphics in the new 'modern' architecture against its previous employ. Graphics has always had a role in architecture, prior to the advent of modernism as an architectural style, it was a superimposition of ornamentation and decoration, stucco for the embellishing of façades.[59]

Thus objects lead a perpetual game which in fact results from a moral conflict, from a disparity of social imperatives: the functional object pretends to be decorative, it disguises itself with non-utility or with transvestite fashion – the futile and indolent object is charged with a practical reason.[60]

Figure 2.16 Café de Unie, Rotterdam, J.J.P. Oud, 1925
Source: Author's own, 1998.

This statement revolves around the history of a consumer society, where the immanent rationale for the justification of an object is its use. Baudrillard believes that the status of an everyday object is a compromise between a puritanical work ethic and an aristocratic otiose morality. The values with which an object is imbued imply that it must dedicate itself to functioning, working, subsequently excusing itself for its previous status as a pure sign of upper-class prestige. Baudrillard then turns on the 'gadget' as the most evil manifestation of this condition. Oud negates any such accusation by the integration of the written word into his facade and the exploitation of typography as an architectural feature, simultaneously the text declares what occurs: 'you can drink coffee here'.

Café de Unie is an exercise in the elevation of the two-dimensional graphic, the relief of the facade only serving to embellish the graphic representation. The on-street presence and the clarity communicated by not the form, but the graphic, firmly establish this building as not only one of the earliest but also, one of the most undiluted examples of the graphic building.

3. *The pure sign*: is an extremely abstracted typological definition for a building that symbolically acknowledges the evident and latent characteristics contained within the activity it houses. The strongest examples of this condition are formally distinctive and unforgivingly unique, a complete material reference to function, the Dominus wine cellar in Yountville, California by Herzog and de Meuron 1998, is perhaps the most amplified example of this condition. The steel frame that forms the structure is subsumed in its meaning by the gabion cages that stack to form the external walls. The gabions (rock) perform the act of bringing the cellar to the surface, inverting a traditional relationship between cool storage and ground datum, whilst enunciating the obvious material reference to cave. The robust rectilinear appearance of the form serves to further allude to the notion of cave as a space that has been carved or eroded from a solid. The building *is* a cellar.

The US Armed Forces Recruitment Station (Architecture Research Office: New York: 2000) is a small box shaped building of approximately 400 square feet in area and 20 feet in height. The two long sides of the box are made of a double-glazed skin which houses coloured fluorescent tubes to form an image of the Stars and Stripes (see Figure 2.17). Sited in the centre of Times Square at the prominent junction between Fifth Avenue and Broadway, the

Figure 2.17 US Armed Forces Recruiting Station, Architecture Research Office, New York, 2000
Source: Author's own, 2001.

building that now sits here is a replacement for what was formerly not much more of a structure than a shed, though serving the very same purpose. This form is as pure and unequivocal example of *building as sign*, as exists. The importance of this building to this chapter is the curious critical ground that the structure has almost innocuously landed itself. The socio-cultural value of the Stars and Stripes has no more been demonstrated than after the events of 9/11. Sales of the flag rose at unprecedented rates, as patriotic and defiant Americans sought to display their national banner in acts of camaraderie, grief and staunch resolution against the disaster bringing down their great nation.

It is a time of mourning and shock across America, but it is also a time for swelling patriotism and old-fashioned allegiance to the flag. The red-white-and-blue motif of the Stars and Stripes has rarely been raised over so many households. The demand for flags was so great that giant department stores were reporting record sales and demand that was sucking supplies dry as soon as they became available. 'I wish I had a truckload,' said Barby Fryer, the manager of a Kmart discount store in Schenectady, New York. Others, including numerous estate agents, were simply giving the flags away.[61]

Figure 2.18 Minnaert Building, Neutelings Riedijk, 1997
Source: Author's own, 2008.

In this respect, the image of the Stars and Stripes on the Recruitment Station signifies the defence of the nation, signing up 'inside' the flag.

Veenman Printers (Neutelings-Riedijk: Ede, NL: 1997) embodies the qualities of the graphic building, its continuous facade is made of serigraphed glass and carries a text by Dutch poet K. Schippers. The building was intended to be seen and 'read' from the passing motorway.[62] The most successful sign-buildings will usually find themselves with characteristics that configure with more than one of the typological definitions made distinct here. This is true of Veenman Printers which may also be defined as a pure sign. Veenman Printers' skin, designed in cooperation with graphic designer Karel Martens, is a typesetting face, the quintessential device that brought about mass production in printing. In the Minnaert building (Neutelings-Riedijk: Utrecht: 1997) it is the interior environment that attracts the attention of critics, predominantly for its seasonally responsive main hall at first floor.[63] The exterior of this building receives less attention for its facade than the Veenman Printers building, yet the Minnaert is as much a sign as the typeset printers elevation: the Department of Earth Sciences with a sprayed concrete skin resembling slumped, red-clay cliffs (see Figure 2.18).

4. *The chocolate box*: the architect-designed designer shop, the ultimate wrapping beyond the tissue paper, box and glossy carrier bag of the most exclusive boutiques, the ultimate package of serious culture as a component of the purchase; it is the true cultural mechanism. Although aided in its definition by examples of retail in designer boutiques, Marni, Sloane Street, and Commes des Garçons NY by Future Systems (see Figure 2.19), Calvin Klein NY by John Pawson, Nicole Farhi NY by Michael Gabellini, the chocolate has wider connotations. The instance of using architecture as the primary attractor to a location, event is intrinsic to modern society, from Crystal Palace to the Festival Hall and the Skylon. Now, as architecture has a more prominent role than it has entertained for decades, this employ is more and more prevalent at a vaster range of scales, from Sloane Street to the Millennium Dome. The true definition of the chocolate box is high design, not limited by budget but by imagination. The value lies in the marvel and the marketing of the architecture and the architect, though anything that varies even a little from the generic will be published somewhere, by the plethora of periodicals that are published each year worldwide.

This typological approach is the most succinct method with which to loosely categorize buildings that are products of their time. The ways in which cited examples of modern architecture have evolved into their genus is dependent on the objectification inherent to human experience, the inception and parasitic growth of the image economy, the translation of material manipulation to articulate presence and message, and the capitalist driven occasions of brand and franchise which in themselves embody *object*, *image* and *message*. The strength of branding in a culture travelling faster than it can understand can be compared to the modern concept that we enter a flow, travel with it and depart

Figure 2.19 Commes des Garçons, New York: Future Systems, 1998
Source: Author's own, 2001.

relatively unscathed. This has produced the modern condition of commerce and manufacture, the 'just in time' philosophy.

The accelerated nature of recyclical cultural processes has reached point zero, where fashion has caught up with itself and has repackaged, reprocessed and represented identifiable stylistic memes so often that the 1960s-1920s-punk-boho-teddyboy-ethno-gangster could well be the next big thing. Essentially, fashion and indeed culture at large, be it art, music, dance or architecture, is no longer necessarily governed within the confines of seasons and movements, although movements are usually an academic postscript to a period of time that may span anything from five to 50 years. Culture is governed by style. In the context of this conclusion, style may be considered as the choice of the individual as to the way they may compose furniture in a living space or clothing for an evening out, or in the field of architecture, how the architect may find 'industrial-baroque' a suitable mode of representation for his latest project. Fashion has become so compressed that everything is in fashion and it is the way that things are juxtaposed that is the new fashion.

In the age of soundbites, sampling and re-edits, image is everything and fashion is composed of everything, issues of context are subsumed by issues of exposure, notions of fashion eroded by the exponents of style. Thus, a tension exists in the production of city branding based on heritage wherein the preservationist protocol overrides any moves that may compromise the heritage brand, thus petrifying cities as caricatures of themselves and leaving no room for flexibility and contingency within the urban model. A further compounding of this condition is the switch from an emergent model to a legislative model for these cities; the cultural and industrial heritage from whence cities' identities are born is emergent and linked specifically to place, time and circumstance, by preserving a city to protect its brand, it is unable to mutate and react to new conditions and thus has the potential for collapse or failure.

The argument as to whether or not brands can alter or impact on city form depends upon which definition of 'the city' is applied. The formal city, the buildings, streets and material of a traditional 'architecture', is governed by capitalism and whilst brand is an intricately woven component of capitalist economics, it is not of sufficient weight to influence form outside of the signature branding of a particular star architect. The type of branded architecture seen in Manhattan, as described by Klingmann, can only be static and thus susceptible to fashion and failure. Moreover, cities governed entirely by brand, those of the New Urbanists, for example, are viewed as curiosities and theme parks, a rejection of the city in favour of a controlled lived experience. If, then, we accept the idea of architecture as experience, then the experiential city is undoubtedly affected by brand. Von Borries' city is one where it is only brand that has the capacity to mutate and adopt rapidly enough to acquire ownership of the visual, thus formal, content of the city. The sign, as the physical manifestation of brand, can be seen to invade all available terrain and to have embedded itself into the fabric of our buildings, each of the typologies defined here are a product of the consumptive city and simply reactions to conditions; they *are* signs, they *are* 'inverted duck-sheds', they are as much embedded in the image economy as any realm of advertising and to acknowledge these objects as without context and accept the sign-object dialectic as an unmistakable force in the production of buildings is vital to contemporary architectural inquiry.

Endnotes

1   See Lefebvre, H. (1991) *The Production of Space* (Oxford: Blackwell) pp. 25-26. (Trans. Nicholson-Smith, D.) from (1974), *La production de l'espace* (Paris: Editions Anthropos) and Baudrillard, J. (1981), *For a Critique of the Political Economy of the Sign* (New York: Telos Press).

2   Mau, B. (2000), *Lifestyle* (New York: Phaidon) p. 11.

3   Lynch, K. (1960), *The Image of the City* (Cambridge, MA: The MIT Press).

4   Despite the stylistic nuances of logos as they are deployed in an array of global conditions, as discussed in Chapter 6, pp. 191–192.

5   Sennett, R. (1990), *The Conscience of the Eye: The Design and Social Life of Cities* (New York: Knopf).

6   Burckhardt, J. (1860), *The Civilisation of the Renaissance in Italy*. Translated by S.G.C. Middlemore (New York: Harper & Row, 1958) p. 143.

7   Burgin, V. (1996), *In/Different Spaces* (Berkeley: University of California Press) pp. 143–148.

8   Choay, F. (1974), 'La ville et le domaine bâti comme corps dans les textes des architectes-théoriciens de la première renaissance italienne', *Nouvelle revue de psychanalyse*, no.9, pp. 239–252.

9   Alberti, L.B. (1443–1452), *De re aedificatoria. On the Art of Building in Ten Books*. Translated by Joseph Rykwert, Neil Leach and Robert Tavernor (Cambridge, MA: The MIT Press, 1988).

10   Lefebvre (1991), pp. 25–26.

11   Burgin (1996) p. 143.

12   Lefebvre (1991) pp. 25–26.

13   Blake, P. (1960), *The Master Builders* (New York: Knopf) p. 195. Sowers, R. (1990), *Rethinking the Forms of Visual Expression* (Berkeley: University of California Press) p. 35.

14   Sowers (1990) p. 35.

15   McLuhan, M. and Fiore, Q. (1996), *The Medium is the Massage: An Inventory of Effects* (San Francisco: Hardwired). First published by Penguin Books, London, 1967.

16   Ibid. p. 8.

17   Venturi, R., Scott-Brown, D. and Izenour, S. (1972), *Learning from Las Vegas* (Cambridge, MA: The MIT Press) p. 135.

18   Baudrillard (1981) p. 188.

19   Marshall McLuhan's *The Medium is the Massage* and Judith Williamson's *Decoding Advertising* both had massive impact on their respective fields and carried the common message of the power of the image.

20   Blake, P. (1963), *God's Own Junkyard: The Planned Deterioration of America's Landscape* (New York: Holt).

21   Venturi et al. (1972) p. 100.

22   Venturi, R. (1996), *Iconography and Electronics upon a Generic Architecture. A View from the Drafting Room* (Cambridge, MA: The MIT Press) p. 127.

23   Klingmann, A. (2007), *Brandscapes: architecture in the experience economy* (Cambridge, Massachusetts: The MIT Press) p. 190.

24   See 'Polar Variables', chapter two of Sowers (1990) pp. 27–32. Sowers discusses monumentality as defined by scale; scale not determined by physical size, but on event.

25   Bayer, H. (1967), *Herbert Bayer* (New York: Reinhold Publishing Corporation) p. 30.

26   www.designmuseum.org/design/jock-kinneir-margaret-calvert [accessed 12 August 2009] The original font had been developed by Hermann Berthold in Berlin and is also widely acknowledged as the precursor to Helvetica.

27   Ibid.

28   Klein, N. (2000), *No Logo* (London: Flamingo) p. 8.

29   Ibid. pp. 12–13.

30   Ibid. p. 13.

31   Ibid. p. 41.

32 Burgin (1996) p. 192.

33 Baudelaire, C. (1978), *The Painter of Modern Life and Other Essays* (New York: Garland) p. 10; Burgin (1996) p. 192.

34 www-03.ibm.com/ibm/history/exhibits/vintage/vintage_4506VV1003.html. IBM scientists discovered how to move and position individual atoms on a metal surface using a scanning tunnelling microscope. The technique was demonstrated in April 1990 at IBM's Almaden Research Center in San Jose, CA, where scientists created the world's first structure: the letters 'I-B-M', assembled one atom at a time [accessed 23 May 2010].

35 Wieden and Kennedy are the advertising agency used by Nike, their 1998 World Cup campaign used an image of Dutch footballer Edgar Davids crashing through the curtain walling system of the tallest building in the Netherlands.

36 Leach, N. [ed.] (1997), *Rethinking Architecture. A Reader in Cultural Theory* (London: Routledge) p. 209.

37 Mau (2000) p. 41, defines the phenomena he feels shapes the global image economy. His categories include: surfaces of inscription, the unstable image, circulation, surveillance, new image infrastructure, camouflage industries, tourism, postscript world, freeway condition, franchise, celebrity, electronic media and violence.

38 Goldman, R. and Papson, S. (1996), *Sign Wars. The Cluttered Landscape of Advertising* (New York: The Guilford Press) p. 14.

39 Ibid. p. 15. Du Pont and Kodak used the same image of flamingos in flight to signify nature and image quality respectively.

40 Ibid. p. 15.

41 Williamson, J. (1978), *Decoding Advertisements* (London: Marion Boyars) p. 43.

42 Goldman and Papson (1996), p. 3.

43 Hirshorn, P. and Izenour, S. (1979), *White Towers* (Cambridge, MA: The MIT Press).

44 Ibid. p. v.

45 Goldman, R. and Papson, S. (1998), *Nike Culture: The Sign of the Swoosh* (London: Sage Publications).

46 Betsky, A. (2000), 'Protosynthesis', *Blueprint*, July, pp. 52–53.

47 *The Mirror* magazine. Saturday 3 March 2001.

48 von Borries, F. (2004), *Who's Afraid of Nike Town? Nike Urbanism and the Branding of Tomorrow* (Rotterdam: Epsiode Publishers). Von Borries dissects the urban marketing strategies of Nike with reference to many of the general remarks made here.

49 Williams, J. (2000) 'Jesus in Nikes', *Guardian*, Saturday 25 March. A review of the biography of Michael Jordan by Halberstan, D. (2000), *Playing for Keeps* (London: Yellow Jersey).

50 OMA/AMO and Koolhaas, R. (2001), *Projects For Prada Part 1* (Milan: Fondazione Prada Edizioni).

51 In fashioning his own compositions of Prada material and mixing the ranges and seasons of the products he selects, Gursky can be seen to have been allowed by Prada to be critical, via an endorsed cultural mechanism, of the very context of commerce within which it exists.

52 Jameson, F. (1984), 'Postmodernism, or the Cultural Logic of Late Capitalism', *New Left Review* no.146, July–August, p. 66.

53   Gavin, F. (2001), 'Put on. Right-on. Come on …', *Blueprint*, March, p. 42. Budweiser are proposed as the first company to use the T-shirt as a marketing tool, in 1965.

54   Groothuis, G. and Oldiges V. (2007), 'Copyright or Right to Copy?', *Mark*, no.5, December/January, pp. 130–135.

55   www.myspace.com/tony_de_marco [accessed 5 August 2009].

56   www.flickr.com/photos/tonydemarco/sets/72157600075508212/ *Sao Paulo No Logo* [accessed 5 August 2009].

57   Burgoyne, P. (2007), 'The Naked City', *Creative Review*, June. The authors were first made aware of this legislation and the resultant physical changes by this article, which also featured the photographs of Tony de Marco.

58   Salzer, M. (1994), *Identity Across Borders: A Study in the 'IKEA-World'* (Universitet Linköping: Doctoral Thesis).

59   Vitt, A. [ed.] (1998), *Architektur und Grafik* (Baden: Lars Müller Publishers) p. 233.

60   Baudrillard, J. (1981), *For a Critique of the Political Economy of the Sign* (New York: Telos Press) p. 32.

61   Gumbel, A. (2001), 'Patriotism', *Los Angeles Independent*, 14 September.

62   www.neutelings-riedijk.com/index.php?id=13,53,0,0,1,0 [accessed 29 May 2010].

63   Lootsma, B. (2000), *Superdutch* (London: Thames and Hudson) p. 147.

3

Networks

There has been a considerable shift from our understanding of that which constitutes 'the city', from the pre-modern model with a single centre and clearly defined boundary, through the subsequent sprawl, as a result of suburbanization, away from the centre thereby differentiating between the core and the periphery, to the emergence of the poly-nucleic model in which the centre and edge of the city are integrated in a variety of urban conditions. This latter model points us towards what many writers now refer to as the 'network city'.[1] This term is, however, rather problematic as there is an implicit tendency to consider the physical landscape to have the capacity and behaviour of digital infrastructures, a comparison further complicated by the commonality of some features and also the applied language by which they are described. In addition, the acknowledged cessation of the fabric

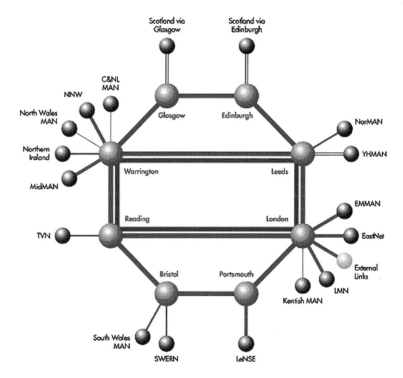

Figure 3.1 Networked Cities
This topology map shows the new SuperJANET4 backbone, as of March 2001.
Source: © JANET[UK].

of the city to the multiplicitous conditions of urbanity has afforded a number of commentators the impulse to focus on various physio-digital analogies and draw connections between the two environments. Whilst such discussion may be useful in certain critical analysis, it does not acknowledge the distinction between the two that has occurred as a consequence of the stacking up and overlays of digital technologies upon extant physical situations to develop a 'multi-layered landscape'.

The bifurcation of 'the city' has developed two fundamentally compelling, if somewhat disorientating, effects. In the first instance, the visualization of 'space', as telecommunications and digital technologies have evolved, has led to the mapping of cities as abstracted networks, frequently favouring topological relationships over topographical ones (see Figure 3.1). Indeed, the widespread availability of online data about any chosen location has led to a presupposed familiarity of terrain that does not exist in a traditional perception of 'place' and has contributed to a diminished sense of awe, invoked by new experience (see Figure 3.2). This condition appears to be one of the factors behind the emergence of urban exploration

Figure 3.2 An example of the Google Street View interface
Source: © Google.

as discussed in the introductory chapter of this book, as people attempt to engage directly with the built environment and its attendant infrastructures as part of an urban experience, even if this behaviour typically relies on navigating marginal space, and as is often the case, results in going underneath the surface of 'the city' both figuratively and literally.[2] The second issue is that of gradual erosion of 'place' in the historical sense and in relation to 'the city'; the term has been supplanted by a hybridized definition that is both in contact and disconnected with the physical space. As Lars Lerup notes in *After the City*, 'The static resistance of traditional architecture in the face of radical mobility demands rethinking rather than escape … The metropolis has replaced the city, and as a consequence architecture as a static enterprise has been displaced by architecture as a form of software'.[3]

This schism between the high degree of connectivity that permeates digital networks versus the increasingly fragmentary nature of the physical urban condition has opened a rich territory for exploitation for artists, designers and other creative practitioners who are involved in navigating this 'in-between landscape'. Networks have emerged in the digital age to pervade societal order and develop new relationships between data, whether as organizing structures, navigational tools, or descriptive mechanisms, for complex matrices of cultural,

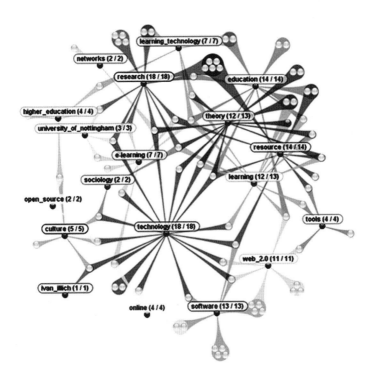

Figure 3.3 Network mapping using the del.icio.us interface
Source: © Joris Klerkx and Erik Duval, 2009.

economic, political or social activity, or a framework that is typically a hybrid of these. The capacity of networks as mapping devices to reveal the configuration of previously unchartered or dynamic relationships is also dependent on a different notion of 'space' that is distinct from the definition that has traditionally enabled urban and cartographic descriptions to be mutually bound (see Figure 3.3). The shift in the nature of the physical landscape towards an increasingly incoherent set of urban conditions and the reciprocal confluence of endless data into a (seemingly) continuous and united system has important implications for the what we might consider to be public domain. In addition to a reconfiguration of the self in relation to how we interact with each other and our environment, the public domain is undergoing transformations that have not been witnessed since the Age of Enlightenment. Georg Simmel observed this phenomenon at the start of the twentieth century, a situation which has only been seen to increase in its complexity and attributes:

> *The relationships and affairs of the typical metropolitan are usually so varied and complex that without the strictest punctuality in promises and services the whole structure would break down into an inextricable chaos. Above all, this necessity is brought about by the aggregation of so many people with such differentiated interest, who must integrate their relation and activities into a highly complex organism.*[4]

The tradition of the public domain as a realm of culture, media and politics is a characteristic that was sustained for more than 200 years, although the gradual deterioration of this performative function through the increased commodification of place as a consumptive environment coupled with a growth in surveillance technologies, has rendered this description largely redundant.[5] The original nature of the public realm within the built environment, as both a receptive and reflexive domain, may now be located in digital networks, that permeate contemporary life, rather than in physical space. The ubiquitous technological presence in our daily communication and other transactions as a correlation of increased growth of broadband in the developed world and the global continuum facilitated by mobile phones, has become manifest in readily accessible, ever-present networks that not only challenge our ideas and experience of 'place' but have precipitated an evolution in relationships of time and distance (see Figure 3.4).[6] This transformation in society has had a number of important implications, but, critical, is the symbiotic relationship we have with these emergent networks as explained by Varnelis and Friedberg:

> *Many different figures are exploring both the networking of space and the spatiality of the network, identifying a series of key conditions: the everyday superimposition of real and virtual space, the development of a mobile sense of place, the emergence of popular virtual worlds, the rise of the network as a socio-spatial model, and the growing use of mapping and tracking technologies. These changes are not simply produced by technology.*

On the contrary, the development and practices of technology (as well as the conceptual shifts that these new technological practices produce) are thoroughly imbricated in culture, society, and politics.[7]

It is tempting to consider the physical disconnection from public space as a comparatively recent phenomenon, correlated to the increased accessibility of technology and its facility to absorb social, cultural and economic exchanges, but the origins of this movement have their roots in the latter part of the nineteenth century, with the advent of widespread physical networks produced by mass transportation. These infrastructures not only had a direct impact on pedestrian mobility by reducing its need in some ways, whilst simultaneously affording greater distances to be travelled in less time, but perhaps equally significant was the corresponding shift in social behaviour. Prior to the development of railways, trams and buses, people had not been in relatively close contact with strangers for sustained periods of time without conversing and as a consequence they typically responded to the situation by disconnecting. This disengagement from the immediate environment was further demonstrated as people moved from increasingly archaic and deprived city centres to the more affluent suburbs. Parallel to this physical shift was the transformation in post-war urban landscapes of people becoming consumers of the city, rather than inhabitants who *lived* in the city and were visible in its public domain. A key evolution of this condition was the 'global

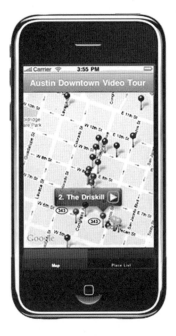

Figure 3.4 iPhone GPS mapping
Source: © Apple.

village' created by the widespread growth of television and its ability to broadcast live information from around the world. An authoritative figure on the effects of media upon lifestyle and communication, Marshall McLuhan provides a defining example the concurrency of place and event offered by the medium, 'After the Apollo astronauts had revolved around the moon's surface in December of 1968, they assembled a television camera and focused it on the earth. All of us who were watching had an enormous reflexive response. We "outered" and "innered" at the same time. We were on earth and the moon simultaneously'.[8] A further influential factor upon the urban environment and our sense of place was the increased mass production and affordability of the car. As a mobile communication device, the car was able to frame the urban landscape through its windscreen, which resulted in a capsular experience and enabled it to act as a mediator of the city. The accelerated growth of physical infrastructure to support the rapidly increasing number of vehicles led to the evolution of new urban networks and conditions that gave preferential treatment to the car rather than the pedestrian. Perhaps nowhere is this more evident than in Los Angeles, which served as a prototype for cities, especially in America, in this regard.[9] One resultant of these new networks was the rise of interstitial zones in and around cities whose predominant feature was one of placelessness and interchangeability (see Figure 3.5).

Figure 3.5 Residual spaces created under the Mancunian Way, an inner-urban motorway
Source: Author's own, 2009.

Throughout the latter half of the twentieth century, urban conditions were steadily eroded of historical character and meaning, as asphalt ribbons – the materialized desires for greater connectivity – dominated urban planning and circumvented traditional material discourse. The sense of 'place' that continued to dissolve as a result of this vacuum had considerable implications for the city as a cohesive and complex structure.[10] Guy Debord lamented the new situation, remarking that there was no longer a 'place where people can discuss the realities which concern them, because they can never lastingly free themselves from the crushing presence of media discourse and of the various forces organised to relay it'.[11] This deterioration of public space, and its interdependent identity of place, accelerated towards the end of the twentieth century, closing with a spatial landscape invisibly pervaded by the neutrality of 'non-place'. The term was coined by the anthropologist Marc Augé to describe transitional spaces that bear no defining characteristics of history or identity. In his acclaimed book, *Non-Places: Introduction to an Anthropology of Supermodernity*, Augé asserts that a historical sense of place, which existed in tandem with humanity, has been challenged by the contingent and temporal, but whilst this description may have initially referred to interstitial components of the urban fabric, the public domain became increasingly subjugated by these features or, perhaps more accurately, lack thereof. He describes the intrinsic nature of this phenomenon as central to our everyday experiences:

> But non-places are the real measure of our time; one that could be quantified – with the aid of a few conversions between area, volume and distance – by totaling all the air, rail and motorway routes, the mobile cabins called 'means of transport' (aircraft, trains and road vehicles), the airports and railway stations, hotel chains, leisure parks, large retail outlets, and finally the complex skein of cable and wireless networks that mobilize extraterrestrial space for the purposes of a communication so peculiar that it often puts the individual in contact only with another image of himself.[12]

If 'non-place', therefore, really *is* the 'real measure of our time' then the projects that afford the terrain for 'non-place'; motorways, airports and malls, may be considered to be as much the architecture of our time as they are the divisive incisors of our cities (see Figure 3.6). The production of interstitial space, now regarded as integral to a reading of the city, is also directly related to this construct and its formal and societal ramifications. If this all appears rather negative for urban conditions then it should be noted that there have been a number of responses to technological developments and the subsequent reconfiguration of 'the city' that have brought much more positive aspects in focus. Although, as the twenty-first century loomed on the horizon, there were a number of theorists keen to depict the annexation of the modern city as a residual effect of the technologies that had infiltrated everyday life, such discourse has proved less substantial over time. William Mitchell's pronouncements on the 'city of bits',[13] whilst engaging, have not been borne out in the development of digital culture, largely due to

Figure 3.6 Arndale shopping centre, Manchester
Source: Author's own, 2009.

the vast increase in the mobility of technology affording freedom of movement and functions, unbounded by context.[14] In fact, rather than necessarily having a corrosive effect on urbanism, there have been transformations due to the rise in network culture that have been highly beneficial. The key difference is that such urban development has been responsive to a global context, shifting the focus from local connections as described by Stephen Graham who argues for a relational and multi-scalar perspective:

> *For discussions of restructuring within cities increasingly must address the changing relations among them, while also being cognizant of the importance of these changing relations within broader systems of geopolitics and geoeconomics. For example, through the logics of the network society, global relational connections can, in certain circumstances, become much more intense than local ones. They can, in fact, be combined with very powerful disconnections. People, machines, institutions, buildings, and urban districts can become intensively woven together across international space through the mediating power of local-global infrastructural networks ... As a result, traditional notions that cities, regions, and nations have any necessary coherence as territorial "containers" become extremely problematic.[15]*

It is also misleading to assume that the apparently formless and invisible digital technologies do not have a material presence that requires extensive implementation within physical urban frameworks to enable their advantages. In their detailed account of the geography of the network society, *Splintering Urbanism*, Stephen Graham and Simon Marvin emphasize the impact of this materiality to facilitate the 'sociotechnical processes' that compose the flows and behaviour of urban life and acknowledge that, whilst fragmentation may be part of the transformations taking place within the urban landscape, there is also an counter-effect of recombination. In the formulation of a response to the primarily corrosive process upon urban conditions, they underline the need to support 'an urban politics of difference that will continue to require embodied and situated presence, proximity and contact – what (some) urban streets and spaces in certain cities have come to stand for and sustain'.[16] This simultaneous process of dispersal and accumulation, via the use of information technologies, which have been transformative in the ways in which we work, learn, socialize and conduct business, has been discussed previously by Manuel Castells in *The Rise of the Network Society*. Rather than eroding the city, Castells views the imposition of technological layers as contributing to the future development of the urban landscape, albeit with an increased mobility as a direct result of rising flexibility in the workplace and social networks. He does not, however, underestimate the degree of reconfiguration that will occur as:

> the interaction between new information technology and current processes of social change does have a substantial impact on cities and space. On the one hand, the urban form is considerably transformed in its layout. But this transformation does not follow a single, universal pattern: it shows considerable variation depending upon the characteristics of historical, territorial, and institutional contexts. On the other hand, the emphasis on interactivity between places breaks up spatial patterns of behaviour into a fluid network of exchanges that underlies the emergence of a new kind of space, the space of flows.[17]

There have been numerous attempts to engage with this emergent situation and architects have been quick to respond to and explore the evolving relationship between media and architecture with practices such as Diller + Scofidio, FOA, Greg Lynn, MVRDV, NOX and Reiser Umemoto engaging with this territory. Prior to discussing the implications of networks in a wider sense, it is worth examining a couple of projects that embrace some of the potential of digital infrastructures and networking directly in relation to architecture and urbanism. The *D-Tower* project designed by NOX for Doetinchem, the Netherlands, 1998–2004 is a multi-platform experience and feedback project that seeks to embed architecture within a larger system of interactive relationships. This system consists of a physical tower, a questionnaire, produced by the Dutch artist Q.S. Serafijn, and a website, all of which are interconnected. Its creator, Lars Spuybroek, describes the concept and intentions thus, 'It is a project in which the intensive (feelings, qualia) and the extensive (space, quantities) change places, where human action,

Figure 3.7 *D-Tower*, NOX
Source: © F.J. Moog.

colour, money, value and feelings all become networked entities'.[18] Conceived as 'a complex alloy of different media',[19] the tower uses data from the website to visualize the emotions of the city on a daily basis via the questionnaire (see Figure 3.7). This translation process is cyclical as the website uses graphics to illustrate the responses of a selection of the city's inhabitants with the selection repeated twice a year to reflect the diversity of the population. The questionnaire gathers information connected to everyday emotions, with questions becoming more and more detailed over time and answers shown as datascapes on the website. The four emotions of hatred, love, happiness and fear are related to four colours of the tower's LEDs which subsequently illuminate the structure based on the dominant emotion of the day as analysed by the website. Through this hybrid media interface, the *D-Tower* has the capacity to disclose qualitative data and reflect the prevailing mood of a street or neighbourhood and demonstrates one way in which the subconscious experience of the urban landscape may be mapped and fed back into its fabric.[20] Whilst this project illustrates an integrative approach to architecture and digital media, the physical object, although unique and alien-like in its formal characteristics, is still relatively static in appearance. An interesting project in a similar vein that predates this work is Nicolas Schöffer's *La Tour Lumière Cybernétique*, 1963, which proposed a 327m high cybernetic tower for La Défense, Paris. Although the work was never realized it sought to connect quantitative data

Figure 3.8 *La Tour Lumière Cybernétique*, **Nicolas Schöffer**
Source: © Eléonore Schöffer.

to qualitative effects and react to the different types of information within the city, including stock exchange, transportation and climatic datasets, and visualize these through a complex system of lighting effects (see Figure 3.8). Perhaps of greater significance is the terminology that Schöffer uses to describe his work, referring to the 'framework', 'coding' and 'programming' of visual and sonic spaces of cities to produce 'cybernetic systems' which enable creative interaction between artist and public via various technologies and media.[21]

In contrast to the above projects, which translate qualitative ephemera into quantitative data and vice versa, the *Blur Building* by Diller + Scofidio develops a response to the increasing abstraction of space and correlating dissolution of place by exploring the role of people in the environment; by creating an alternative experience. The project was constructed on Lake Neuchâtel, Yverdon-les-Bains, Switzerland, for the Expo 2002 and whilst the architects have been engaged with research and design concerning new media technologies for many years, the *Blur Building* represents something of watershed for the confluence of their ideas.[22] The built element of the project consists of an ellipsoidal tensegrity structure on

Figure 3.9 *Blur Building,* **Diller Scofidio + Renfro**
Source: © Diller Scofidio + Renfro.

columns above the lake, but it was the total immersive experience produced by the combination of traditional building components and electronic media that made the concept and design such a sensation. Using water pumped from the lake and fed through a dense array of high-pressure nozzles, the resultant effect was an artificial fog that, unlike entering a building, afforded visitors the sensory experience of moving through a medium that, much like the Internet, was 'formless, featureless, depthless, scaleless, massless, surfaceless, and dimensionless' (see Figure 3.9).[23] Distinct from many immersive environments that typically integrate high-definition visual characteristics, *Blur Building* provided a departure by rejecting the Cartesian principles of space and submerging the visitors into new, suspended territory devoid of form, function or meaning. The technological ingenuity within the project enabled it to minimize the physical fabric and material quantities in favour of the experiential qualities, giving the feeling that visitors were floating inside a cloud. In the original design, people were intended to wear smart raincoats, or 'braincoats', as the architects referred to them, that would track visitors and facilitate interaction between them via LEDs whose behaviour would respond to the answers provided to a pre-entry questionnaire. A highly successful integration of architecture and new media, this project signals the potential for new negotiations between material and space and allows us to reconsider the open territory that has been exposed in the shift in the nature of the physical landscape. However, whilst the triumph and experiential aspects of these projects should not be underestimated, they do highlight their production as bespoke objects of architectural high culture rather than addressing a broader context of typical urban conditions.[24] Perhaps of greater significance, in the context of these chapters, is to emphasize that this shift towards networks of abstracted 'space' rather than urban physical 'place' is not simply driven by technology but is embedded in developments across society (see Figure 3.10). Networks have now permeated traditional hierarchies within commerce, politics, economics and other organizations, along with their top-down communication systems.[25] A key indication of this growth is the prevalence of 'network' in the linguistic terminology of everyday life, being used to describe all manner of connections and organizations, albeit with

Figure 3.10 *KM3, Gotham,* **MVRDV**
Source: © MVRDV.

blurred definitions. However, it is important to iterate here that whilst the level of interest in and use of topological relationships is increasingly widespread, aided and abetted by the growth in use and developments of digital technologies, this may not be quite as radical as it first appears. As Manuel De Landa explains in *A Thousand Years of Nonlinear History*, the networks of online individuals and communities may be much more 'destratified' than with other forms of media but this does not necessarily mean they have replaced existing structures and modes of connection and communication.[26] Instead, such relationships may actually serve to augment existing hierarchies through reconfiguration, facilitating restratification of the networks in the process. Before we become too absorbed in this issue, let us consider the move from urban place to abstracted space a little further through the work of several creative practitioners. This naturally raises questions regarding the visualization of these systems as 'an art of networks' rather than territories, as described by media theorist and software designer Warren Sack.[27]

Terraswarm are one such partnership exploring these structures and modes.[28] A pseudonym, or alter ego, for the architects Aranda/Lasch, Terraswarm was developed as an urban research practice, or as they put in their own words, 'as a way to not do architecture'.[29] The first project they collaborated on was the

Figure 3.11 *Brooklyn Pigeon Project* **apparatus, Terraswarm**
Source: © Terraswarm.

Brooklyn Pigeon Project, 2004, contemporary with the widespread accessibility and engagement with online descriptions of physical territory at the time, such as Google Earth. Developed from an initial concept to create a satellite, but one that leaves the grid system of the city in favour of mapping other data, in this scenario the dynamic behaviour and view from a flock above the city. Using small tracking devices and cameras attached to a number of pigeons, the various flight patterns, both as an individual trajectory and in relation to the flock, were observed and measured (see Figure 3.11). These flight paths were then subsequently mapped and visualized to reframe and offer a new understanding of the city below. Aranda and Lasch's desire to capture the dynamic patterns of urban phenomena is clear when describing their interest in flocking, 'If one considers the city a dynamic in which systems of flow–such as traffic, circulation of goods, or crowd behaviour–can be applied to any urban transformation, then flocking provides a vital model of complex coordination that describes these material shifts'.[30] By documenting and illustrating the patterns through which the pigeons flock, the project not only discloses a new vision or structure of urban space but affords the mode of its communication to have greater agency, facilitating narrative and interpretation. Whilst the resultant images were relatively abstract, influenced by the flying motion of the pigeons, the representation of the city brought new revelations to bear on the nature and description of the urban landscape.

In terms of mapping, this project has an underlying critique of prevailing urban systems and our attachment to the imposed ordering of the 'grid'. Rem Koolhaas, writing about Manhattan in the influential *Delirious New York*, highlights the superficiality of the grid: 'In spite of its apparent neutrality, it implies an intellectual programme for the island: in its indifference to topography, to what exists, it claims the superiority of mental construction over reality.'[31] The flight path of an individual pigeon is much more complex and variable than the orbit of a satellite which navigates in a predictable loop and direction. By using cameras as opposed to a global positioning system (GPS), the emphasis of the project is in mapping new networks rather than referencing conventional organizations of the urban landscape. The images captured through this process raise some important issues on how we view maps and the manner in which our cities and landscapes are communicated. The aerial photography that is now such a familiar method of looking at urban space, due to its accessibility in Google Maps and other software applications that has become part of our regular interface with the Internet, is amalgamated from a myriad of separate images that are carefully stitched and treated in post-production to give the illusion of a continuous landscape. Any arbitrary information that contradicts the larger context is removed or 'corrected' to show the 'real' world, undistorted by the actual curvature of the earth. In resolute

Figure 3.12 Visual material produced by *Brooklyn Pigeon Project*, Terraswarm
Source: © Terraswarm.

contrast to this process, the *Brooklyn Pigeon Project* illustrates the entropic nature of an emergent system, removing the element of control even further away from any inherent hierarchy in both the structure and content of the resultant images. In this sense the project embraces Koolhaas' notion that 'the Grid's two-dimensional discipline also creates undreamt-of freedom for three-dimensional anarchy. The Grid defines a new balance between control and de-control in which the city can be at the same time ordered and fluid, a metropolis of rigid chaos'.[32] The highly effective mapping capability of birds has long interested researchers, and this project reflects the current trend for visualizing the urban landscape as a series of dynamic flows. Perhaps more pertinently it also demonstrates a re-mapping of familiar urban conditions, affording a mode of inquiry and description of the environment that gathers data without imposing regulatory systems of control (see Figure 3.12). This opening up of new perspectives is critical in the development of discourse concerning the urban in the manner described by Italo Calvino, 'The city, however, does not tell its past but contains it like the lines of a hand, written in the corners of the streets, the gratings of the windows, the banisters of the steps, the antennae of the lightning rods, the poles of the flags, every segment marked in turn with scratches, indentations, scrolls'.[33] It is possible to simultaneously reject and accept this position, if we consider work such as *Brooklyn Pigeon Project* as illustrative of the reframing of old thinking with new eyes.

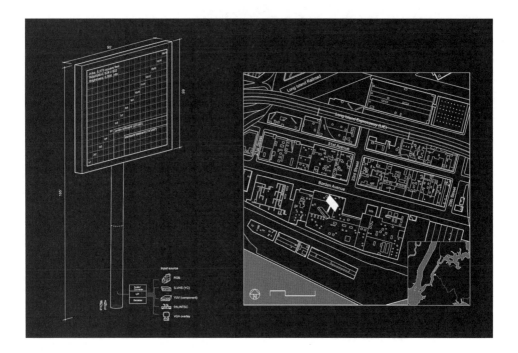

Figure 3.13 *Color Shift*, billboard dimensions and location, Terraswarm
Source: © Terraswarm.

The study of pattern in the work of Terraswarm is primarily concerned with analysing the built environment and breaking it down to reveal new relationships. Taking the dialogue between universal themes and experiential states, that they explore across their work, they describe its indeterminate nature as being reflexive to the surrounding urban conditions, 'It is a boundless and inspiring conversation, one that reminds us that designing can be about communing between two worlds: one entirely abstract and coded, the other very real and alive, like what we find through our interactions every day with people, communities, and cities'.[34] In their *Color Shift* project of 2007, Terraswarm appropriated the largest video billboard in North America, owned by Fresh Direct grocers in the borough of Queens, New York. By substituting the usual stream of advertisements with an algorithm that fed a sequence of colours the billboard was transformed and reconfigured the ephemeral nature of its immediate environment. As each colour was programmed to sequentially reach its maximum saturation and, given the physical prominence of the billboard, the urban landscape glowed in deep reds, yellows and blues within a two-mile radius (see Figure 3.13). This project had a pronounced effect on the city as the urban landscape reconfigured through the gradual cycle of colour, illuminating the context in different ways by virtue of the generated level of hue, brightness and saturation. In addition, *Colour Shift* communicates the capacity for transformations of the built environment without construction but by intervening

Figure 3.14 *Color Shift*, temporal landscape, Terraswarm
Source: © Terraswarm.

in urban space in a temporal, non-physical manner. Beyond the immediate aspects of sculpting the city through light, and the reinterpretations of the context that this afforded, the project also sought to address the role of media in the urban environment. The contemporary city, with all its streams and pulses of lights, slogans and images, often driven by advertising demands, can appear illegible and disorientating, particularly at night. However, our familiar engagement with such modes of communication does not account for other possibilities that are dynamic and harmonious rather than passive and discordant. The networks of media that influence behaviour and events in the urban landscape are restructured here into an experience that is at once recognizable and abstract. Considered in this manner, *Color Shift* responds to the prevalent trend for the city to be subsumed by management practice in favour of political or cultural phenomena by creating such an experience that redefined 'place', albeit in a temporal and intangible way (see Figure 3.14).[35] The billboard's typical audience of drivers moving along the infrastructure of the Long Island Expressway is extended due to the scale and effect of its transmissions but in this case the typical flicker of branding is supplanted by ethereal transitions of colour, a process that accentuates the perception of colour depth by moving between related hues.

Mapping Networks to Decode New Territories

Maps operate in an interstitial zone between territory and visualization. They are not indiscriminate communication tools, representing data and knowledge as an image or other type of media. Furthermore, maps may be analysed and interpreted, thereby providing new discourse on existing situations or revealing latent characteristics. In this sense the critical observations made in Fredric Jameson's essay, 'Postmodernism, or the Logic of Late Capitalism', concerning the state of post-modern society and culture, resonate even deeper now than when they first appeared over 25 years ago. His suggestion that we might adopt cognitive mapping 'to endow the individual subject with some new heightened sense of its place in the global system', rather than a total comprehension of the situation, offers an open dialogue between any territory and mappings of it.[36] The transformation from data to knowledge is an experiential cycle that perpetuates further value and information. By providing a legible visualization of often hybrid and complex information, the instrumental aspects of maps also enable us to develop tactics and strategies for future implementation. Indeed, they are communicative tools that afford the user to project their ideas. Traditional cartography is intrinsically bound to the physical landscape, data that is typically both measurable and finite in scale. It is here that the challenge of mapping digital networks becomes apparent. As a datascape, the Internet has a vast quantity of information that is both complex and continually evolving. In addition, the mapping of Internet 'space' is problematic as it does not exist in a material sense but is omnipresent across the physical landscape (see Figure 3.15). This issue

Figure 3.15 A 3D hyperbolic topology of the Internet (circa 2001)
Created using the Walrus visualization tool developed by The Cooperative Association for Internet Data Analysis (CAIDA).
Source: © 2002, The Regents of the University of California. All Rights Reserved.

underpins all attempts to navigate between network space and urban place, as acknowledged by Dirk van Weelden:

> *The thorniest aspect of network mapping is still the poorly understood relationship of digital space to the physical world. As soon as this dilemma is acknowledged, the task ceases to be just a matter of intelligently visualising the traffic of bits. Rather, it becomes a question of graphically visualising the Internet as a specific part of human society. How do you depict connectivity as a special kind of social activity? The most straightforward model of network*

maps is as encyclopaedic tools, which undertake a form of data mining geared
towards – the critical study of the world, harnessing the specific realities of
cyberspace.[37]

Mapping networks has powerful implications beyond the description of a
datascape in conventional terms as it also reveals relationships and the extent
of connectivity. In particular, the mapping of networks describes the ecological
mutuality between digital and physical landscapes, especially with regard to social
behaviour and patterns. This 'social' data is an extrapolation of that which exists
in the real world, i.e. a confluence of cultural, political, economic and religious
datasets that both explicitly and implicitly explain how we interact within and
across systems as well as with each other. The complexity of the datascape is
increased further as these relationships evolve and form new patterns and
networks in their own right. Whilst the dynamic exchange between physical and
digital landscapes continues to develop, mapping these networks offers fertile
ground for creative research and dialogue. In his compelling essay, *The Anti-
Sublime Ideal in Data Art*, media theorist Lev Manovich discusses the advantages
of dynamic data visualization and mapping using digital technologies as 'meta-
media',[38] which has provided new modes of inquiry for artistic practice.[39]

Media and communication networks form the primary territory across which
artist Lisa Jevbratt operates. Her work is concerned with systems and collectives
and is pertinent in this context given the intrinsic invisibility of the behaviour and
events that occur within digital networks. Writing about the emergence of 'systems
art' in the 1960s, Jack Burnham describes the shift in culture and the corresponding
reaction from artists, 'In the past our technologically-conceived artifacts structured
living patterns. We are now in transition from an *object-oriented* to a *systems-
oriented* culture. Here change emanates, not from *things*, but from the *way things are
done*'.[40] Through a series of projects exploring the nature of networks, Jevbratt has
developed modes of inquiry to enable interpretation of the navigation of Internet
users. Interestingly, given the intangible and dissolute character of digital space,
she is keen to connect the projects with more defined techniques. Concerning the
nature of her work and the network environment Jevbratt asserts that:

> *artist programmers are more land-artists than writers; software are more*
> *earthworks than narratives. The "soil" we move, displace, and map is not the*
> *soil created by geological processes. It is made up of language, communication*
> *protocols and written agreements. The mapping and displacement of this*
> *"soil" has the potential of inheriting, revealing and questioning the political*
> *and economic assumptions that went into its construction.*[41]

With this perspective in mind, Jevbratt's work offers a very different sense of
data. Through projects such as *1:1*, 1999/2002, and *Infome Imager Lite*, 2002–2005,
the mapping of dataset to image is an unambiguous process of translation that
attempts to utilize graphic visualizations to disclose latent structures of the dataset.
In *1:1*, a crawler or automated web-browser, was employed to catalogue more than

Figure 3.16 *1:1*, Lisa Jevbratt
Source: © Lisa Jevbratt.

200,000 Internet Protocol (IP) addresses from a huge database of those available between 000.000.000.000 to 255.255.255.255 (see Figure 3.16). If a site was found it was added to the database regardless of whether it was publicly accessible. When the project was first initiated approximately 2 per cent of the IP addresses were searched and 186,100 sites stored. However, in late 2001 when the project was reignited, the Web had developed and altered considerably. Rather than survey the entire Web, five interfaces or mappings were produced to visualize the variants in the database: *Hierarchical, Every, Random, Excursion* and *Migration*. This database of selected IP addresses was then mapped by assigning a pixel of colour to each IP address. The lowest IP address is located in the top left corner and the highest in the bottom right. The different colour values that emerged through the mappings are a direct correlation of the red, green and blue mixed in relation to the parts of the address. The variables inherent in the dataset are used to produce several different maps by implementing numerous rulesets and observing the visual effects, for example the *Hierarchical* interface of data maps only the top level domains, i.e. .com, .gov, .edu, etc. whilst the mapping of *Every* is inclusive of all possible IP addresses. This produces a filtering system of the dataset, allowing us to view it from various positions as dynamic mappings through which we can turn various layers of information on and off. Visually we are confronted with a series of complex striated patterns of colour whose varied and non-uniform organization have a direct relationship with the topography of numerical space and density.

However, the *1:1* project has other implications beyond mapping as it enables us to consider the visualizations as tools in their own right, revealing inherent structures and providing the capability to navigate or, perhaps a more appropriate word here, *enter* the dataset in a variety of ways. This is no coincidence as Jevbratt describes: 'When working on *1:1* I realised that the interfaces/visualizations were not maps of the Web but were, in some sense, the Web. They were a new kind of image of the Web, and they were a new kind of image. These images are "realistic" in that they have a direct correspondence to the reality they are mapping.'[42] This process of translation or mapping is interesting as the resultant visualizations are not interpretations but are objects for interpretation in their own terms, as she continues:

> *Instead of representing data symbolically by filtering it through known visual forms, the collected data should be represented by leaving an imprint; the images are 'rubbings', indexical traces of reality, and they are reality. The reason why this minimal 'indexical' method of visualization occurred to me was because I wanted to make images of the whole Web, making it visible and accessible in one glance. There were no room for three-dimensionality with its overlapping shapes; pixels spent on anything purely 'decorative' or in-between spaces. Every pixel mattered.*[43]

The subsequent project, *Infome Imager Lite,* develops some of the themes of *1:1* by directly engaging the viewer, or user in this instance, in the construction of the dataset and visualization process. By enabling the audience to control the mapping that feeds into the visualization, the user is effectively integrated into the process. The visualizations produced are interfaces that directly correlate to the sites crawled, in a similar manner to *1:1* the main difference exists in the open yet personal dialogue between user and the mapping process (see Figure 3.17). As a result, the software has explicit connections with a user's experience by illustrating personal networks and choices. This raises another key difference between the *Infome Imager Lite* which is localized and contextual whereas by contrast *1:1* is overtly macro and global. This brings us to a theme that we will return to throughout this book, in which mapping either by the protagonist or spectator reveals latent patterns within space and the negotiative patterns of its infrastructure. In this context such activity fundamentally acts as a locative device in an apparently infinite and ever-mutating topological framework. A central theme in the content of the artist's work is the hidden information and structures of network data that may be revealed and explored to provide new understandings of the social as well as technical landscapes intrinsic to the Web. Jevbratt defines the term 'Infome' to describe the entirety of computers and code along with their inherent networking capabilities. The opening of these networks through data that has a material presence allows her projects to capture complex and dynamic realities for observation and discussion as

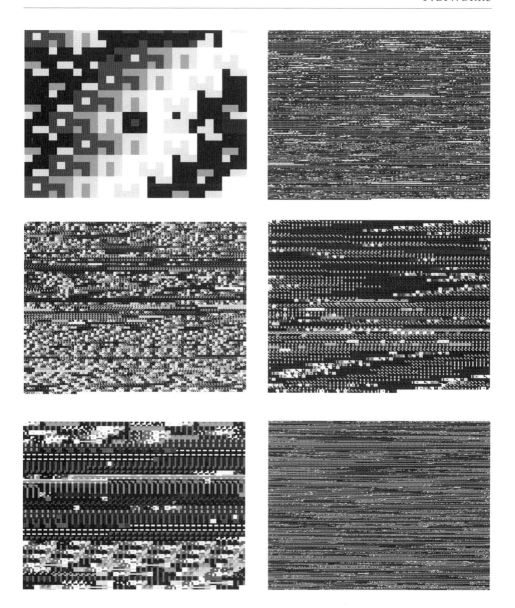

Figure 3.17 *Infome Imager Lite*, sample of dataset visualizations, Lisa Jevbratt
Source: © Lisa Jevbratt.

described by Mitchell Whitelaw: 'The Infome is real, concrete, not a Platonic ideal or a cyberspace of pure thought, and it is tightly coupled to the societies, cultures and technologies that create it; as Jevbratt shows we apprehend it by working, concretely, in it; writing code, initiating processes that themselves inevitably alter the Infome's terrain.'[44]

The work of Jevbratt therefore echoes that of the architects and urban designers that have sought to intervene and communicate notions of the city, the only shift is one of context that is both autonomous and interdependent to the physical urban landscape. Far from the dissolution of the public domain that has been described earlier in this chapter, urban conditions may just simply be renegotiated and interpreted when combined with emergent networks that demonstrate an influential yet intangible bearing upon our everyday experience. This generosity of exchange and community may have evolved from the ancient agora in traditional architecture terms but its functionality and significance to 'place' may just require our communication to be considered in slightly different terms:

> *The world wide web could be described as a complex intermingling of spaces with varying degrees of public-ness, from seemingly private to explicitly public ... In the single isolated moment, this space might appear as a tool for private entertainment and consumption, but if we expand our perspective just slightly, we see that over time and space, it is a place we share with others, dispersed geographically and from the past to the future. It is a public space where we constantly leave traces of our actions, thoughts and opinions.*[45]

If this brings us back to themes of 'place' and navigation then it is worth considering the implications of networks for mapping and their ability to provide intelligent maps that are dynamic, reflexive and complex with respect to the information they synthesize. In *The Invisible City: Design in the Age of Intelligent Maps*, Kazys Varnelis and Leah Meisterlin explain the ubiquity of mapping as software-driven interfaces afford new relationships and visualizations of datasets that favour cartographic invention over convention. Emphasizing their role as an important element of network culture, they suggest that 'In this condition of total urbanity, maps as navigational tools for the physical traversal of space are supplanted by intelligent maps for navigating a contemporary space in which the physical becomes a layer of data in a global informational space. If that space is created by society, it is also a space that, in its massive complexity, has become unknown to us, a second nature simultaneously also a second city and the space in which today's identities are being formed. Much of this world is invisible and it is the task of the designer to help us understand it'.[46] As we have previously discussed in this book, maps do not simply represent physical territories nor is the practice of cartography confined by its tradition and conventions. Engaging with the data of digital networks and exploring new methods for communicating this information, whether directly associated with the urban landscape or not, has become a focus for a number of creative practitioners.

One such figure is Stanza, a London-based artist whose interest in networks and the visualization of data gathered from cities has led to the production of alternative maps to reveal latent characteristics of, and interrelationships within, urban conditions. A key aspect of his work is the tripartite relationship of handling data in terms of its collection, visualization and display. Pertinent in this context is the feedback loop created with the urban landscape as the artist states, 'Data from security tracking, traffic, and environmental monitoring has been used to make artworks. These investigations have created new ways of comparing, conceptualizing and then visualizing complex concepts related to the relationship of emergent data and real space in the built environment'.[47] The integration of digital technologies with the public domain reveals further relationships, and, as such, the datasets he explores provide catalyst not only as a creative medium in themselves but as instruments to inform new urban experiences. In his project *Soundcities*, 2003–2008, Stanza recorded found sounds and 'soundscapes' from a number of cities around the world through his interest in how such data is expressive of the identity of particular geographic locations. Developing the notion of the identity of the city through aural data, the project explores the inhabitation of different places as experiential: 'These sounds also give clues to the emotional and responsive way we interact with our cities. The sounds of cities evoke memories and as globalization fractures our images of specific locations we find things that appear the same the world over.'[48] Whilst highly engaging as a piece of work, *Soundcities* is of specific interest here due to the way in which its creator has evolved and networked its content (see Figure 3.18). The data-collecting technology comprises of a system of

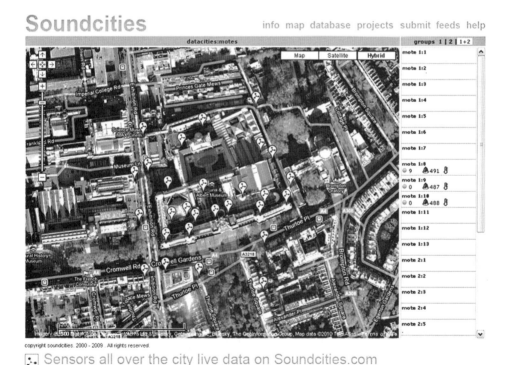

Figure 3.18 *Soundcities*, **London, Stanza**
Source: © Stanza.

microphones with GPS and wireless capacity, whose sounds are streamed live to an online server. Keen to retain the fluidity and transformations characteristic of cities, Stanza has developed an interactive website, soundcities.com, to facilitate the ongoing nature of changes in the global urban landscape and enable the public to participate with it. Based on the principle of 'open source' software, the website allows its users to create their own mixes of the audio data and upload them into the database for other listeners. Conceived as a series of online mixing desks coupling images from the various locations, the data will be used to create visual collages connecting architecture and people to the specific sounds, further augmenting this digital archive. The resultant collages or cityscapes form mappings of live data from the geospatial world, reassembled online:

> *A number of special generative codes re-arrange these natural street sounds, this is the sound of the urban, the true sound of the street. This literally is the sound of the street. Included here is a system that allows the use of generative audio systems to play online. So the city sounds are placed in an ongoing generative environment.*[49]

Stanza's interest in the interplay between the urban landscape, online networks and surveillance culture is more explicitly demonstrated in his project, *Sensity*, 2004–2009. The series of artworks in this project are produced using data from the built environment: the flows of people and traffic, levels of air pollution, along with the sounds and vibrations of buildings. *Sensity* then displays the 'emotional' state of the city it has recorded through visualization and sonification of real time spaces as offline installations and artworks. Describing the intentions of the project, the artist emphasizes the significance of this type of work to aid our understanding of the urban landscape, 'I want the public to explore new ways of thinking about interaction within public space and how this affects the socialization of space. The project uses environmental monitoring technologies and security based technologies, to question audiences' experiences of the event and space and gather data inside the space'.[50] Using a series of small wireless sensor boards or 'motes' to collect data and upload it to a central server, *Sensity* gathers huge quantities of information directly from the city and affords new interpretations and reconfigurations of urban space by providing access to 'invisible' but important qualities of the city. The project therefore attempts to map and visualize the live real time city through a physical network of motes that then communicate this data to a digital network, enabling users to work with it in an open source environment (see Figure 3.19). Through the interaction across the digital network, the data may be used to reform and reinterpret experiential aspects of the city and explore its characteristics and their flux. The connection and networking of information, both physically and digitally, evident in this work illustrates the ability to capture, analyse and synthesize data to not only inform our knowledge of the built environment but to establish a platform upon which we may develop strategies and tactics for the design and evolution of it. As Stanza puts succinctly, the project 'leverages these real time data cities and represents it online, showing the life of the system, opening up the system, and

Figure 3.19 *Sensity*, **Brixton, Stanza**
Source: © Stanza.

then publishing emerging changing behaviours of the space'.[51] With the potential to run this type of system in cities around the world, the project has the capability to link real time global information and provide monitoring of the urban landscape as public domain data resource as well as use this data as a medium for creativity. Projects such as *Sensity* offer a rich platform across which we may be able to better understand our urban landscape by increasing our knowledge of the ebbs and flows that occur around and within the more fixed elements of buildings and infrastructure.

The disclosure of the complexity and information of the data in projects such as these affords us the opportunity to think in visual terms and uncover unknown territory. Our familiarity with extant networks should not therefore be assumed, as the *experience* of these, whether physical or digital, may provide significant tools for discourse and design. Returning to the assertion of Manuel Castells, the implications of networks are not exclusively technological but incorporate the social, economic and political and it is within this hybrid space of flows that we need to evolve creative practice that is responsive to this emergent condition and its (dis)location across the physical urban landscape. Anthony Burke summarizes the contemporary situation thus:

> In contemporary architectural terms, network practices have been couched in an almost single minded techno-utopian revival of a happy and inevitable past-future, with a Marimekko patterned aesthetic to match. However by attempting to continually synthesize the complexities of the political and material aspects of networks, by embracing this dynamic, architecture is able to construct a new form of generative and creative practice, perhaps even while coming to terms with its new subject. While being overwhelmed by a tsunami of technical affordances, architecture needs once again to critically interpret their human value through the spatial consequences and opportunities of the flows that have been put in motion by the technologies we have so eagerly consumed.[52]

The proliferation of digital networks as temporal infrastructures of contemporary cityscapes reveals a connectivity of latent information and public domain that is at best discreet if not completely submerged in the physical urban landscape. The inclusion of this data into the design protocols of architecture and urbanism, both pedagogic and professional, may afford greater discourse as it allows us to consider the experiential aspects of the city and incorporate many societal issues that are perceived as lost through the decline of traditional public space. It is through understanding the everyday integration of actual and digital space that we may inform and expand discourse in architecture and provide a shared space that responds through effective modes and structures to the changing urban conditions that surround us. Indeed, as Bruno Latour suggests, 'there is an Ariadne's thread that would allow us to pass with continuity from the local to the global, from the human to the nonhuman. It is the thread of networks of practice and instruments, of documents and translations' that provides intermediary systems or assemblages that afford greater interaction.[53] If, as Bill Hillier has suggested, 'buildings are among the most powerful means that society has to constitute itself in space-time, and through this to project itself into the future' then the way in which we consider our 'environment' (in social, economic, political and ecological terms) as a space of flows becomes even more pertinent and potentially less reliant on built form alone.[54] However, perhaps the greatest obstacle in this regard is the manner in which digital networks and the physical landscape are described. There is a tendency in recent critical theory and literature on the subject to assume that omnipresent and influential computer technologies have taken over the urban realm and that architecture simply cannot keep up. Of course, the key aspect of this perspective is that digital networks and physical conditions are distinct layers which infers a process of capillarity between the two in which the digital networks siphon the characteristics of the real world, emptying it of meaning and value. Is this actually true? Perhaps, as Aurigi and De Cindio suggest, the radical transformations that appear possible are not actually borne out in reality:

Both utopia and dystopia have been heavily involved in predictions on mega-scale transformations of society, cities and space. And yet, when we observe things around us we can notice how cities are not giving any sign of obsolescence, how people are still people who just happen to use technologies, how space has not been replaced by virtual environments – despite the recently renewed hype on phenomena like Second Life – and basically how 'embedded' digital technologies have become, and how 'real' their functions feel.[55]

This reinforces an important feature of networks that, despite a number of proclamations and diverting theories through ongoing technological developments, they form an interdependent part of urban conditions. As Graham and Marvin state, 'the development of multicentred, fragmented cities or home-centred social life is supported by both the development of tele-communications networks in electronic space and the development of transport networks and suburbs in urban places'.[56] If anything this should reassure designers who now face the twenty-first century city as a mediated landscape of networks, nodes and fluid systems of density, programme, and urban space (see Figure 3.20). Whilst the previously held

Figure 3.20 Digitally tagged city, David Rainbird
Source: © David Rainbird, 2001.

legibility of spatial order may now be very difficult to establish, if even identify, due to the constant temporal layering of infrastructural elements, both upon and within existing territories, the integration of mapping and networks provides some clues to future development. Indeed as Liz Mogel emphasizes: 'The way we visualize spatial and personal relationships has also radically changed–the absolute centrality of the Internet to metropolitan citizens, saturation of electronic communication, and increased mobility have taught us to understand information as embodied in map/networked form, rather than through linear narratives.'[57] Therefore, rather than contributing to a reduced sense of awe, networks have the capability to enrich and extend our everyday experience and understanding of the city. By providing useful tools to describe and extrapolate ideas about the city, networks afford us the opportunity to explain urban conditions by giving us some objectivity and critical distance as Silver and Balmori suggest: 'The idea of the network itself becomes the infrastructure for a reality that extends well beyond the reach of a single author. The network encourages interaction, thus preparing the way for emergent phenomena and the complex interactions of a variety of forces, entities and subjects ... Rather we might understand it as a parallel universe intimately connected to the vicissitudes and flux of our physical environment.'[58] Considered in this way, networks should be seen as advantageous as they enable things to be symbolically brought into a proximity that negates geographic location and facilitates wider discourse. As J.J. King has observed, 'Information and knowledge have always figured and refigured how we experience space, but the stitch-and-suture recombinations that occur when physically-distant locations are networked is novel and noteworthy'.[59]

It is therefore much more useful to engage with networks as multi-scalar devices that further the dialogue around our relationships to, across and within urban landscapes. The 'networked individualism'[60] that affords each person to construct his or her own community as a bespoke infrastructure with relevant connections affords a mode of structuring and restructuring relationships that goes far beyond what is capable in purely physical terms. Despite this, such connectivity should be seen as an attribute that reinforces our integration with urban conditions rather than separating us from them. As Benjamin H. Bratton suggests, it may be much more useful if 50 per cent of all architects and urbanists globally, ceased designing buildings and physical infrastructure or 'hardware' of the built environment and turned their abilities towards the design and programming of the 'software' to develop more effective use of the systems and structures that already exist.[61] He posits that such application of architectural expertise may afford us to regenerate the city in a manner that directly addresses rather than ignores or places little value on networks:

> *Architecture's programming expertise must participate wholeheartedly in this assignment, replicating, condensing, mobilising, diverging and converging the small and large interfaces that constitute the social ... The design frameworks are protocols that ensure a predictable malleability of information flow. For example, the street grid is a protocol, a dumb fixed standard that allowed*

the modern city to emerge as a dynamic network. If it had been animate or idiosyncratic it would not mediate the maximal churn that it does. Taken to its radical logic, Archizoom's No-Stop City was a rendering of this modernity in its purified form – the city as an infinite protocol.[62]

Our perception and experience of the networked city is becoming further nuanced with the development of locative media and handheld devices that enable us to be connected to digital networks and the urban situation at the same time. Already an area of considerable research and discussion, such technology will continue to evolve our relationship with the digital/physical hybridization of features we now call the city and develop appropriate design responses.[63]

Endnotes

1   For an extensive discourse on this transformation see Boyer, M.C. (1996), *Cyber Cities: Visual Perception in the Age of Electronic Communication* (New York: Princeton Architectural Press).

2   The imaginative appeal of underground networks and derelict architectures is discussed further in 'Chapter 2: The Underground' from Manaugh, G. (2009), *The Bldg Blog Book: Architectural Conjecture, Urban Speculation, Landscape Futures* (San Francisco: Chronicle Books) pp. 51–116.

3   Lerup, L. (2000), *After the City* (Cambridge, MA: The MIT Press) pp. 22–23.

4   Simmel, G. (1903), 'The Metropolis and Mental Life', in: Wolf, K.H. (1950), *The Sociology of Georg Simmel* (New York: The Free Press) pp. 412–413.

5   Though, has been explained elsewhere, this decline was largely the result of a confluence of a number of developments that were unfortuitous rather than driven by aspirations of a control state. For an overview of this process see Brook, R. and Dunn, N. (2009), 'The Control of Space: Mediating Fear in the Urban Condition', *Isolative Urbanism: An Ecology of Control* (Manchester: bauprint) pp. 7–14.

6   One example of a project that produced a mapping of a latent network within the physical landscape is Janek Schaefer's project *Recorded Delivery*, 1995. The project consisted of sending a sound-activated tape recorder as a nondescript parcel through the British postal system. The tape recorder was sound reactive, enabling it to automatically edit the entire journey into a recording that was subsequently exhibited at the parcel's destination as a sound installation. While conceived as an art project, it is interesting to note that Schaefer was studying architecture at the time of *Recorded Delivery* and was concurrently designing a new Post Office building. He has acknowledged the revelatory aspects of this project as part of his research into the inner workings of such a building and its attendant network. More details are available at: www.audioh.com/projects/recorded_delivery.html [accessed 14 December 2009]

7   Varnelis, K. and Friedberg, A. (2008), 'Place: The Networking of Public Space', in: Varnelis, K. [ed.] *Networked Publics* (Cambridge, MA: The MIT Press) p. 15.

8   McLuhan, M. and Powers, R.B. (1989), *The Global Village: Transformations in World Life and Media in the 21st Century* (New York: Oxford University Press) p. 4.

9   For an exhaustive analysis of this prototypical development see Banham, R. (1971), *Los Angeles: The Architecture of Four Ecologies* (London: Allen Lane).

10   The parallel decline in both public space and the identity of 'place' is a key aspect of the argument put forward by Jane Jacobs in her highly influential book of 1961, *The Death and Life of Great American Cities* (New York: Random House).

11   Debord, G. (1998), *Comments on the Society of the Spectacle*. Translated by Malcolm Imrie (London: Verso) p. 19.

12   Augé, M. (1995), *Non-Places: Introduction to an Anthropology of Supermodernity*. Translated by John Howe (London: Verso) p. 79.

13   In this book, William J. Mitchell reassesses the nature of architecture and urbanism in light of ongoing progression and innovation in digital technologies. Key to this argument is the notion of electronically mediated environments that provide the springboard for a number of speculations with regard to the near future. Whilst it makes for engaging reading, much of these pronouncements occupied an almost sci-fi terrain and were quickly superseded by further technological developments. Mitchell, W.J. (1995), *City of Bits: Space, Place and the Infobahn* (Cambridge, MA: The MIT Press).

14   By contrast, in his later book, *e-topia*, Mitchell addresses the broader opportunities of networks and their capacity to enable cities to 'work smarter, not harder'. Mitchell, W.J. (1999), *e-topia: 'Urban Life, Jim – but not as we know it'* (Cambridge, MA: The MIT Press).

15   Graham, S. (2002), 'Communication Grids: Cities and Infrastructure', in: Sassen, Saskia [ed.] *Global Networks, Linked Cities* (London: Routledge) pp. 73–74.

16   Graham, S. and Marvin, S. (2001), *Splintering Urbanism: Networked Infrastructures, Technological Mobilities and the Urban Condition* (Oxford: Routledge) p. 408.

17   Castells, M. (2000), *The Rise of the Network Society*. 2nd edn (Oxford: Blackwell Publishing) p. 429.

18   Spuybroek, L. (2004), *NOX: Machining Architecture* (London: Thames and Hudson) p. 158.

19   Ibid.

20   For further details on the mapping and visualization process of the *D-tower* including a live webcam feed visit: www.d-toren.nl/site/manual_en.html.

21   Even though at the time of his writing in 1978, the computational technology was not being used for parametric design in the contemporary sense, Schöffer was fully aware of its potential for generative design and as a responsive tool, 'Today all this is made considerably easier by the use of computers, those powerful electronic extensions of mankind, conceived by humans. Here the notion of "the creation of creation" becomes an obvious reality. The computer can explore and choose, or can at least easily and rapidly present us with, series of combinations by which our own choice is facilitated to create and recreate multiple solutions in multiple directions, each having the trademark and quality of the basic programmes while differing fundamentally from them'. Schöffer, N. (1978), *Perturbation et Chronocratie* (Paris: Editions Denoël-Gonthier, Grand Format Mediation), as referenced in Schöffer's essay, *Sonic and Visual Structures: Theory and Experiment*. Available from: www.olats.org/schoffer/savs2.htm [accessed 31 March 2010].

22 For an overview of Diller + Scofidio's earlier work, many projects of which include an explicit integration with media technologies see Diller, E. and Scofidio, R. (1994), *Flesh: Architectural Probes* (New York: Princeton Architectural Press).

23 Incerti, G., Ricchi, D. and Simpson, D. (2007), *Diller + Scofidio (+ Renfro): The Ciliary Function* (Milan: Skira Editore S.p. A) p. 144.

24 By contrast, the work of Forays explores the role of networks within the public domain through 'open-ended minor architectures and the modification of everyday infrastructure'. Experimental in nature, their projects such as *The Edible Excess Machine*, 2007, and *Prototype for Bent Infrastructures*, 2008, examine the possibility of new resources by repurposing and connecting to existing infrastructures in cities. For more information visit: http://forays.org.

25 For an engaging example of a project that addresses global networks in this manner, see Martin, R. and Baxi, K. (2007), *Multi-National City: Architectural Itineraries* (Barcelona: Actar).

26 For an overview of his synthesis, the reader is referred to 'Conclusions and Speculations' in De Landa, M. (1997), *A Thousand Years of Nonlinear History* (New York: Zone Books) pp. 257–274.

27 Sack, W. (2010), 'Aesthetics of Information Visualization', in: Paul, C., Vesna, V. and Lovejoy M. [eds] *Context Providers: Conditions of Meaning in Media Arts* (Bristol: Intellect, 2010).

28 The various boundaries of such structures within networks are considered further in 'Negotiation and Connectivity: A Boundary Approach to Multi-layered Landscapes', by Isabelle Doucet in: Healy, P. and Bruyns, G. [eds] (2006), *De-/signing the Urban: Techno-genesis and the Urban Image* (Rotterdam: 010 Publishers) pp. 330–345.

29 McGuirk, J. (2008), 'Aranda/Lasch: Cracking Architecture's Code', interview with Justin McGuirk, *icon*, 56, February, p. 61.

30 Aranda, B. and Lasch, C. (2006), *Tooling*. Pamphlet Architecture; 27 (New York: Princeton Architectural Press) p. 64.

31 Koolhaas, R. (1978), *Delirious New York: A Retroactive Manifesto for Manhattan* (New York: Oxford University Press) p. 20.

32 Ibid.

33 Calvino, I. (1974), *Invisible Cities*. Translated by William Weaver (London: Secker and Warburg) p. 11.

34 Sakamoto, T. and Ferré, A. [eds] (2008), *From Control to Design: Parametric/Algorithmic Architecture* (Barcelona: Actar-D) p. 195.

35 The widespread growth of the 'experience economy' and branding of cities is discussed in 'Affective Architecture in the Branding of Cities', by Søren Buhl Hornskov in: Marling, G. and Zerlang, M. [eds] (2007), *Fun City* (Copenhagen: Arkitektens Forlag/ The Danish Architectural Press) pp. 143–157.

36 Jameson, F. (1984), 'Postmodernism, or the Cultural Logic of Late Capitalism', *New Left Review*, 146 (July/August), pp. 53–92.

37 van Weelden, D. (2006), 'Possible Worlds', in: Abrams, J. and Hall, P. [eds] *Else/where: Mapping New Cartographies of Networks and Territories* (Minneapolis: University of Minnesota Design Institute) p. 27.

38   Manovich, L. (2002), *The Anti-Sublime Ideal in Data Art*. Available from: www.manovich. net/DOCS/data_art.doc [accessed 5 December 2009].

39   This movement can be seen as mirroring Judith Williamson's 'meta-structure' in advertising and signalling the critical confluence of art and commerce, no longer exclusively within a symbiotic economic relationship, but sharing notions of a new idiom. Williamson, J. (1978), *Decoding Advertisements* (London: Marion Boyars).

40   Burnham, J. (1968), 'Systems Esthetics', *Artforum*, September.

41   Jevbratt, L. (2006), 'Inquires in Infomics', in: Corby, Tom [ed.] *Network Art: Practices and Positions* (Oxford: Routledge) p. 75.

42   Lisa Jevbratt being interviewed about her projects in *A Minima*, no.14. Espacio and Publicaciones, S.L. Spain, 2005. Available from: http://aminima.net/wp/?p=93 andlanguage=en [accessed 29 December 2009].

43   Ibid.

44   Whitelaw, M. (2008), 'Art Against Information: Case Studies in Data Practice', *Fibreculture*, issue 11. Available at: http://journal.fibreculture.org/issue11/issue11_whitelaw.html [accessed 5 January 2010].

45   Jevbratt, L. (2007), *Searching Traces of We – Mapping Unintended Collectives*, Swedish National Public Art Council's Annual Catalogue no.38.

46   Varnelis, K. and Meisterlin, L. (2008), *The Invisible City: Design in the Age of Intelligent Maps*. Available from: www.adobe.com/designcenter/thinktank/tt_varnelis.html [accessed 12 March 2010].

47   Artist's statement, available from: www.stanza.co.uk/about/statement.html [accessed 29 March 2010].

48   Project description, available from: www.thecentralcity.co.uk/info/soundcities.html [accessed 12 March 2010].

49   Ibid.

50   Interview with Stanza, March 2010. Available from: http://we-make-money-not-art. com/archives/2010/03/do-you-have-a-photo.php [accessed 29 March 2010].

51   Project description, available from: www.stanza.co.uk/sensity/index.html [accessed 12 March 2010].

52   Burke, A. (2007), 'Redefining Network Paradigms', in: Burke, Anthony and Tierney, Therese [eds] *Network Practices* (New York: Princeton Architectural Press) p. 74.

53   Latour, B. (1993), *We Have Never Been Modern*. Translated by Catherine Porter (New York: Harvester Wheatsheaf) p. 121.

54   Hillier, B. (1996), *Space is the Machine: A Configurational History of Architecture* (Cambridge: Cambridge University Press) pp. 403–404.

55   Aurigi, A. and De Cindio, F. [eds] (2008), *Augmented Urban Spaces: Articulating the Physical and Electronic City* (Aldershot: Ashgate) p. 1.

56   Graham, S. and Marvin, S. (1996), *Telecommunications and the City: Electronic Spaces, Urban Places* (London: Routledge) p. 329.

57   Mogel, L. (2008), 'On Cartography', in: Thompson, N. [ed.] *Experimental Geography: Radical Approaches to Landscape, Cartography, and Urbanism* (New York: Independent Curators International and Melville House) p. 107.

58   Silver, M. and Balmori, D. [eds] (2003), 'Networking Maps: GIS, Virtualized Reality and the World Wide Web', *Mapping in the Age of Digital Media: The Yale Symposium* (Chichester: John Wiley and Sons Ltd).

59   King, J.J. (2006), 'The Node Knows', in: Abrams, J. and Hall, P. [eds] *Else/where: Mapping New Cartographies of Networks and Territories* (Minneapolis: University of Minnesota Design Institute) pp. 44–49.

60   Wellman, B. (2001), 'Physical Place and Cyber Place: The Rise of Networked Individualism', *International Journal of Urban and Regional Research*, 2(2), p. 238.

61   Bratton, B.H. (2009),'iPhone City', in: Leach, N. [ed.] *Digital Cities*, Architectural Design (London: John Wiley and Sons) pp. 90–97.

62   Ibid.

63   For example, this subject was the focus of a major international conference; *The Mobile City: A Conference on Locative Media, Urban Culture and Identity*, Netherlands Architecture Institute, Rotterdam, 27–28 February 2008, and has since developed into a cross-disciplinary platform for researchers, academics, practitioners and organizations exploring the relationships between architecture and new media technologies and the implications of these as part of the design processes that may shape the twenty-first century city. For more information: www.themobilecity.nl [accessed 14 February 2010].

4

Films

As has previously been discussed, the city as a prevailing framework; socially, culturally, economically, politically, etc., has attracted a considerable degree of analysis and speculation, with particular regard to what many view as the failings of the modern city. These urban conditions are not, however, simply the organization of the built environment but also represent a 'site' of confluence across which a number of disciplines continue to address urban issues and develop modes and structures for engaging with these. Whilst Chapter 3 dealt with the advancing abstraction of space and the mutual decline of place, for most of us the city still exists in relatively conventional terms – as a largely well-defined system of elements, some of which are static whilst others are in flux. As the urban geographer David Harvey has noted, the transformations that have occurred across the physical environment post-Second World War have meant that it is no longer possible to refer to previous spatial categories that provided a clear taxonomy of urban and rural landscape conditions.[1] Instead, we are now presented with urbanized space in many different guises through which the distinction between centre and periphery is constantly renegotiated resulting in a lack of definition regarding boundaries and form. However, as Richard Skeates suggests, such conditions provide fertile ground for investigation: 'It is not only theory that has been mapping this blurred terrain. Representations, in particular in film, but also in certain forms of fiction, can be found of a city that appears to be fragmenting, mutating and generally evading old definitional categories.'[2] Furthermore, the aerial overview of cities that provides us with a typically coherent, albeit deceptive, structure is significantly contrasted by the experience 'on the ground'.

Whilst contemporary urban landscapes may often be presented from above, the spatial organization and fragments are actually consumed from below, i.e. the *lived experience* of urban conditions. This contrast between the relatively static order of the system and the high degree of mobility and temporality of life on the streets reminds us of the duality of cities and their ability to shift between the objective and the subjective. As the sociologist Fran Tonkiss writes, 'Alongside a conception of the city as defined by built forms or demographic facts, might be posed an alternative version that understands it in terms of modes of consciousness or experience. People's experience of the city is not only or always determined by larger social or economic structures, but also fashioned by their individual perceptions, mental maps and spatial practices' (see Figure 4.1).[3] It is here that we are able to identify the narrative nature of these conditions with particular reference to moving images that may afford exploration and understanding of urban space and event as filmic mappings. The many benefits of mapping as an activity with which to engage and reveal characteristics of the city have been discussed, but relevant here is the use of films as mapping devices that describe transition, behaviour and event as described by Andrew Webber:

> *The mapping of urban space at once fixes locations and provides a basis for motion around them and along the channels between them. And the technology of the moving image is, in part, an advanced cartographic apparatus, combining the act of location and the enabling and tracking of motion and locomotion ... Such cinematic plot maps show the city as a place of movement both orderly and disorderly, a place of assignation and appointment, but also of random encounter and traumatic accident.*[4]

Since the development of film as a medium architecture typically served as its central protagonist, connecting us to the fabric of the city. This initial association developed into a reciprocal, if not always beneficial, dialectic.[5] Although the earliest filmmakers used stationary cameras, they very quickly developed methods for attaching their equipment to moving vehicles, affording the audience the sensation of a variety of transitions through space, cities and landscapes (see Figure 4.2). The incorporation of tracking shots alongside panning and cut-up techniques enabled vehicular motion to be directly perceived and the montages of the urban landscape to be experienced. The significance and popularity of film as an art form and medium of communication has resulted in an intricate dialogue with architecture that has not only transformed our understanding of the built environment but our *experience* of it. This relationship has afforded us with the ability to view the moving landscapes within films as experiential mappings that have an inherent mobility that is psychogeographic in nature. Writing about this mapping capability of films, the film theorist Giuliana Bruno asserts, 'A frame for these cultural mappings, film is *modern cartography*. It is a mobile map – a map of geo-psychic differences and cross-cultural travel. A voyage of identities in *transito* and a complex tour of identifications, film is an actual means of exploration: at once a housing for and a

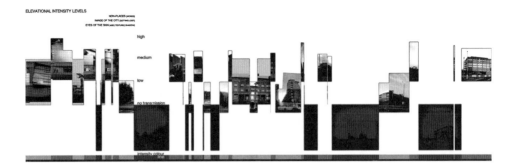

Figure 4.1 Sound mapping of Whitworth Street, Manchester, Johnathan Djabarouti, 2009

Source: © Johnathan Djabarouti.

Figure 4.2 The phantom ride
This involved either a camera being attached to the front of a train, tram or other form of transport or the camera operator filming the journey. The effect of which was to make the audience feel like they were actually experiencing the ride for themselves (see Railway Ride Over the Tay and Glasgow Trams 1902). These phantom rides were very dramatic for an audience witnessing moving pictures for the first time.
Source: © Scottish Screen Archive at the National Library of Scotland.

tour of our narrative and our geography'.[6] This theme has been developed further by François Penz who compares the legibility or disclosure of the urban landscape in films as complementary to the imageability that Kevin Lynch sought to identify in his early research on understanding cities.[7] Furthermore, films have the capacity to render the city as a narrative in a reflexive relationship as described by Roy Strickland, a relationship that:

> *consists of people claiming, occupying and mapping urban form and space. In return, urban complexity enables people to construct highly personalized relationships with their environment that foster intimacy, social exchange, introspection and conflict … In cities, where exterior and interior, public and private, may be separated by little more than a wall or window, minor variations*

in form, down to the curb, sidewalk or step, can exert powerful influences on people's behaviour, providing a rich vein for exploration in urban design.[8]

Architecture has long held a fascination with film, keen to apply the terminology, visual motifs and techniques that filmmaking offers as being analogous, if not literal, to the direction of materials, form and light within the discipline. That a number of notable architects including Coop Himmelb(l)au, Rem Koolhaas and Bernard Tschumi have previously embraced the glossary and methods of film as part of their descriptive and explorative modes of inquiry, the majority of such attachment only served as part of the many foibles of Deconstructivism (see Figure 4.3). Indeed, writing in *Architecture and Disjunction*, Tschumi asserts:

Yet architecture is inhabited: sequences of events, use, activities, incidents are always superimposed on those fixed spatial sequences. These are the programmatic sequences that suggest secret maps and impossible fictions, rambling collections of events all strung along a collection of spaces, frame after frame, room after room, episode after episode.[9]

Indeed such connections are made even more explicitly by Koolhaas who opines that he may still be a scriptwriter in some sense, writing of architecture and filmmaking that 'there is surprisingly little difference between one activity and the other … I think the art of the scriptwriter is to conceive sequences of episodes which build suspense and a chain of events … The largest part of my work is montage … spatial montage'.[10] However, as Kester Rattenbury has discussed, whilst there may be similarities between the two, the interesting territory lies in the complementary differences.[11] As a rich and evolving dialogue between the two subjects continues apace, the proliferation of educational programmes, research and related theoretical material expands along a number of different trajectories. Therefore, it is important to clarify the position from which we are to consider films here. In this context we view films as narrative and interpretative tools that typically are concerned with spatial sequence, editing and revelation within the city. They use allegory, narrative and structural patterns to unfold ideas and tell a story. The story of how a space is used, in relation to character and action, may reveal a latent history of the role of space within the city. Space can even be used as a character, acting independently within the narrative itself and, as such, films may map a version of the city that is manifest of networks, urban subtexts and occasional nodal collision. Indeed, films may provide us with 'the preconditions of another life' that Henri Lefebvre referred to in another context.[12]

The prevalent mode of treatment in relation to the interface between film and architecture is that of societal phenomena through which the city is viewed, rather than as a medium of experience that frames the urban condition and facilitates various scenarios to be played out before the viewer. In this sense we may consider the use of narratives to be a valuable instrument that enhances our understanding of urban form and social life and which underpins the *performative* nature of the built environment. The limitations offered by urban conditions across a range of scales

Figure 4.3 Bernard Tschumi, filmic sequence, *Manhattan Transcripts,* **1979–1980**
Source: © Bernard Tschumi Architects.

such as district, street, doorway, etc., provide a series of spatial demarcations that create a rich and typically complex system of public and private space encoded with various definitions, social claims and activities dependent on the temporal lens through which they are occupied or used. Conversely, the sheer intricacy of the city as a phenomenon reminds us of Walter Benjamin's suggestion that film may be the only medium to come close to being able to capture all its different qualities:

> *Now the city turns into a labyrinth for the newcomer. Streets that he had located far apart are yoked together by a corner like a pair of horses in a coachman's fist. The whole exciting sequence of topographical dummies that deceives him could only be shown by a film: the city is on its guard against*

him, masks itself, flees, intrigues, lures him to wander its circles to the point of exhaustion. But in the end, maps and plans are victorious: in bed at night, imagination juggles with real buildings, parks, and streets.[13]

This notion of inhabitation raises an important issue with regard to the role of city as a narrative 'background'. The use of various cinematographic techniques posit the protagonists *within* the urban fabric as they occupy the time and space of the city. Considered in this manner, the spatial fragmentation of the cinematic experience actually mirrors our own physical relationships with the built environment as we course strategic trajectories across the cityscape with purpose rather than as an impromptu act with its inherent accidental encounters. The *situation* of the city provides an extensive series of cues from which we can develop design ideas and speculations on the future of urban space and form. Viewed in this manner we seek to use the underlying socio-political infrastructures ingrained

CITY OF MANCHESTER   *   CENTRAL AREA

REFERENCE

1. TOWN HALL	4. ALBERT SQUARE	7. MASONIC TEMPLE	10. TRINITY STATION ANNEXE	13. CATHEDRAL	16. ART GALLERY	19. RETAIL MARKET
2. PROPOSED EXTENSION	5. POLICE HEADQUARTERS	8. COURTS OF LAW	11. SAINT ANN'S CHURCH	14. CHETHAM'S HOSPITAL	17. AMUSEMENT CENTRE	20. BUS STATION
3. EXISTING EXTENSION	6. RYLANDS LIBRARY	9. EXHIBITION HALL	12. ROYAL EXCHANGE	15. COMMERCIAL CENTRE	18. PICCADILLY GARDENS	

Figure 4.4 City of Manchester 1945 Plan: a modernist utopia
Source: © Manchester City Council.

into the material surfaces of the city as a tool to engage with *actual* urban conditions rather than adopting a bird's eye perspective as the all-pervasive designer with a 'correct' solution. This latter approach has characterized the majority of attempts to bring order to cities through planning, regulation and legislation (see Figure 4.4).[14] The landscapes of exchange of which the city is comprised afford its actors a myriad of opportunities and circumstance that may be brought to bear on the perception of 'place'. Memory, gender, ethnicity and socio-economic factors are interdependent parameters that are also inextricably linked to the various physical territories within the cityscape. Viewed in this manner, Giuliana Bruno asserts the connections between the urban landscape and its actors since 'the streetscape is as much a filmic construction as it is an architectural one'.[15]

The critical appraisal surrounding Situationism has brought focus to the 'unitary urbanism' aspect of their practice with particular relevance on the ambiance and lived experience of the city.[16] This recalls the filmic narrative of Ralph Rumney's *Psychogeographic Map of Venice*, 1957, which consists of a sequential montage of street views and captions to illustrate an urban drift (see Figure 4.5). As such, Situationist mapping explores the lived experience of urban landscapes as *mobilities*, physical and emotional, through which narratives and further descriptions may evolve which disclose the temporal and visceral flows amongst built fabric. We are reminded at this juncture that the city is no longer an object, but rather it is a superorganism within which our routines, traversals and experiences are subjective 'texts'. In *The Practice of Everyday Life*, de Certeau sought to describe how such texts were made in the built environment despite the regulatory bodies and codes that indirectly bore

Figure 4.5 Ralph Rumney's *Psychogeographic Map of Venice*, 1957
Source: © Ralph Rumney.

upon them. The 'spatial stories' he refers to are the mappings of everyday users of the city and in this sense they exist, if indeed at all, as residual traces that are barely detectable yet document detailed experiences of living in the urban realm. These narratives are temporal and contingent and thus mirror the filmic versions we encounter. In both situations, we inhabit the urban landscape in a fluid manner, far removed from the fixed and objectified view of buildings and much closer to the dynamic discourse of location and event in which 'Space melts like sand running through one's fingers' as described by Georges Perec.[17]

Of particular significance here is the value of films as diagnostic instruments that afford us the opportunity to describe and understand urban conditions. With specific reference to the 'everyday' in terms of our interactions with the built environment, films have the capacity to illustrate the *experience* of living in the city. They are able to convey the dynamic, temporal qualities of the city as a superorganism with its countless narratives, events and fluctuating systems. As Paul Virilio has noted, 'Since the beginning of the twentieth century, the classical depth of field has been revitalised by the depth of time of advanced technologies … The screen abruptly became the city square, the crossroads of all mass media'.[18] However, this is not to suggest that such films necessarily need to adopt a stringent social realism in order to be useful, but rather that the content may facilitate a discourse that relates to the urban landscape. Equally, while much has been made of the speculative near-futures offered in films such as *Blade Runner* and *The Matrix* these detachments from the contemporary cityscape, despite providing subjects for fervent dissection, soon become as lumbered if not obsolete as the many sci-fi projections made for the year 2024 at *Futurama II*, New York World's Fair, 1964–1965.[19] Therefore, although 'film architecture' in this latter sense may offer 'reflection and commentary on contemporary developments, as a testing ground for innovative visions, and as a realm in which a different approach to the art and practice of architecture can be realised', it is important that we do not become seduced by these projected cities as a form of escapism.[20] This is not to infer that films may not have any element of fantasy but rather that the negotiation between physical terrain and narrative is as lucid as our own. The architectural historian Mitchell Schwarzer elaborates further: 'Film can reveal to us architectures that exist only in the mind, architectures composed of sensation but also memory and imagination; and such film architecture yields insight into the perception of real architecture.'[21] Indeed it is the ability of the camera to move through space and place that facilitates the articulation of these architectures, allowing us to perceive the *lived* experience of the films in a visually rich manner, compressing the complexity and density of information into a coherent sequence. This in turn may facilitate a more responsive architecture and urban design to emerge that acknowledges the lived experience of the city. The influential film theorist Ricciotto Canudo was particularly receptive to the lived experience that films could describe, stating that film 'achieves the greatest mobility in the representation of life'.[22] It is here that we may see the cogent parallel between films and architecture in their ability to articulate spatial and temporal situations, i.e. the social and cultural activities and structures of life. Such experiences are fundamental to the way in which we exist, perceive and behave within urban landscapes as Juhani Pallasmaa describes:

> *Lived space resembles the structures of dream and the unconscious, organized independently of the boundaries of physical space and time. Lived space is always a combination of external space and inner mental space, actuality and mental projection. In experiencing lived space, memory and dream, fear and desire, value and meaning, fuse with the actual perception. Lived space is space that is inseparably integrated with the subject's concurrent life situation. We do not live separately in material and mental worlds; these experiential dimensions are fully intertwined. Neither do we live in an objective world. We live in mental worlds, in which the experienced, remembered and imagined, as well as the past, present and future are inseparably intermixed.*[23]

Envisaged in this way, the modes and structures through which film and architecture both express urban conditions and provide comprehension of the interactions within them are very similar. However, given the tension between the two subjects it is worth reiterating that we do not propose to adopt the language or techniques of filmmaking, but rather consider films as narrative and interpretative instruments that may tell us more about cities than the frequently sanitized and idealized views that are held up through the wide range of communication media that is typically used in architecture (see Figure 4.6). The cropped, stylized and unoccupied 'places' of architectural photography remain a consistent portal through which many of us view architecture in a highly object-orientated way and are not the focus here. By contrast, the capacity of films to illustrate the lived experience of the physical landscape is both arresting and revelatory. Filmmakers have, since the inception of the medium, been keen to utilize the symbolism and spatialities of architecture to provide both rich discourse with universal themes and facilitate narratives to be woven into their structure.[24] The reciprocity that exists between the two disciplines, coupled with their innate ability to inscribe place with event is put succinctly by the artist and filmmaker Peter Greenaway: 'for architecture, write film; for architect, write filmmaker.'[25] However, the apparent synchronicity between architecture and film does not necessarily offer a coherent understanding of either subject. The developments in media throughout the twentieth century have clouded the situation as described by Anthony Vidler, referring to architecture and film as 'entirely different media utilizing their respective technologies, the one to simulate space, the other to build it, now, by contrast, the increasing digitalization of our world has rendered them if not the same, at least coterminous'.[26] It therefore becomes apparent that the position from which we view the relationship between these subjects is paramount. The urban landscapes depicted in films translate the actual living city, imbuing them with heightened effects and narratives and thereby providing reflections, albeit in a transformative manner. As John Orr writes:

> *In a way, the cinematic city always imitates urban life. City dwellers not only live in a world planned for them by designers, builders, and architects,*

they also create their own life-worlds within, saturated in the symbolic, which is drenched and varied. The metropolis is thus never the sum of its physical parts but an accretion of living tissue, of both humdrum activities (work, commuting, shopping, eating, and sleeping) and public spectacle (the festivals, celebrations, riots, and demonstrations which define flowing history). A film is both representation of that living tissue and an integral element within it.[27]

It is here that we may see the advantages of films as descriptive tools that proffer synthesis of the 'urban'. Furthermore, the opportunity that films provide as analytical and transformative mappings that develop and translate our exploration of the urban landscape is inherent in the medium, as Walter Benjamin wrote: 'Couldn't an exciting film be made from the map of Paris? From the unfolding of its various aspects in temporal succession? From the compression of a centuries-long movement of streets, boulevards, arcades, and squares into the space of half an hour? And does the flâneur do anything different?'[28] A critical aspect of films is their ability to address the discontinuities and voids of the fragmented cityscape and (re)define these as part of a narrative that reminds us of the presence and

Figure 4.6 Manchester Civil Justice Centre
Source: © Daniel Hopkinson.

influence of such urban conditions. Key to this characteristic is the representation of ungoverned niches and the porosity between interior and exterior. The isolation of urban fragments, as settings for the temporal and visceral, refracts the use and transactions that may occur in our cities. Furthermore, these 'fictions' of the city are pivotal to the architecture of lived space as Giuliana Bruno asserts:

> *Architecture is neither static structure nor simply just built. Like all tangible artifacts, it is actually constructed–imaged–as it is manipulated, 'handled' by users' hands. And like a film, architecture is built as it is constantly negotiated by (e)motions, traversed by the histories both of its inhabitants and its transient dwellers. Seen in this way, architecture reveals urban ties: the product of transactions, it bears the traces of urban (e)motion and its fictional scriptings. A relation is established between places and events that forms and transforms the narrative of a city: the city itself becomes imagined as narrative as sites are transformed by the sequence of movements of its traveller-dwellers.*[29]

The use of an unoccupied council estate in South London by Gary Oldman for *Nil by Mouth*, 1997, is a deliberately raw statement, both literal and metaphorical, of the situation in which its characters find themselves located. We use the term unoccupied here, rather than uninhabited, as the depiction of decrepit high-rise, with its foreboding transitional spaces of corridors and concrete walkways, creates a sense of desperation and neglect on those remaining, people who *exist* on the margins of society, rather than *live* (see Figure 4.7). The everyday in this composition

Figure 4.7 Aylesbury Estate, London, the setting for *Nil by Mouth*
Source: © Matt Kimemia.

131

is a familiar drudgery with no spectacle in the positive sense. The restlessness of the film's protagonist to find his next fix only serves to echo the unwelcoming nature of the environment that surrounds the social underclass. The marginalized nature of the film's characters isn't simply illustrated by the residual spaces they move through but also via the criminal and illicit networks they negotiate and their volatile relationships with one another. Equally, the endless background noise of the film whether from the pub, club, traffic or television, returns us to the condition of the contemporary urban landscape as an oppressive place without respite. Across these situations, everything – built environment, interiors, people, emotions – show traces of wear and tear: 'As a narrative that is in part a memory film, *Nil by Mouth* brings back to life the recently disused and discredited – the modernist high-rise became instant slum, deserted by most of its dwellers, and then closed down. ... The sequence of its use transforms it cinematically into an image of living death.'[30] The subsumption of the characters by their immediate surroundings serves to illustrate the direct correlation between the materiality of dwelling and urban phenomena with particular regard to the effects of weathering and neglect upon both the built fabric and the psyche. In this context the city is described as both placeless yet inescapable, with the situation of the urban landscape providing the undertow for the conditions of its occupants.

This placelessness of the contemporary urban condition also permeates Mike Leigh's *Naked*, 1993, with the continuous relocation and traverses of its central character, Johnny, who is always on the move as he laments, 'I've got an infinite number of places to go. The problem is where you stay'. The film follows the main protagonist after he flees his home city of Manchester for London to find refuge with his former girlfriend. Intelligent, lyrical and reckless, Johnny encounters the dark underbelly of Britain's capital city as he embarks on an odyssey, espousing his views to any given audience regardless of the consequences. A series of chance meetings and events culminate in the further dislocation of him from the world, leading to his rejection of, or indeed by, others. The displaced, and frequently despairing, society illustrated in the film reflects the fragmentary existence of many people within our cities, with the streets being worn out and any spectacle far from the privileged point of view so enticing to Debord.[31] The everyday rhythms present here eschew the typical systems of movement in the city, instead occupying a gritty nichescape of London's alleyways, doorways, and other spatial interstices that provide negligible comfort, surreptitiously pushing the characters on (see Figure 4.8). Whilst there may be a number of subtexts to the film in relation to the plight of its characters,[32] the situation they are inextricably embedded into is overtly political: 'There is no question that *Naked*'s dark, metaphysical vision is shaped by the general pessimism and sense of malaise and social decline that dominates post-Thatcher England.'[33] This endless motion is an explicit motif within the film, as Leigh described at the time of its release: 'The fabric of society is crumbling in England, there are people all around the streets ... Although there are plenty of homeless people in England, I didn't want to make a documentary about homelessness. In a sense, I think the film crosses the park of homelessness without actually dealing with it as such. Although, everybody in it, in a manner

Figure 4.8 Johnny in the wasteland of London, *Naked*
Source: © Mike Leigh, Thin Man Films, 1993.

of speaking, is rootless, or at least displaced.'[34] Such restlessness is both literal and metaphorical in this film, offering an untouched portrait of the world. Indeed the director himself has commented, 'I felt in some way that I could make a film that could express the future through a bleak, urban landscape, by creating the world as it actually is now'.[35] The resultant experience is realistic though undoubtedly heightened through a dominant visual style that, specifically in this film amongst Leigh's oeuvre, reflects the chaotic, complexity, dirt and messiness of living in cities:

> *Watching his films is less like learning about something (with stylistic signposts telling us what is important and what things mean) than living through unassimilated experiences, the way we do in life. Moving through Leigh's scenes is a lot like having things happen to us in life. We are taken on a voyage without a road map to guide us. We are denied shorthand or abstract ways of knowing. We are put on the qui vive, forced to figure things out step by step. The films don't simply refer to, summarize, or offer conclusions about experience. They offer experiences that test our powers of perception in the same way experiences in life do.*[36]

Inherent to both these films is the use of the urban scene as ungoverned, providing its own ecology of configuration and event. Most significantly, the figures' constant movements highlight the volatile nature of the urban landscape and the duality of their relationship with it, which is at once disconnected and ingrained with no respite. This serves to emphasize the intensification and condensation of the everyday that is replete with the behaviour and events so acutely mapped in films such as *Nil by Mouth* and *Naked*. Rather than address a wider perspective of the urban landscape, the tight, weaving narratives in these films provide an intrinsic mutuality between the occupants' mobilities within their environment.[37] The transgressions depicted across the cityscapes in these films are balanced by the corresponding forces such environments have upon the people within them. It is here that the lived experience of the contemporary urban landscape is explicitly held up for our inspection, as the many failings of the modern city are evident and the environment subjugates the individual.

On a related trajectory, but with a different theme, is Andrea Arnold's *Red Road*, 2006. Set around the housing apartment blocks of the same name, in the inner suburbs of Glasgow, the flats were the tallest residential buildings in Europe at the time of construction but soon fell into social and physical decline as poverty, crime, fear and despair coagulated (see Figure 4.9). The coeval detachment of people from the municipal space they live by reflects a broader attitude to the levels of

Figure 4.9 View of the Red Road Estate
Source: © James Burns, 2007.

control, governance and surveillance culture. Instead of an urban landscape we are offered the 'scanscapes' of the CCTV network, mediating and stitching the piecemeal spatial experiences of figures together into an event narrative. Arnold's filmmaking is fluid and engaging, albeit often unsettling. Rather than favouring a more traditional narrative with central performances, the characters in *Red Road* live their lives 'around the film's edges, which vividly recreates the buzz of urban life'.[38] In this sense, the actual protagonists are the housing blocks themselves, which have an emblematic and looming presence throughout the film. The lack of public amenities between and around these blocks is synonymous with many similar housing projects around the world. The ensuing nature of the public realm in this regard is characterized by the 'mass absence', described by Albert Pope as those spaces that are designated by the lack of an urban collective.[39] Instead of public facilities and social behaviour, the cityscape provided here affords its users negotiated and appropriated niches for ambiguous and fleeting events and transactions.

Red Road illustrates the contemporary 'landscape of fear' as defined by Mike Davis' *Ecology of Fear* (1998) and described by Brook and Dunn in which 'The city and its suburbs were classified and perceived as dangerous. There are two visible reactions to this emergent physical context; one is the rise of technological controls on space, the increased use of CCTV, the growth of gated communities and such, the other is the burgeoning social and spatial fragmentation dependent on economic means'.[40] Critical to the mapping of urban space that this film provides is the bypassing of social relations through their artificial replication of social control functions via surveillance technologies.[41] The dissected public

Figure 4.10 CCTV control room, *Red Road*
Source: © Andrea Arnold, Advanced Party Scheme, Sigma Films, 2006.

135

domain therefore becomes a heavily recorded and scrutinized landscape that, rather than enabling activities, actually becomes entirely bereft of social interaction (see Figure 4.10). The complexity of the interface between the 'multiple screen aesthetics' of CCTV and physical conditions alongside the relationship between the surveiller and surveilled has a number of affective dimensions as discussed by Patricia Pisters. Of particular relevance here is her assertion that films such as *Red Road* present surveillance technologies as capable of 'affection-images rather than paranoid panoptic images', which underscores their assimilation into everyday life.[42] This allows us to reconsider the value of such technologies and how they reshape our perception of the built environment. Far from being the omnipotent eye that demarcates and regulates urban space, the rising use of CCTV and other surveillance media has simply precipitated in the creative appropriation and enclosure of residual space, by individuals, subcultures and communities. The severance and fragmentation of the cityscape has therefore enabled greater cultural identification through the navigation and inhabitation of these 'in-between' spaces as a reactionary mechanism. In a number of ways this points us towards an inversion of the public domain – rather than focusing on the increasingly homogenized formal and aesthetic language of the centre and periphery, it is possible to identify a responsive nichescape of places that become defined by particular uses and experiences – which facilitates the actions, needs and desires of those inhabiting the urban landscape (see Figure 4.11).

Figure 4.11 Unregulated urban intervention, New York, 2009
Source: Author's own, 2009.

Continuing the shift from city centre to periphery, *La Haine*, 1995, affords the opportunity to explore themes of identity, alienation and appropriation across urban conditions. Directed by Mathieu Kassovitz, amongst the backdrop of considerable unrest within the Parisian outer suburbs at the time, the film illustrates three protagonists' intrusion into and ejection from accepted norms, i.e. the spaces of commerce and the establishment, which only serves to demonstrate their apparent lack of place in society. The competition for urban space permeates the film throughout with the values of inner city realm versus the outlying *banlieues* being depicted as 'the fiercely guarded space of the metropolitan centre of Paris under threat from its "others" placed out in housing schemes on the city's outskirts. Here, urban space is always contested and a site of potential conflict; through violence and resistance, the appropriation of this space by the centre is made explicit'.[43] Understood from this perspective, it becomes clear that the alienation from the built environment is a product of numerous complex constructs largely underscored by economic and social status, whether legal or otherwise, that are exploited further by those in pursuit of order and control. *La Haine* maps a Parisian suburb through event with the sets being characterized by singular or collective action. This enables the film to convey the foibles of its characters, which provides us with what de Certeau described as the 'little space of irrationality' in the everyday.[44] The use of the city as a singular entity from which they are temporarily locked out only serves the momentum of the protagonists' behaviour as they are forced to sleep in the non-place of a shopping centre prior to the intense conclusion. Using a 24-hour cycle as a temporal setting, the first half of the film is based in an outer suburb or *banlieue* of Paris, which is at once both symbolic of the isolation of its occupants

Figure 4.12 *La Haine*, banlieue
Source: © Mathieu Kassovitz, Canal+, 1995.

and representative of the increased mobility and growth of the city. In addition, the film illustrates this living environment as a set of urban conditions that are under considerable pressure from authorities to gain order and maintain governance. The continuous drifting of the protagonists throughout the film highlights the disparity between their limited private interiors and the external environment that provides spaces for exploration and transgression, even if they have nowhere to go with purpose (see Figure 4.12). As a mode of experience the communal aspects of these outer suburbs are clearly evident in the appropriation of space, such as rooftops, wherein the characters maintain temporary control and create boundaries from the restrictive milieu of the ground conditions. Perhaps even more so than in the other films discussed in this chapter, the cinematography in *La Haine* is used to create major contrast in the characters' relationship with their surroundings. By shooting the first half of the film using wide angle with considerable depth of field, the inhabitants become integral to the urban conditions and there is a clear sense of belonging.[45] Even the extensive floating, panning shot across the terrain of the *banlieue*, to the sound of a DJ mixing KRS1 and Edith Piaf, represents a dream-like quality within the urban landscape in which the inhabitants are able to experience reverie and chance, surreal encounter. Such interdependency between people and place evokes the realism that makes the film provocative yet believable, as suggested by François Penz:

> *The cité is not revealed to us per se, as in a documentary, but through the careful staging of the dramatic action. And yet there are sufficient elements to (re)present an architectural/urban coherence, to restore to the viewer a sense of 'being there'. A large part of the cinematography in the cité consists of such sequence shots, some lasting two to three minutes, and reinforces this immersive feel. While this a tough strategy for the actors, it allows the audience to experience the space in real time, to get a feel for the topography of the place, its levels, its thresholds, conveying a more realistic sense of time and distance and of the overall scale of the environment.*[46]

In direct opposition to this strategy during the second half of the film, in which the three protagonists find themselves in the centre of Paris, a number of methods are used to reinforce the sense of alienation and rejection. Firstly, the characters move across a series of interiors that are inhospitable and, coupled with the generic and anonymous external environment, contribute to the atmosphere of detachment. Even their arrival into the city centre is communicated with a specific camera technique to establish this disconnection, 'Indeed, the Paris sequence starts with an unusual compensated zoom which signals an alien environment as the city behind them becomes a blur. They do not belong to Paris and they do not know the city' (see Figure 4.13).[47] Secondly, by using a static camera rather than tracking or sequence shots which feature heavily in the first half of the film, the motion, or lack thereof, posits the characters into a world which is fragmentary and foreign in nature rather than fluid and intrinsic to their behaviour. These framing and editing techniques are further enhanced by the third element of the event narrative which shifts the

Figure 4.13 *La Haine*, Paris city centre
Source: © Mathieu Kassovitz, Canal+, 1995.

balance of control from the protagonists, who are very much part of a community integrative to their domain in the *banlieue*, to the authorities and dwellers of the city centre who repeatedly discredit and exclude them. The combination of these methods have resulted in a mode of representation of the geographical and socio-cultural context of the *banlieues* that has led *La Haine*, along with other films, to be considered as embodying a sub-genre of filmmaking in their own right.[48]

If we allow ourselves to zoom out from the relationship between centre and periphery and consider the conditions *across* the contemporary city, then we are able to examine it as a superorganism which affords a myriad of strands and fragments to exist and be (re)connected. *Dirty Pretty Things*, 2002, directed by Stephen Frears, represents the city as a multi-scalar system comprising of various components and 'unseen' networks, and uses the fractured urban situation as a set of conditions for exploitation and selfish profiteering. Indeed the splintering of urban space and narratives within the film provides residual niches that the characters are able to occupy, however fleetingly, to further illustrate their position in the margins of society. Rather than depicting the prevalent view of London at the time, which favoured a 'sanitized fairy-tale city' with predominantly white middle-class characterization, the film's setting is one of a contemporary multicultural city.[49] This is furthered by the narrative that chronicles the relationship of two immigrants in the city, one illegally seeking refuge whilst the other is awaiting the results of her application for asylum. The political furore that surrounded these issues is well documented and the film's treatment of supposed 'hospitality' and 'safety' in Britain has already been examined in detail.[50] In the context of this chapter, the pertinence of the film's subject matter is its ability to communicate a much more

Figure 4.14 Taxi rank, *Dirty Pretty Things*
Source: © Stephen Frears, British Broadcasting Corporation, 2002.

familiar view of an international city, as a lived experience of those who inhabit it, rather than a series of iconic tourist postcards. As Nick Roddick has observed, the London depicted in *Dirty Pretty Things* 'always seems to be just around the corner from the one most of the British audience know ... convey[ing] the feeling of the whole quasi-invisible civilization created by the needs of a modern tourist-cum-business metropolis' (see Figure 4.14).[51]

Indeed, the city offered here is one of latent networks that are carefully navigated by those who need them in order to survive and remain hidden from the scrutiny of authority. Consequently, the characters occupy a series of 'in-between' spaces, primarily the service zones of a hotel that facilitate the comfort of others, through which they are regularly exploited. The majority of the film's narrative takes place in unconventional hours and places with constant referencing to the time and muted colours of settings in the half-light of either dawn or dusk to reinforce the characters' positions as servile to mainstream society (see Figure 4.15). The infrastructures that provide the figures with mobility in *Dirty Pretty Things* are cultural, social and economic which are typically invisible to the everyday experience of the city, bearing illegible traces of existence. As with *La Haine*, the grime and mess of the city, that is so often romanticized as pivotal to its atmosphere, here provides the context for 'living' – a reality that is actually tense and frightening. Instead of the freedom of movement across the urban landscape so often taken for granted, the people within these networks are in continual mobility, which is far from privileged and only facilitates a lived experience on the edge of normative society:

Much of the film's power comes from the carbuncular pockets of the city, shadowy and backstage, that it depicts: hospital crematoria, private cab firm backrooms, underground car parks, prostitute chambers, illegal sweatshops … Even the hotels and hospitals, places where sterilized cleanliness is part of the deal, look shabby. Everything, even the fleeting shots of the Millennium Dome in the distance, is off-white.[52]

This perpetual motion is punctuated by brief respite but the lack of private space in conjunction with the awkwardness of domestic scenes in the film further

Figure 4.15 CCTV and scan, *Dirty Pretty Things*
Source: © Stephen Frears, British Broadcasting Corporation, 2002.

underscores the tension and fear of those being surveilled. As the director acknowledges even the inherent benefits such as a socialized organization of health care is a potential trap, 'For illegal immigrants, it's more complicated. They don't want to have anything to do with the system; they're terrified by the system, so they just keep away'.[53] However, the fluidity of urban experience afforded by the networks the characters in *Dirty Pretty Things* use directs us to consider the cityscape as a porous entity, providing space if not necessarily 'place' for people and their vagaries, rather than a fixed object. Although the events within the film construe to provide a coherent structure, we are actually faced with fragmented and piecemeal lives that are threaded together by circumstance and the dearth of identity, as succinctly posed when one of the protagonists is told, 'You don't have a position here. You have nothing. You are nothing'. The non-places of contemporary urbanism depicted here are further accentuated by the use of an airport for the first and final scenes of the film which reminds us of the constant mobility and consumption of space over place in the amorphous, transitory and anonymous generic city. Whilst an unquestionably provocative film that does not offer any easy answers, *Dirty Pretty Things* excels at a description of a major set of urban conditions that are recognizable for their ability to displace, demarcate and shelter both communities and individuals in spite of (rather than because of) its organization and attempts for control.

Of course, for many of us the city is not an environment in which we attempt to carve out such a literal and desperate mode of survival. Instead, for the vast majority of those that inhabit it, the city affords a lived experience with its attendant features and forces, both negative and positive. Therefore, for the last film in this chapter let us consider Michael Winterbottom's *Wonderland*, 1999, which shows a living city; busy, claustrophobic, noisy, and reflective of the urban conditions with which many of us are familiar. Using speeded-up sequences to provide an impressionist and immersive experience of the city as streaks of colour, time and space, the film is able to convey a sense of the fluidity of urban conditions and those that engage with them (see Figure 4.16). The film actually returns us full-circle to the domain of *Nil by Mouth*, but the emphasis here is beyond the cramped living conditions and towards a much more globalized view of a large metropolis. By using handheld cameras and recording the city 'as it is', with minimal lighting, radio mikes and no extras in the exterior scenes, contrasted with the tight framing of interior scenes, the film conveys a contemporary cityscape very effectively. These filmmaking strategies serve to reinforce the multiple narratives of the film, resonant with the reality of urban life: 'We recognize, however, that this extreme spatial restriction has itself some diagnostic value with respect to a now globalized world: like a photographic negative, the film's representation of circumscribed journeys prompts inference of the reverse, of more expansive flows and mobilities elsewhere.'[54]

Of particular interest here is the film's attempts to integrate dramatic events with a documentary aesthetic, which permits *Wonderland* to describe domestic melodrama within a fragmented and chaotic city. These personal dramas are woven throughout the continual fabric of the city, reinforcing its conditions and by coupling the images with Michael Nyman's evocative soundtrack the overall effect

Figure 4.16 Street flux, *Wonderland*
Source: © Michael Winterbottom, British Broadcasting Corporation, 1999.

is one of 'changing the type of time and space of the film from a very particular set of events in one character's life to a more general, abstract meditation on city life'.[55] In *Wonderland* the icons of London are always part of the cityscape and are not highlighted or distinct from their context but become narrated as 'private' places for contemplation or intimate event, albeit in the public realm, rather than sights. The city is portrayed as an everyday experience suffused with routines, encounters, stories and interpretations all of which are held in balance by urban systems, situations and the lives they enclose (see Figure 4.17). This film, perhaps more than any of the others discussed here, highlights the diminished legibility of spatial order in the city, instead illustrating the lived experience as one that negotiates networks, systems and nodes of fluctuating programme, density and urban space. Most significantly, *Wonderland* reinforces an understanding of the identity of the city as being inscribed by its inhabitants and vice versa, favouring personal narratives that are at once vital to the individuals concerned and meaningless to the world beyond them. This balance is effectively depicted throughout the film as Charlotte Brunsdon has noted: 'Now while on the one hand we have been clearly shown that this is Saturday night London nightlife, on the other the disassociation of the mise-en-scène encourages us to read at a more general level. Although we know exactly what has happened to Nadia, we are also encouraged to see Nadia as just one person in a huge city.'[56] The intertwined

Figure 4.17 Personal reflection in the 'iconic' city, *Wonderland*
Source: © Michael Winterbottom, British Broadcasting Corporation, 1999.

complexity of everyday behaviour, as first defined by Jane Jacobs in *The Death and Life of Great American Cities*, illustrates the flows of people and the city as a confluence of lived experience and urban conditions. The networks precipitated by social interaction and lived experience actually form as a result of both necessity and contingency, but, most pertinently, in spite of the built environment, rather than because of it. Living in cities, as with any location, predicates routines and behaviours that are often functional and not necessarily sublime, a feature that *Wonderland* successfully depicts. A deliberate paucity of phenomena is instead replaced with the minutiae of everyday life but the importance of such activities should not be underestimated as the anthropologist Tim Ingold writes: 'A place owes its character to the experiences it affords to those who spend time there – to the sights, sounds and indeed smells that constitute its specific ambience. And these, in turn, depend on the kind of activities in which its inhabitants engage. It is from this relational context of people's engagement with the world, in the business of dwelling that each place draws its unique significance.'[57] In this sense, the city is an organic body in which the seemingly mundane and banal are where the points of interest lie. The experience of most people living in an urban landscape is just this type of relationship; unremarkable yet inseparable from the city's built fabric. Perhaps most critically, our ability to flow through urban systems and engage space in different terms has resulted in the city becoming intrinsic yet muted to urban living as Richard Sennett as noted: 'Today, as the desire to move freely has triumphed over the sensory claims of the space through which the body moves, the modern mobile individual has suffered a kind of tactile crisis: motion has helped desensitize the body. This general principle we now see realized in cities given over to the claims of traffic and rapid individual movement, cities filled with neutral spaces, cities which have succumbed to the dominant value of circulation.'[58] The strengths of *Wonderland* are in its capacity to show us the mappings of individuals that accumulate and form a collective text of urban conditions. By using parallel narratives, the film is able to convey the contingencies and realities of urban existence through a series of events that imaginatively, but also essentially, capture the mutuality between the city and those that live in it (see Figure 4.18).

Films, therefore, provide us with a highly engaging mode of inquiry and structure that affords description and critique of the contemporary city and its various permutations. Never static or easily defined, the urban conditions of films allow for the multi-scalar framework of the city to be navigated and narrated in a manner that is at once both personal and detached. Films also allow the city to be described as a dynamic and realistic series of spatial demarcations that create a rich and typically complex system of urban space ingrained with various definitions, social claims and activities dependent on their occupation or use. Considered in this way, it is possible to see films as mappings that correlate with Lefebvre's social

Figure 4.18 Everyday urbanism, market, Madrid, 2009
Source: Author's own, 2009.

production of space, i.e. they illustrate an intersection between the three modes: spatial practices, representations of space, and representational spaces. This has implications for urban systems as it is a medium that may capture the marginalia that is fragile and fleeting yet so endemic to life in cities.

It should also be emphasized that this type of work is not simply limited to cinematic representations either, with a vast array of artists working with film media to explore the urban environment. Doug Aitken is one such figure who has created video installations that are wholly immersive in their physical layout and filmic content. In his installation work, *Electric Earth*, 1999, the viewer is presented with a multi-sectioned walk-in experience that uses the gallery sequence of space as representational of urban space with a narrative in a conventional sense (see Figure 4.19). As Michael Speaks observes '*Electric Earth* becomes real when we become part of its image flow ... We are surrounded by "perceptions" actualized in a space where the dancer's subjectivity divides in two placing us at the centre of his world. We are exposed to the very same images he is exposed to—all the "background" images that do not result from but cause his reactions. But we are also exposed to his actions perceived as images—his trek across the city'.[59] However, it also possible to see the narrative of the installation as having a different relationship, with a clearly demarcated beginning, middle and end set of conditions. The filmic transition from the initial confined space, via an open street view, towards the final tunnel perspective also recalls a classic American motif of the twentieth century, the highway to the horizon. Perceived in this manner, *Electric Earth* resonates with

Figure 4.19 *Electric Earth*, Doug Aitken, 1999
Source: © Doug Aitken, *Electric Earth* 1999, Venice Biennale, courtesy of 303 Gallery, NY.

Figure 4.20 Times Square = city life, copied and pasted around the globe, New York, 2009
Source: Author's own, 2009.

the wider context of the urban environment in a much more general sense, offering the viewer a direct physical narrative parallel to the film's thematic content and shift. The *experience* of film in this regard is, as discussed at the beginning of this chapter, perhaps the closest we may be able to engage with urban life other than reality itself. As the artist himself has stated, 'I think the experience of nonlinearity and fragmentation is with us all the time. They are sometimes seen as dangerous and are often associated with chaos. But in many ways, they're truer to reality'.[60] This reminds us not only of the more permanent physical layout of the city but also the systems and elements that are in flux. The value of this for architects and urbanists is significant as films facilitate translations and reinterpretations that may reveal aspects and patterns that are latent and buried deep within the temporal state of cities. Viewed in this manner, films become instrumental in edifying our understanding of urban form and social life and highlight the performative aspect of the built environment (see Figure 4.20). The power of films as devices that disclose the temporalities of urban conditions should not be underestimated as Isabelle McNeill has suggested:

Like the city wanderer moving through inhabited streets and architecture, the subject navigates through the contemporary landscapes of media, memory and the metropolis. But these representational zones rarely 'map onto' one another with perfect coherence. Rather, they fuse to create a multi-dimensional, mobile space where disorientation is a constant possibility. As we move through time and space, the mental maps we produce of our mnemonic, urban and media environments are constantly subject to redistribution and sometimes to complete disintegration and fragmentation. But rather than understanding this as a growing threat to the spatio-temporal anchoring of the modern subject … I would suggest that the geography of our social representations have always held the possibility of dislocation, but that this phenomenon can be reconceived and represented anew through contemporary artistic media, including film.[61]

Films afford a mapping and descriptive technique that explicitly addresses the temporal features of the lived experience in cities. In addition, they facilitate the mapping of versions of the city that consist of urban subtexts, networks and nodal collision. By chronicling personal narratives, films have the capacity to explore the mutuality between the environment and those within it. Through the production and analysis of such maps, which acknowledge the lived experience of the city, architecture and urban design may be more responsive to its inhabitants and users. The inclusion of this information may develop our understanding of urban interstices and provide us with the opportunity to explore unchartered terrain, physical and hypothetical, in architecture and urbanism. The films discussed here illustrate interpretations of urban space and seek to make sense of such space, no matter how dire the conditions or events. This is a significant issue as urban space is intrinsic to those that engage with it and far from a benign influence or backdrop to the behaviour and interaction of people. The contribution to our knowledge of the physical and time-based characteristics of the urban landscape that films offers us should therefore further equip and enhance our strategies for addressing it.

Endnotes

1   Harvey, D. (1990), *The Condition of Postmodernity* (Oxford: Blackwell).
2   Skeates, R. (2003), 'Those Vast New Wildernesses of Glass and Brick: Representing the Contemporary Urban Condition', in: Laplace, P. and Tabuteau, É. [eds] *Cities on the Margin; On the Margin of Cities* (Besançon Cedex: Presses Universitaires Franc-Comtoises) pp. 25–42.
3   Tonkiss, F. (2005), *Space, the City and Social Theory* (Cambridge: Polity Press) p. 113.
4   Webber, A. and Wilson, E. [eds] (2008), *Cities in Transition: The Moving Image and the Modern Metropolis* (London: Wallflower Press) pp. 2–3.
5   For example see the overview of the birth of the film city in Barber, S. (2002), *Projected Cities* (London: Reaktion Books).

6   Bruno, G. (2008), 'Motion and Emotion: Film and the Urban Fabric', in: Webber, A. and Wilson, E. [eds] *Cities in Transition: The Moving Image and the Modern Metropolis* (London: Wallflower Press) p. 26.

7   Penz, F. (2008), 'From Topographical Coherence to Creative Geography: Rohmer's *The Aviator's Wife* and Rivette's *Pont du Nord*', in: Webber, A. and Wilson, E. [eds] *Cities in Transition: The Moving Image and the Modern Metropolis* (London: Wallflower Press) pp. 123–140.

8   Strickland, R. (2006), 'Background into Foreground: Film as a Medium for Teaching Urban Design', *Places: Forum for Design of the Public Realm*, 18(2), pp. 44–51.

9   Tschumi, B. (1994), *Architecture and Disjunction* (Cambridge, MA: The MIT Press) p. 157.

10   Toy, M. [ed.] (1994), *Architecture & Film*, Architectural Design, No. 112 (London: Academy Group, 1994) p. 7.

11   Rattenbury, K. (1994), 'Echo and Narcissus', in: Toy, M. [ed.] *Architecture & Film*, Architectural Design, No. 112 (London: Academy Group, 1994) pp. 34–37.

12   Lefebvre, H. (1991), *The Production of Space*. Translated by Donald Nicholson-Smith (Oxford: Blackwell) pp. 189–190.

13   Benjamin, W. (1985), *One-way Street and Other Writings*. Translated by Edmund Jephcott and Kingsley Shorter (London: Verso) p. 179.

14   See, for example, Hall, P. (1988), *Cities of Tomorrow: An Intellectual History of Urban Planning and Design in the Twentieth Century* (Oxford: Basil Blackwell).

15   Bruno, G. (1997), 'Site-Seeing: Architecture and the Moving Image', *Wide Angle*, no. 19, p. 12.

16   Tom McDonough has compiled all the key work of the Situationist International with particular emphasis on the connections between the city with their theories and practices: McDonough, T. [ed.] (2009), *The Situationists and the City* (London: Verso). Also noteworthy in this regard is Simon Sadler's compelling book on the Situationists in which he analyses their critique on the built environment and their principles for the city and the lived experience of it: Sadler, S. (1998), *The Situationist City* (Cambridge, MA: The MIT Press).

17   Perec writes about the fragility of space in relation to time and memory, suggesting that both serve to distort, if not erode, 'places' as they are containers for events and behaviour which are transient in nature: Perec, G. (1999), *Species of Spaces and Other Pieces* (London: Penguin Books Ltd.) p. 91.

18   Virilio, P. (1991), *The Lost Dimension*. Translated by Daniel Moshenberg (New York: Semiotext(e)) p. 25.

19   For example see Benjamin, A. (1994), 'At Home with Replicants: The Architecture of Blade Runner', in: Toy, M. [ed.] (1994), *Architecture & Film*, Architectural Design, No. 112 (London: Academy Group, 1994) pp. 22–25.

20   Neumann, D. [ed.] (1996), *Film Architecture: Set Designs from Metropolis to Blade Runner* (Munich: Prestel-Verlag) p. 7.

21   Schwarzer, M. (2004), *Zoomscape: Architecture in Motion and Media* (New York: Princeton Architectural Press) p. 230.

22   Canudo, R. (1911), 'The Birth of a Sixth Art', in: Abel, R. [ed.] (1988), *French Film Theory and Criticism: A History/Anthology 1907–1939*, Vol. 1 (Princeton: Princeton University Press) p. 61.

23 Pallasmaa, J. (2001), *The Architecture of Image: Existential Space in Cinema* (Helsinki: Rakennustieto) p. 18.

24 For a contemporary exemplar of this tradition it is worth considering the body of films produced by Peter Greenaway. His treatment of architecture as both a structuring device as well as a metaphorical vehicle for events in his cinematic work is well documented. For further discussion on this aspect of his films see Elliott, B. and Purdy, A. (1997), 'Flesh on the Bones: Architecture as Allegory', *Peter Greenaway: Architecture and Allegory* (Chichester: Academy Editions) pp. 45–62.

25 Peter Greenaway interviewed by Marcia Pally (1991), 'Cinema as the Total Art Form', *Cineaste*, 18(3), p. 9.

26 Vidler, A. (1993), 'The Explosion of Space: Architecture and the Filmic Imaginary', *Assemblage*, no.21, pp. 44–59.

27 Orr, J. (2003), 'The City Reborn: Cinema at the Turn of the Century', in: Shiel, M. and Fitzmaurice, T. (2003), *Screening the City* (London: Verso) p. 285.

28 Benjamin, W. (1999), *The Arcades Project*. Translated by Howard Eiland and Kevin McLaughlin (Cambridge, MA: The Belknap Press) p. 83.

29 Bruno, G. (2002), *Atlas of Emotion: Journeys in Art, Architecture, and Film* (London: Verso) p. 66.

30 Orr, J. (2003), 'The City Reborn: Cinema at the Turn of the Century', in: Shiel, M. and Fitzmaurice, T. (2003), *Screening the City* (London: Verso) p. 284.

31 The context of Leigh's operations in relation to contemporary urban conditions are discussed in detail in: Watson, G. (2004), 'In Pursuit of the Real', *The Cinema of Mike Leigh: A Sense of the Real* (London: Wallflower Press) pp. 25–32.

32 For an incisive analysis and treatment of *Naked*'s characters see Whitehead, T. (2007), 'The Future is Now: Naked', *Mike Leigh* (Manchester: Manchester University Press) pp. 90–113.

33 Carney, R. and Quart, L. (2000), *The Films of Mike Leigh: Embracing the World* (Cambridge: Cambridge University Press) p. 237.

34 Carr, J. (1994), 'Naked: English Director Mike Leigh Turns His Uncompromising Vision on the Way Things Are', in: Movshovitz, H. [ed.] (2000), *Mike Leigh: Interviews* (Jackson: University Press of Mississippi) p. 56.

35 As quoted in: Fuller, G. (1995), 'Mike Leigh's Original Features', *Naked and Other Screenplays* (London: Faber and Faber) p. xxxviii.

36 Carney and Quart (2000) p. 242.

37 For a thematic overview of films connected to the representation of contemporary urban conditions see: Blandford, S. (2007), 'Last Orders in Wonderland: England and Cinema', *Film, Drama and the Break-up of Britain* (Bristol: Intellect Ltd.) pp. 19–46.

38 Review by Rich Cline. Available at: www.shadowsonthewall.co.uk/06/redroad.htm [accessed 13 February 2010].

39 Pope, A. (1996), *Ladders* (New York: Princeton Architectural Press) p. 232.

40 Brook, R. and Dunn, N. (2009), 'The Control of Space: Mediating Fear in the Urban Condition', *Isolative Urbanism: An Ecology of Control* (Manchester: bauprint) pp. 7–14.

41 Nock, S.L. (1993), *The Costs of Privacy: Surveillance and Reputation in America* (New York: Aldine De Gruyter).

42   Pisters, P. (2008), 'Multiple Screen Aesthetics, Neurothrills and Affects of Surveillance', *Cartographies of Sensation – Between Emotion, Feeling and Affect in Art, Philosophy and Science*. Vienna, 14–15 November 2008.

43   Mahoney, E. (1997), 'The People in Parentheses: Space under Pressure in the Post-modern City', in: Clarke, D.B. [ed.] (1997), *The Cinematic City* (London: Routledge) p. 183.

44   De Certeau, M. (1984), *The Practice of Everyday Life* (Berkeley: University of California Press) p. 111.

45   For a detailed account of these cinematographic techniques and the urban conditions they represent see Higbee, W. (2001), 'Screening the "Other" Paris: Cinematic Representations of the French Urban Periphery in La Haine and Ma 6-T Va Crack-er', *Modern & Contemporary France*, 9(2), pp. 197–208.

46   Penz, F. (2007), 'The City Being Itself? The Case of Paris in *La Haine*', in: Marcus, A. and Neumann, D. [eds] *Visualizing the City* (Abingdon: Routledge) pp. 150–151.

47   Ibid. p. 148.

48   See Higbee, W. (2007), 'Re-Presenting the Urban Periphery: Maghrebi-French Filmmaking and the *Banlieue* Film', *Cineaste*, Winter, pp. 38–43.

49   As projected in films such as *Four Weddings and a Funeral*, 1994, and *Notting Hill*, 1999. For further discussion on this representation of London and the United Kingdom see Monk, C. (2001), 'Projecting a "New Britain"', *Cineaste*, 26(4), p. 35.

50   See Gibson, S. (2006), '"The Hotel Business is About Strangers" Border Politics and Hospitable Spaces in Stephen Frears's *Dirty Pretty Things*', *Third Text*, 20(6), pp. 693–701.

51   Roddick, N. (2002), 'Dirty Pretty Things', *Sight and Sound*, 12(12), p. 45(1).

52   Sandhu, S. (2002), 'The City's Secret Heartbeat', *Daily Telegraph*, 13 December.

53   Lucia, C. (2003), 'The Complexities of Cultural Change: An Interview with Stephen Frears', *Cineaste*, pp. 8–15.

54   Dix, A. (2009), '"Do you want this world left on?": Global Imaginaries in the Films of Michael Winterbottom', *Style*, 43(1), pp. 3–25.

55   Brunsdon, C. (2004), 'The Poignancy of Place: London and the Cinema', *Visual Culture in Britain*, 5(1), pp. 59–74.

56   Ibid.

57   Ingold, T. (2000), 'The Temporality of the Landscape', *The Perception of the Environment: Essays on Livelihood, Dwelling and Skill* (London: Routledge) p. 192.

58   Sennett, R. (1996), *Flesh and Stone: The Body and the City in Western Civilization* (London: Faber and Faber) p. 256.

59   Speaks, M. (2002), 'Doug Aitken's Temporal Ecology of Images', *Doug Aitken A-Z Book (Fractals)* (Philadelphia, Pa.; Zürich; Ostfildern-Ruit: The Fabric Workshop and Museum; Kunsthalle Zürich; Hatje Cantz).

60   Daniel, N. [ed.] (2006), *Broken Screen: Expanding the Image, Breaking the Narrative: 26 Conversations with Doug Aitken* (New York: Distributed Art Publishers) p. 8.

61   McNeill, I. (2008), 'Transitional Spaces: Media, Memory and the City in Contemporary French Film', in: Webber, A. and Wilson, E. [eds] *Cities in Transition: The Moving Image and the Modern Metropolis* (London: Wallflower Press).

5

Marks

The marking of space and the battle for space has become paramount, as artwork within the public domain, however executed or finished, has collided with the privatization of space. The critical debate around the making of marks on, between, around and within built space has moved from questions concerning the morality and motivation of the act, to a discourse around the demarcation, control and ownership of space. The predominant characteristic of a visual culture is the predatory regime of inscription. As a human characteristic, inscription clearly has its roots firmly grounded in pre-history, however painted narratives found in caves bear little relation to a seemingly futile culture of grafting a sign with no meaning onto any available urban surface. In this respect graffiti can be directly compared to branding, not to cave painting, and subsequently bound within a post-modern context.

When writing about any form of subculture and subcultural expression it is almost impossible not to get caught up in the ethics and politics that define a particular scene. Many of the guiding morals in this context are shared between disciplines and concern 'respect' within any given community, regardless of any outward display, or otherwise, of 'respect' for society at large. The, largely unwritten, nature of these scene-specific rules of engagement also mean that for the observer or recorder, some form of proximity, participation or absorption is necessary to be able to interpret or engage. This need to transcend politics and garner acceptance is far more amplified when studied from a sociological position or within other disciplines that concern themselves with the nature of society. Here, the interest lies not in the morally driven societal impact of activities that involve leaving marks in places construed or defined as private, but in the very act of making the mark and the sequential patterns of movement and behaviour through particular urban landscapes. To this end, the artists interviewed and referenced for this chapter have been specifically selected from the plethora of 'street' and graffiti artists that have emerged since the 1960s.

The artists that choose to perform in public and use the city as their canvas can be placed firmly into two camps: those that use the street to make money by virtue of legal public performance and those that use the street exclusively as a form of illegal expression. One of the first contemporary issues exposed when the term 'illegal' is uttered is that of the ownership of space. Whilst the paragraph above affirms a lack of concern, here, for the societal impact of these expressions, it is impossible not to discuss the impositions that policy and economics, and their perceived physical manifestations, make on the inhabitants of the city. The apparent control of the city, or a lack of, may account for a personal experience of a location as welcoming or threatening, friendly or hostile, safe or dangerous. Mark making and the act of graffiti can be construed as an indicator of lawlessness and a loss of control and is frequently cited as such when discussed by those that form and uphold the law, and even those that participate in the act:

> *I think graffiti disturbs because of a matter of disorder/mess. A big diagonal tag will always disturb more than a horizontal one. Then comes the saturation and most of the time more disorder with it. But, I don't know if you remember the shops shutters in the 90's in Paris, people were painting their tag following the lines of the shutter in a very arranged way and I think that way less people were disturbed by graffiti.*[1]

The control of urban space is possibly the defining characteristic of the early twenty-first century, many citizens of the United Kingdom would recognize their urban environment as composed of conditions that are elements of the fictional dystopian futures of the twentieth century, *1984*, *Logan's Run* (see Figure 5.1), *Total Recall*, *A Brave New World*, are all filled with technocratic mechanisms of control, supposedly to the benefit of the greater good, but having read, watched and understood the anxieties presented by such visions, how have we walked into a version of our future that we authored with such derisory fear? The answer is, incrementally. A slow, but steady, collision of ideologies and modes of production through the twentieth century has made manifest the state of control. The confluence of modernism and capitalism has created a series of urban landscapes that impose control through surveillance and fear and their respective perception.[2] The heavily surveyed and internalized spaces of our cities were formed as a result of reactionary policy to the exurban peripheral development of shopping centres during the post-war era. The coincidence of the exclusion of certain types of individual and activity, usually perceived as undesirable or antisocial, from these spaces, is just that, a coincidence, but the privatized nature of public space within these confines promotes sensations of comfort and security that effectively makes a 'better'

Figure 5.1 Film still from *Logan's Run*
Source: © Michael Anderson, Warner Brothers, 1976.

consumer. It may be considered that the heightened sense of reality induced by the internalized landscapes of the modern retail environment is in fact responsible for our apparent detachment from the very nature of the city.

We view the city as niche-space. Our lives have become sufficiently mobile to enable an experiential sequence concerned with jumping from one specific physical context to another in the most direct and most perceptibly 'safe' way possible. The notion of mobility and its proximity to urban experience is not a new one and has indeed concerned architectural discourse for the better part of half a century, since *View from the Road*.[3] The perceived directness of the urban consumptive experience related to motor driven mobility has only been amplified by the addition of communication technology to this construct. Where once one would drive to the urban centre and browse amongst a determinate number of locations for a particular product, the act of browsing is now performed conveniently via the Internet and the act of physical purchase, if at all, is one of a very direct 'retrieval'. If then, the predominant mode of experience is consumptive and occurs in niches, albeit still spaces of encounter, what is the resultant impact on the reading of the city? The sequence described above is largely prohibitive to components that are outside of the control of the participant, it is not the experience of the city of 100 years ago. The grime and gritty reality of aspects of the city are excluded from this mode of experience and viewed with fear and suspicion. A burgeoning gap between rich and poor in Western society is fast becoming the type of dystopian order of the have and have-nots perceived as abhorrent in fictional accounts.

Anthropologist Mary Douglas sheds some light on the societal constructs that go some way to informing the social orders within which activities such as Outsider Art may exist. Her group and grid theory[4] proposes four principal types of social organization plotted onto a graph. The four are said to exist in all societies with varying degrees of dominance, yet individually opposed and incompatible in terms of status, behaviour and social control (see Figure 5.2).

The terms 'group' and 'grid' are defined as a general boundary around a community and the control of individual behaviour by regulation respectively. A member of traditional society, said to be dwindling in numbers, could be described as *Positional*, a family orientated structure with strong religious beliefs. The *Individualist* is weak in group and grid and characterized by the private benefit and capitalist consumptive cultures of the West. The *Isolate* is highly controlled but often without community, asylum seekers can be seen to be part of this typology, typically the *Isolate* attracts little attention. An *Enclave* is a small group living in a hostile environment from which they have withdrawn, they recruit amongst the *Isolates*.

Douglas predicts that the Enclaves could be considered as all sorts of subcultures, both benign and destructive, and that their strength is stimulated by a general sense of disillusionment of the mainstream. Those who practice art illegally in the street may be viewed as of this set, the pertinence of this model is that it makes no other account for motivational reasoning other than a need to disassociate with perceived conventional societal constructs and, as such, negates any moral debate about a particular activity. It is perhaps pertinent here to introduce artists that are accepted

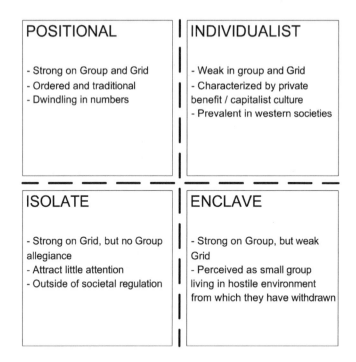

Figure 5.2 Diagram to illustrate the sectors and factors within Douglas' *Group and Grid* **theory**

Source: From original produced by Rick Dargavel, Manchester School of Architecture, 2009.

within the contemporary art world that share practice with those emerging from a subcultural context. The discourse and commentary applied to 'legitimized' practice within conceptual art is accessible and appropriate and neatly avoids any distractive negativity in its dissection.

Daniel Buren is one such artist who has worked in a breadth of environments and sustained a method of work that has consistently maintained a dialogue with space. Techniques of repetition of content, form and placement have perpetuated as he has developed an exchange between his material and the matter within which it exists. Perhaps subject to the ravages of commodification, Buren has unfortunately been labelled as 'the Stripe Guy', due to his use of striped material as a recurrent motif within his work. It is his work outside and within marginal spaces, and his approach and attitude to context that is relevant to this examination.

The width of the stripes upon a range of materials in Buren's work is an unwavering constant. The 8.7cm dimension of the strip was inherited from work with striped fabric which invariably had stripes gauged between 8.5 and 9cm. Buren actually qualifies his own gauge and tolerance as 'Striped bands, alternately white and coloured, each 8.7cm wide, plus or minus 0.3cm',[5] this 0.3cm deviation the only variation in 40 years of practice. The striking aesthetic of the banded material affirms the implicit character of the interventions as necessarily transformative to facilitate an exchange with context that is consistent, yet site specific.[6] He began to utilize printed paper as his medium in the external environment and commenced the anonymous act of placing striped posters around Paris by night, as he perceived it as being 'safer', a notion he eventually rejected in favour of working in daylight. Paris in the 1960s was a hotbed of political activism in reality as much as within art theory, the city was covered with ad hoc adverts and manifestos and Buren's act and product slipped into this landscape without challenge. He acknowledges that after May 1968 the police became more interested in his activities; any act in the street was viewed with suspicion following the riots.[7]

In a conversation recorded between Pierre Huyghe and Buren in 2001,[8] Buren considers the break he made from painting vertical lines on canvas and his move into the wider urban environment. He characterizes that leap as a wholesale shift in practice, in ideology and critique. Whereas the repetitive motif of the 8.7cm wide line upon the finite surface of a canvas was calling into question the limits of convention and the mode of artistic production in the avant-garde, to transpose the motif to an external, non-gallery position immediately altered the role of the line, the composition and the signification of the works. Perversely it was the successive and repetitive nature of the act of painting canvas that led Buren to the street, but the street that inverted the striped identity of his 'signs' from provocateurs to negotiators. Buren himself, in the course of the interview, refers to the motif as a 'visual tool', an important distinction to the artist and here. His 'tool' or 'sign', as he describes, is his alphabet and is a long way from any inscribable notion of 'logo': 'A logo is a complete and indivisible whole outside of which it cannot exist. It is an autonomous object. A neutral sign allows reading, rereading and connecting. It contradicts or emphasizes its surroundings.'[9]

Whilst maintaining a position that holds Buren's work, importantly, as a mutating sign, that implies specificity but has associative properties by virtue of its constants, it is also important to understand that whilst the stripes enable readings and re-readings this was not their primary function. The act of working 'in-situ' and without a studio was paramount to Buren as he initiated his field experiments and it is the choice implicit in doing so that subsequently informed the reading of the work and the work as a reading. The term 'in-situ' is most commonly used in architectural dialogue to precede the word concrete, and by its virtue implies a sense of permanence not associated with the term 'pre-cast', for example. Buren uses the term in its truest and most literal sense to describe 'a work which not only has a relationship with the place in which it finds itself, but also which has been made entirely in this place'. To qualify this Buren used to precede the phrase with the word 'made' on the invitations to his private view. Doherty discusses the role of the term 'in-situ' in the titles and in his own descriptions of his working methods. She proposes that this is indicative of his concerns of site specificity and place. Quoting Massey, she writes, 'what gives a place specificity is not some long internalised history but the fact that it is constructed out of a particular constellation of relations'.[10]

This condition is exemplified by his 1995 reworking of a 1970 work *Bus Benches*, this time curated by the Temporary Contemporary gallery, an annex of the MOCA, Los Angeles. The original piece was advertised by means of a postcard without a title, carrying the statement 'There are visible, alternate vertical stripes, white and blue, from 15th June to July 30th day and night on 50 bus benches'.[11] In his revisiting of this piece Buren used his stripes, this time in white and green, to coat the back of concrete benches at bus stops across the city, a space usually reserved for advertising (see Figure 5.3).

This instantly presents the viewer with a conceptual image of the infrastructural networks of the city that are connected at these locations and invites participation in pursuit of an aesthetic vision of the conceived whole. The manner in which one negotiates the city to view some or all of the sites requires the navigation of abstract representations of forms of the city; stylized transport maps are notoriously disconnected from geometric space. In his 2004 programme, *Map Man*, Nicholas Crane illustrated this point by walking between two tube stations in London and then travelling between the two stations underground, the disparity between the actual physical proximity and the abstracted diagram of Beck's 1933 tube map is illustrated by the amount of time taken on the two journeys, walking being a fraction of the time of the tube journey and that implied by the tube map.

Should the viewer choose to move between the *Benches* sites by a method other than by bus, he establishes new formal networks between the pieces and a pedestrian viewer, unfamiliar with the terrain, is inadvertently participating in the practice of dérive. This imposed or implied dérive has more credence and content than other subjective and referential art practice contemporary to this piece. Buren himself talks, though without definite intent, about the complementary nature of the works as assembled groups or comparative negotiations of their contexts. The linking of heterogeneous objects or spaces, and the reading of these, as contradictory between locations is an express goal of Buren, though he acknowledges that it is not successful at every turn. There also exists in this work commentary about the ownership of space, the prevalence of the sign, branding and the everyday.

Buren uses the term 'photo-souvenir' to describe images of his work recorded at a particular moment in time. Adopting a tourism term to its own ends, Buren explicitly elevates the viewer to participant; the act of recording one's own souvenir or purchasing another's vision of the same implies concern, critical or otherwise, with context. By so branding the image, the role of the viewer as participant is crystallized, without their consultation. It is a powerful assertion that places Buren's work, not exclusively as providing a reading, but legible in its own right, it is in fact the objectification of the work that Buren would seem to have spent years trying to avoid. It is, however, inevitable that his work would become objectified in the capitally driven art market and it may be argued that the application of the word 'souvenir' charges the record of the work with the heavily subjective articles of memory and nostalgia, thus negating any such imposition by critics or academics and retaining the role of mediating and shifting sign.

In an interview with Hans Ulrich Obrist,[12] Buren, when asked to consider his works in rural locations, makes explicit his understanding of a process driven

Figure 5.3 *Bus Stops*, Los Angeles, Daniel Buren, 1995
Source: © Keith Schoenheit, 1995.

landscape of human intervention, stating that he can be responsive to any built condition and his work is as contextual in a rural setting as an urban setting. He dismisses the notion of working in a desert, as the land artists of the 1960s did, as he perceives it as without encounter and without a human history and it is the constructed environment on which he draws when entering a negotiative discourse of line, form and space. This statement makes clear the intent of Buren to engage directly with other forms of human intervention, whether as activism, prevalent in his early work, or as discursive. His work is not about the exploration of the limits of space, as Smithson et al.,[13] but a negotiation about place using intervention in real space to expose latent characteristics of the city; political, social and institutional.

Whilst Buren would eschew the political content of his work he acknowledges that once a work is within the public domain its politicization is not in the hands of the artist, but in the hands of the public. In an early work, which perhaps subverts his apparent quest for the ambivalence or neutrality of the act, Buren illegally posted pink and white striped paper over a significant portion of Bern's billboards after having been rejected from participation in a collective exhibition, *When attitudes become form* (1969 Bern, Switzerland).[14] This may be viewed as principally a provocative act in the context of the invited exhibition that Buren sought to either append himself, or challenge. This aside, the deliberate use of such a charged and corporate space across such a broad domain is undoubtedly calling into question issues concerning the demarcation and ownership of space in the city.

When asked directly about architecture Buren is less confident of his relationship with such and it would appear that his default position is to objectify context using a visual language: 'Architecture and architectonic elements are formal anchoring points among others. The furniture, the colour … are visual elements which are jut as indicative as the architecture itself.'[15] It is assumed here that he refers to his direct association with buildings that he considers carry the label 'architecture', in which he has performed installations, indeed the interview progresses to such a conclusion. It is of note that Buren does not defer to a position concerning the role of architecture in the production of space, his primary field of operation. It is within this dialectic, between form and space, that his interventions provide comment or readings.

The development work associated with *The Eye of the Storm*,[16] a large installation at the New York Guggenheim, actually exhibits Buren's concern with the city much more explicitly than he would appear to be able to separate 'architecture' and 'the city' in discussions concerning his own work. The descriptions and phrasing in the exhibition catalogue piece, *Along the Ways: From Plans to Realisation*, are demonstrative of Buren's inherent grasp of the relationship between interior and exterior space, between positive and negative space and the operative characteristics of the urban grid. He also managed to embed memory and memorial in the narrative surrounding the proposal, as it unfolded. The use of a frame to describe the orthogonal nature of the grid and thus expose the negative space of Frank Lloyd Wright's imposition would also call to mind the scaffold originally installed to facilitate the spiralling form of the building. This work, more importantly its development, might be said to affirm the thematic content of earlier pieces in the street and of the city. The product of the city is space and memory and the presence of these, whilst abstracted, is evident, from posters to bus stops to buildings, in this examination.

Rorimer writes of the close association of Buren's work with architecture[17] and cites his project in the Art Museum of the University of Berkeley in particular as being an architecture in its own right and simultaneously permitting a reading of the architecture within which it exists. In this context though it is undoubtedly his earlier works in the street that have resonance with other navigational practice that mediates the latent networks of the city. Even Buren's gallery pieces, which negotiate interior and exterior architectural space, speak less of the 'city' and more of a specific and constrained context than the *affichages sauvage*,[18] which speak 'with' the street, rather than 'of' the building. It is this unanticipated and chance driven incident that allows the work to be read beyond the act of its placement and as a barometer of the city by virtue of its placement and its immutable form.

The unquestionable ephemeral nature of all works on the street cannot be denied, but the temporality of such is not always conceived of in terms of its decay. The convention within graffiti is that better paint and an absurdly inaccessible spot will ensure longevity, increased visibility and thus greater kudos. Latterly, in the work of artists like Swoon (see Figure 5.4), the deliberate engineering of fragility

Figure 5.4 Swoon cut out drawing amongst tags on a doorway, New York, 2009
Source: Author's own, 2009.

and guaranteed degradation was integral to pieces applied to a street context. The *affichages sauvage* of Buren inadvertently raised these questions as a critical concern, amplified by the apparent need of the participant to read the posters as a group or series and the indiscriminate forces of removal, over-posting and weathering continually acting upon the 'series'. Buren embraced the role of dissident artist but was distinctly aware of the potential discourse thrown up by his actions and that he had not preconceived the wealth of issues associated.

The term 'street art' is often considered derogatory within the community of artists working in public, and, effectively, a byword for 'amateur' by those who consider themselves to be 'true' graffiti writers. Eltono, a Parisian living in Madrid, uses the term 'public space artist'[19] to describe his practice and Invader, a Parisian in Paris, has coined the useful term 'invasion'[20] to describe his work. The semantics of the ascription and the associated implications thereof are important in this context. Whether or not artists who practice non-traditional forms of graffiti are indeed 'art fags'[21] is not pertinent to this inquiry and rests, as an argument, within a long and complex series of unwritten, ever shifting rules concerning the practice of graffiti. In its initial forms when geographically confined predominantly to the subways of New York and within a relatively small group of practitioners, who had regular contact with one another, the code of graffiti was a more overt and discernible entity and is described with unequivocal precision and clarity in the 1982 publication, *Getting Up*.[22] The global proliferation of the act and the virulent consumption of every available surface has led to infighting and splintered ethics dependent upon specifics; online forums are frequently peppered with annals of opinionated diatribe concerning morals and authenticity of acts and works, when in fact, after nearly 40 years in existence, authenticity has all but vanished from graffiti.

One of the reasons for the negative implications attached to the term 'street art' is that it unfortunately acts as a coverall description and is commonly used to describe any form of mark making that cannot be classified within the conventions of graffiti. Despite the oppositions within the disciplines, the edicts of a strong work ethic[23] persist and commitment and subsequent exposure still carry cachet across the community. Many artists began their engagement with the urban realm practising the conventions of the tag, throw-up and piece before making the transition to working with other methods or means; it is therefore not unusual to transpose cultural codes from graffiti to art in the urban environment. In an unusually candid and direct essay, Steve Powers, known as ESPO, describes this shift and his personal politics:[24] 'Graffiti writers can make good artists. They've endured being beat, buffed and cuffed, and have come back for more.' In this sense he is simply acknowledging the requisite resilience of both the artist and the writer, and he goes on to try to explain the tacit ethics and his difficulty overcoming such: 'Graffiti and art are separate languages, and for years I was looking for a translation between the two. It was important to me that I kept the dialogue I had with the graffiti crowd going, and when I didn't see a way of creating art that spoke to my crowd, I just kept writing.' Powers is relevant here as his work has assumed a commercially acceptable, almost nostalgic, aesthetic

Figure 5.5 Espo (Steve Powers) 'T' for the *New York Times* magazine, 2006
Source: Author's own, 2009.

whilst continuing to subvert and challenge conventionally held ideas. He works in a strongly graphic style (see Figure 5.5) and has assumed the techniques and motifs of traditional sign-painters. His appropriation of the sign-writers' visual language permits perceptive socio-political commentary within a familiar visio-spatial context, the opposition between medium and message only serves to amplify the intent. Many artists, like Powers, who have wide appeal and acceptance, within and outside of the graffiti community, served their time as illegal practitioners.

Eltono explains that his method of application, with masking tape and a brush, rarely attracts the attention of authorities, whereas he suggests that painting with a spray can carries much more negative associations. Whilst painting in Madrid Eltono has never been arrested or asked to stop or move by the police, he considers his technique as 'benign'[25] and attributes his lack of problematic instances to the manner in which he applies paint to surfaces and the territory he chooses upon which to practice. Eltono clearly has a fascination with the orthogonal, his chosen sites are consistently rectilinear in form that allows his signature to be consistently applied, despite the site-specific nature of each intervention. 'So first comes the site and then the image, I draw and compose the painting depending on the main lines I found on the spot (windows, doors, colour change, light boxes…). I usually

Figure 5.6 Eltono, Manchester, 2002
Source: Author's own, 2008.

improvise the design in my head and then draw it directly with the tape, I almost never draw a sketch before.'[26]

Eltono and Nuria, both residents of Madrid, draw and work within themes discussed here in the practice of other artists, but have made themselves distinct in the adoption of that which Buren rejected, the logo. It is perhaps the logo as motif, as an alternative to the conventional letter-based tag, that epitomizes the shift in art practice in the streets since the turn of the twenty-first century. At its worst this can be a crassly conceived character that is made into a sticker or paste-up poster, at its best it can be a mediator between place and space, it can sustain political discourse, it can be a map, a network and a game. Eltono and Nuria use abstracted forms of a repeat 'icon'[27] a 'tuning fork' (see Figure 5.6) and a 'lock and key' (see Figure 5.7) respectively, which are adapted to the site in which they are placed. Their early practice has an archaeological resonance, both in practice and in record, and is distinctly tied to openings, niches and crevasses of the urban fabric.

> *Empty space is as important as painted space, actually, in my paintings, the painted stripes are the same size as the unpainted space between them so half of the painting is empty. It is something that I used to criticize in traditional*

graffiti, the fear of emptiness, it is very usual that graffiti artists fill all the space, without using the wall as a background and in a way canceling it.

Boundaries are also important in my work, I need elements on the wall to define the area where I'm going to paint. If there are no elements on the wall, no lines to work with, I usually want to go big and use the limits of the walls as the main lines for my design.

I need existing lines and boundaries to frame my work, if not, I will expand the painting until I found them.[28]

Eltono also rejects conventional letterforms[29] in favour of a minimalist device with which to negotiate space. Doors, blank panels, relief spaces in façades are all typical of the sites that Eltono and Nuria exploited in their initial post-graffiti[30] forays. These spaces, usually neglected or derelict, were chosen not to necessarily form any commentary on development or estate, but because a mark in an unmaintained location is likely to have greater longevity. They do however reveal a pattern of dereliction in the city and Eltono acknowledges the gentrification in 2009 of many areas that were undeveloped and keen spots for practice in 2000.[31]

Figure 5.7 Nuria, Liverpool, 2002
Source: Author's own, 2002.

I am affected because when a building is getting too old, and before being destroyed, it will be an art opportunity surface. Then, most of the occidental cities are changing to cleaner, this means less inspiration and less sites to paint for me. During the past three years, I did most of my paintings in Latin America.[32]

This is really part of the urban mechanism rather than any direct relation, but, in the cyclical transformation of the city, the scars are as valuable as the surgery. Eltono recognizes this and, as time passes, this value of his work becomes increasingly valuable as both as a metaphor for, and as part of, the city.

As I am painting on fixed elements in the street, I never own my artwork. This means they are not in a studio, protected by a plastic bag and everything can happen to them, from cleaning, painting, signing to poster pasting over. This is actually something I love. I love to see my painting evolving, it seems to me that the artwork is alive, painting street related art on a canvas is for me like a kind of stuffed art, like some art conservation process. I use to document my paintings each time I see it, to compare it with earlier pictures.[33]

A series of photographs published online chart the effects of time, action and reaction between Eltono, other mark makers and the cleaners on the metal panel of a newspaper kiosk in Madrid (see Figure 5.8). This can easily be referenced as a form of urban archaeology and both Eltono, and blogger Guillermo,[34] make reference to such. As the site has been cleaned with solvents, the two Eltono pieces, one on top of the other, have been remixed to create a battle-scarred new version. This is not unlike an earlier work by Eltono in Milan, which accelerated the same process by subtly inviting the public to take part.

In my gallery work I always give a big place to the public to interact with the artwork. I like to not control the whole process of creation, I like to be surprised by the result, I think it is an interesting way to learn about my own work.[35]

By binding three posters together, yet leaving the corners of the upper-leaf turned, as if to invite the act of peeling, and posting them in the street, Eltono was able to generate random and interactive remixes of his work. The project was inspired by the accumulation of layers that illegal posters and glue create on a site as they are repeatedly papered, and speaks of such, but the disposition, subsequent record, collection and representation of the entire work can be associated with the displacement of site, the ownership of space and ideas about chance and random event (see Figure 5.9). Of the original 16 posters, eight were recovered, four were left in-situ and four were stolen or removed.

Lykkeberg (2008) suggests that the distinction between conceptual art and graffiti is the same as that which binds them; writing. Both practices are concerned with writing, about their work or embedded within their work, although this point of common departure rapidly fissures as conceptual artists adopted simple

Figure 5.8 Eltono, Madrid, 2005–2009

Mutation or remixing of the two layers of the artist's imposition by other forces of the street, namely cleaning with solvents.

Source: © Eltono and Guillermo, 2005–2009.

Figure 5.9 Eltono, *Pubblico*, Milan, 2007. Poster that has been torn by passers-by
Source: © Eltono, 2007

fonts to permit focus on content and graffiti artists deconstructed the alphabet to attain distinction. The inability of critics to place graffiti within any art tradition or existing theory has allowed freedom for the graffiti writer to comment on the city in any way they see fit and often raise challenging ideas about the nature of space without intent.

> *I believe writers destroyed and rebuilt the alphabet to suit themselves, and ironically, by destroying the communicative aspects of letterforms, they succeeded in making letters icons, thus even in Hungary they know who SEEN is. The first time I saw somebody paint their name as a font, it was SANE, and it was a complete shock.*[36]

Here Powers asserts the reclamation of type in the graffiti canon. As ESPO (Exterior Surface Painting Outreach), Powers played an interesting game through the 1990s, in New York, using a visual language that paralleled the legitimized formal expression embodied in the practice of sign-writing. Powers' mode of practice was deliberately critical and distinct from other graffiti by its wider discourse concerning the legitimacy of the demarcation of urban space. ESPO often paints boldly in a 'mural' style, wearing boiler suits and looking vaguely official, he recalls, 'I'm in the home stretch with no hassles, when I hear a police radio squawk. I nearly fall off the ladder, but keep composed when the cop on the beat asks, "What do you get paid for this?" I said "$17.50 an hour, plus overtime". He nodded and walked on'.[37]

The selection of particular sites that were so visible, that the application of paint could not be naturally perceived as anything but legal, was one small part of this construct. The aluminium roller shutters of store fronts were one such space serially marked by Powers in a style that was far removed from that which had come to be associated with the aesthetic of graffiti. The adopted moniker of ESPO mutated in Powers' hands from a collection of letters into a self-styled corporate identity. A website, essentially a marketing tool composed from specific images of ESPO's work that were referential to some form of community outreach and environmental improvement by mural type work, carries the following statement:

> *The Exterior Surface Painting Outreach is a not-for-props volunteer organization dedicated to making the world a different place. We accomplish sweated-status by stepping up and seizing space wholesale, and selling it back to the public at retail. After paying pound royalties to Revs, and reinvesting in Home Depot Futures, the rest is pure profit. We tax toys, stay tax-exempt, and hold slackers in contempt. Currently we have over 28 sites on visual lockdown in the 5 boroughs of New York. In order to demonstrate the effectiveness of the come-up, grate keepers are dispatched at all hours, and have a get-over rate of 96.5%. That's over 62% more dope than the leading brand. The bottom line for ESPO is oil-based Gloss Black, and the future holds nothing but Aluminum for the stockholders of this fine company. (Mark Surface CEO, from the annual stockholders meeting keynote speech)[38]*

This linguistic parody of commercial terms, combined with slang, is typical of the playfulness that persists in this work. It is grounded in a history of irreverence in graffiti, which permits the projection of a flippant, couldn't-care-less, sarcastic critique of commercialism that simultaneously carries a weight and seriousness that is bereft from conventional modes of contemporary art. Powers manages to make his mark, treading a fine line between brandalism and corporate engagement, he acknowledges that to emerge from an illegal art practice to working with commercial entities is full of paradox, but doesn't necessarily allow any politicized concern of these apparent conflicts to pervade or dilute the content of his work.

An even greater irony exists specifically with ESPO; there is a prevalent concern amongst practitioners who recognize their work as no longer being 'graffiti', of being perceived as having 'sold out'. As ESPO, Powers had already exploited a commercial language to stand out, thus perhaps having already dealt with the prescient issues of identity, brand, ownership and authenticity and many of the nuances between. An essay by Powers for a catalogue published to accompany the Sponsorship exhibition at Los Angeles' BLK/MRKT gallery speaks of his attitude to working with corporations:

Don't be a tool.

Do something worthwhile or don't bother.

The first means that you have to put your needs ahead of the company you are doing work for. If they want you to rip yourself off for an ad campaign, tell them they're better off getting an intern to bite your style. The second quickly follows the first in that if the company is ready to let you be yourself, deliver the goods effectively without any internal conflict. Make art, show your good side, invoice promptly, repeat until tired.[39]

An ESPO work sponsored by Nike in Los Angeles is a case in point. He volunteered to paint over graffiti in the city in the style of the state-employed painters. This act usually involves the application of a paint that is similar, though rarely matching, in colour and tone to the surface upon which graffiti has been applied; the 'buff'[40] often assumes the formal envelope of the illegal mark in an orthogonal patchwork. ESPO, adopting this tactic, painted highly stylized, minimal versions of his letters, E S P O, over existing graffiti with the permission of the authorities via the legitimacy of a corporate sponsor (see Figure 5.10). There is an air of futility about the entire work, the supposed environmental improvement, valuable to the authorities, would have been temporary at best, the sponsor really saw little attention for its intervention and the very act of 'going over', albeit within a greater conceptual frame, is contradictory to the background of the artist in graffiti. Yet, the explicit aim of the work was to expose this futility and its resultant futile presence only serves to reinforce a position concerning the worth of space and its implied ownership by the marks applied to its surfaces.

The notion of graffiti as antisocial is easily understood; it is evidence of a lack of control. However, if we understand control and social order as the imposition of not the state, but of a capitalist consumptive system without the moral order of religion, then it is easy to see how apparently uncontrolled marks can be daubed upon the surfaces of the city without this accounting for, or being representative of, societal collapse. Graffiti did emerge in New York and Philadelphia at a time of economic depression and perhaps its virulent spread was attached to large numbers of young people without purpose or employment, but it has persisted as an art form through years of plenty and, indeed, has become a commodity in its own right. Perhaps graffiti does signal a lack of control, but when it directly challenges authority by virtue of the actual content this is often symptomatic of much wider unrest towards a situation. Spin's piece 'DUMP KOCH' in 1982, famously pictured in *Subway Art*[41] carries the tagline '*When will he learn the art will _never_ die?*' (see Figure 5.11). The work is a direct response to New York City Mayor, Ed Koch, and his campaign to rid the city of graffiti, amongst other clean-up measures. A photograph of the train carrying the message is presented to Koch in the film *Stylewars*,[42] his response: 'I guess I must be getting to them.' This reply typifies the flippant and dismissive attitude of Koch to wider social unease. Koch was held in contempt by a significant number of New York's minority communities for his unwillingness to engage with

Figure 5.10 ESPO, *Community Service,* **Los Angeles, 2002**
Source: © Steve Powers, Espo.

them and his apparent Manhattan-centric view, this attitude is epitomized by the character Sonny in Spike Lee's *Do the Right Thing* who expresses his dislike for the mayor during the montage concerned with racial prejudice.

Whether or not graffiti is morally acceptable is not for discussion here, and is such subjective territory that to promote discourse is relatively futile. The above

Figure 5.11 *Style Wars* **film still**
Mayor Koch reacts to photograph of Spin's piece Dump Koch, 1982.
Source: © Wienerworld, 2007.

seeks to inform a position wherein the general perception of a 'good' society is one of conformism and obedience to a context that has not been created by democratic freewill, but by economic forces outside of the control of governance. The act then, of making a mark, within this context may be seen as immediately calling into question the demarcation and ownership of space, whether as a deliberate act of defiance or simply a convenient place to perform.

In respect of convenience and surveillance, it is not in the interests of the artist to be caught as this will usually result in some sort of imposed punitive measures, it is therefore typical to find that hotspots for the practice of graffiti are often marginal spaces that are between periods of development or simply in decline. That isn't to say that the entire city may not be viewed and researched as a canvas, simply that there is a relationship between risk and proliferation that is related to authoritarianism and uncontrolled, unobserved spaces provide a calm territory for the artist to practice without fear of castigation. The hardcore of graffiti practitioners would not necessarily agree with this reading as truly reflective of the graffiti scene, indeed those that only paint on the street and do not run the risks associated with train yards may be held in contempt by others who see trains as the pinnacle of any writer's career. The painting of trains in the UK has become an increasingly complex activity requiring considerable commitment and planning, to an extent that would seem disproportionate to any person not fully indoctrinated and consumed by the act of making these particular marks.

The burgeoning Urban Exploration scene discussed in the introductory chapter, perceived as risky and cutting edge by some, could be compared to a tea dance when one considers the risk and penetration into forbidden and unused parts of the city by decades of graffiti protagonists. The 2009 book *Crack and Shine*[43] documents the London graffiti scene from the 1980s to the present day and celebrates the act of infiltration, in particular the section on Teach DDS, which contains a series of images of Teach ascending access hatches from various underground locations and the artist proudly opening a locker full of keys to the Bakerloo line tunnels. This constantly shifting game of cat and mouse is composed of action and reaction, mischievous accounts of 'playing' on the tube all day and deploying buttons and switches on the trains just to find out what they are for and whether or not the resultant action is useful in the arsenal of the writer in his battle to 'get up', forms some of the narrative. Artists' demonstrable knowledge of vast tracts of London's hidden space is brought to the fore in Sky Travel's 2004 series *The Tube*, where engineer Andy Hog qualifies the penetrative navigational skills of writer Tox and his knowledge of the London Underground network, stating, 'even I don't know how to get into these places'.[44] The desire to paint is such that in seeking new spots writers often are putting their lives at risk and it is not unknown for young people to have died in the act of reaching or painting. The security that now surrounds most urban railways is such that a determined writer must now be even more persistent and obsessively dedicated to gaining access to forbidden places; security

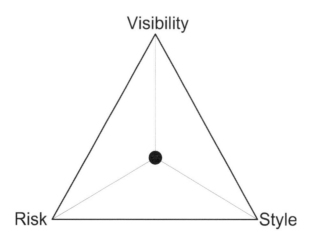

Figure 5.12 The Burner Triangle
A piece that satisfies all three criteria equally may well be considered a true burner.
Source: Author's own, 2010.

means risk and risk combined with visible presence, carrying a 'style' weighting, is the currency of kudos within the, predominantly male, community of graffiti (see Figure 5.12).

KR, Craig Costello, using his two letters has taken rooftop practice and placement as perhaps the primary concern of his illegal work. Commercially successful with his own ink, KRINK, Costello is said by Powers to be 'a minimalist in his medium, concentrating his efforts on tags throw ups and straight letters'.[45] This was in 1999 and referring to his work predominantly in San Francisco. On return to New York, KR established a strong visual presence by the use of inherently simple letterforms in extraordinary and provocative places, alongside ESPO, Cost and Revs, amongst others. Here, KR places his unmistakable letters so that they are visible from PS1 in Queens, at a time when large parts of MOMA are closed to the public for the new extension and some of their collection exhibited at the Brooklyn gallery (see Figure 5.13). Whilst contemporary art cannot really fathom graffiti, here is graffiti poking fun at it. Costello's concern seems to be with form and space; photographs in his monograph show blank marks in abstract shapes,[46] not related to any graffiti, in various urban contexts. His work with his own ink has become increasingly abstracted, as he works no longer with product, but with resultant, the drip. The drip has a history within graffiti related to bad application or cold weather and the excuses tagged alongside poorly executed

Figure 5.13 KR, visible from PS1 Gallery, Queens, New York, 2001
Source: Author's own, 2001.

Figure 5.14 KR, various, New York, 2009
Source: Author's own, 2009.

pieces,[47] the mistake was often deliberately drawn into letterforms themselves as if the characters were melting. KR allows his drip to be the work itself; the ink finding its own path, through over-application, down the surface to which it has been applied. USPS mailboxes, doors and the insides of trusses are afforded new spatial definition as the ink mediates their surface and form in the manner of Smithson's *Asphalt Rundown* (see Figure 5.14).

This ultimate gesture towards form over style can be perceived as contradictory to the traditional governing rules of graffiti and, despite being embedded within the KRINK brand, it is reductive to the point of uselessness and the typical absence of commentary from the artist reinforces its futility to the public. Despite this, the art fraternity has bought the brand KR and KR has increasing association with established galleries (see Figure 5.15). The drip pieces are contextual insofar as their motion and rest are concerned but, as described, they have cultural resonance and the proximity or lack of distinction between the branded version and the art version of Costello's practice epitomizes the contemporary cultural landscape.

The common aesthetic between the artists discussed here is one of reduction, of a retreat from the conventional visual language of graffiti. It is this relocation that sets these artists apart and either their continued ethical balance or previous history that sustains their credibility amongst their peers and external critics alike. Despite their self-extraction from graffiti, all of these artists choose to be publicly known and allow their practice to fashion some form of existence whilst preserving their integrity; this is in marked contrast to Revs. As KR and ESPO, Revs developed his practice through the rejection of traditional, yet obtusely imposed, rules of graffiti.[48] His work is such a rejection of style that even lovers of graffiti struggle to grasp his intent, he is without ambition for fame and now positively avoids publicity or any form of self-promotion.[49] Several interviews and texts contain accounts of an attempted suicide by Revs, and the rejection of that act as having shifted his

Figure 5.15 KR, Eyebeam Gallery, New York, 2007
Source: © FW18, 2007.

attitude towards production in the street to 'the point of a pure primal grunt'.[50] Revs has rejected style completely in favour of content, whether it is hidden work[51] or work in ultra-exposed spots. Revs is known to have painted subways where no one would ever be able to fully read his emotional narrative outpourings. It was his intention to record a verse in every subway tunnel in New York, he completed 235 before his arrest in 2000.[52] In his case it is a *complete* rejection of earlier more traditional letterforms, Revs used to be known as Revlon, a respected writer of trains throughout the 1980s. The stylistic shift between the two identities is so extreme 'that most spectators think it's two different people'.[53] In an examination of Revs' work that is currently accessible,[54] which is clearly a small fraction of his production, the eschewing of style, in favour of material permanence, becomes apparent, 'which is the point, after all'.[55] This is not, though, indicative of his early practice that initially moved away from conventional modes of graffiti.

With Cost, during a sustained period in the early 1990s, Revs went 'all-city' like no one before, using stickers, posters, rollers, disguises and any other ammunition available, the pair went on an express mission 'to change philosophies a bit. Change everyday life',[56] with the assertion that 'graffiti's changed in the '90s; nowadays writing your name on walls, just putting it up everywhere, is the same old same old. Scrawl on the streets, writ on the trains then it gets cleaned the next day, talk a lot of garbage ... You've got to try something different'.[57] They used an answering

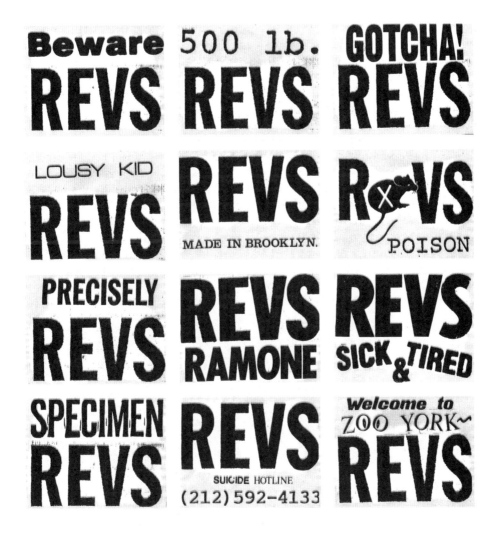

Figure 5.16 REVS, various posters
Source: © REVS.

machine with messages from 'Graff's Grandma', an old lady's voice espousing a twisted wisdom, to communicate with the public, who called the numbers printed on their posters. It was this period too that saw the development of extendable paint rollers used to form simple, but huge, letters high on the sides of buildings, a diversification of method as well as message; as Revs says, 'graffiti writers do have a message. It's just that nobody knows what it is. It's not a strict statement, it's a way of life'.[58] Cost's statement concerning the everyday has a resonance with other post-modern reactionist activity that counts a heightened reality as more valuable than a closer inspection of the norm. The adoption of this broad range of media to cover every available surface moved their version of graffiti firmly into art territory, but remained 'unauthorized, not for profit, public art'[59] and Revs and Cost maintained a work ethic equal to that of any illegal writer.

Their posters were apolitical or contained direct cultural jibes albeit in obsequious and confusing textual dispositions, some of which Revs readily admits were meaningless.[60] Nonetheless, the unsettling nature of the overtly disenfranchised voice screaming from the page in stark black capitals raised questions about commercialization and its impact upon society (see Figure 5.16). Though the socio-political context within which these provocative acts occurred are not as relevant here as the physical relationship between practitioner, tool, media and site. The limits of graffiti were conventionally bound by the body and space, but these productions superseded any such limits,[61] by the use of scaffolding and ladders, alongside their modified tools. A new measuring device against the scale of the city, particularly in their roller works, typically executed on brick gable walls, the divisible space shared between the letters, as if on a page (see Figure 5.17). The conceived whole of Revs' life story scattered through the subway tunnels as a metaphor for the fragmented existence in and of the nichescape city is too

Figure 5.17 REVS COST, New York, 2009
Shortly after this photograph was taken, the letters, which had been up for more than 10 years were cleaned as part of the new High Line park development.
Source: Author's own, 2009.

Figure 5.18 REVS, micro-sculpture welded to post, Bushwick, New York, 2009
Source: Author's own, 2009.

alluring a proposition to discard, regardless of the motivation for this act; Revs gets about as far as stating, 'this is my way of documenting everything'.[62]

In a further expedition into hidden space, but at a micro-scale, Revs also produces tiny steel cutout versions of his letters and welds them into almost invisible or seemingly innocuous locations, predominantly in edge space, be it post-industrial or riverside, these are places that are not ordinarily trodden (see Figure 5.18). Here too is a mapping of the residue of late capitalism of modern ruin, and a fossilized marker that simply alludes to the fact, 'I watched this happen'. This text stops deliberately short of trying to impose a reading of Revs' work without a discourse that involves him. The description of how his work exists within that which we have defined as the contemporary urban landscape and how this work may be conceived to be part of that landscape is of value here, as is the rejection of style. The perceived lack of skill, deliberately practiced by Revs and Cost and a hundred artists behind them, has actually now become a part of graffiti culture, and thus absorbed by that which it strove to escape. When accepted as a norm and on collision with the hardcore this scrawled version can debase graffiti to the simple nature of 'smash it all', largely in response to measures designed to prevent vandalism.

They can no longer create beautiful vandalism due to the London Underground's zero tolerance policy, so they will vandalise in the most disgusting way they can. Economics has now crept into the realm of the vandal as all aspects of a secret war are considered.[63]

The above statement accompanies a photograph of a tube train with two wide lines of black paint dragged, without design, across the length of four carriages. The perceived war over space means that all opportunity to mark, no matter how crude, will be asserted by certain 'dedicated' practitioners. The constant battle between those making marks and those motivated to remove them is reduced to a physical appropriation of space by layer upon layer of paint, alternatively the practitioner and the cleaner. The association of the forms of these marks is a narrative about the nature of the particular site. The tag is always a trace of the mediation between the actor, his tool and the space to which it is applied, the over-painting invariably assumes an orthogonal patchwork quality and serves only to cover the extents of the mark rather than the repainting of the entire space. This layer of paint subsequently forms a new spatial canvas inside of the original and often governs the mediation of the next act of marking. This cyclical process of mark and re-mark, other than keeping cleaners employed, is about the control of space as much as any other discourse.

The territorial nature of graffiti is perhaps less evident or prominent in Western Europe and indeed in the United States than it was at its inception, and continues to be in parts of Central and South America. The idea of crews 'owning' an entire subway line and being 'up' more than any other was one of the defining characteristics of the early days of graffiti in New York as documented by Chalfant and Cooper,[64] phrases like 'stay off my line' were commonplace and do persist to this day, but are now more within the realm of nostalgic paraphrasing than any gang related territorialism. Rivalry in the form of written insult, if not 'crossed out' or 'gone over' (see Figure 5.19) may be perceived as a healthy challenge, driving crews with a common aim to cover as much surface as possible. Crossing out may indicate that a personal spat has arisen between individuals or crews, but is largely attached, in the West, to minor perceived misdemeanours within the code of graffiti and misplaced adolescent, testosterone driven, anger. 'Beefs'[65] do exist, and do run on for years and can result in physical confrontation, but they are not usually attached to gang related culture or to a truly territorial context wherein the ownership of the walls indicates the ownership of the street and its (illegal) economics. There *is* an increasing amount of gang related graffiti on the streets of Britain, and this may be construed as actually reinforcing some of the stereotypical associations of fear and lawlessness, but the predominant marking of the street is made by those with a creative bent and a mild appetite for risk. It would be unrealistic to disassociate risk and the endorphin and adrenalin rushes attached to such from the act of working on the street, but again, this aspect of the act is sufficiently explained here by the notion of the act as 'political' and the breadth of motivations that this coverall provides. It is however necessary to make mention of

Figure 5.19 Evidence of rivalry, Ballard, Seattle, 2009
Source: © Jetpack McLeod, 2010.

the association of territory, risk and politics of graffiti in order to discuss the most spatially composed sector of urban marking, *pixação*.

Pixaçãoes is the Brazilian expression for tags, and the territorial nature of the work of the *pixadores* is second to none in its application and its scaled up typographic approach to the space of the city. The phenomenon has been discussed in the Western media via the work of Francois Chastanet, primarily in *Eye* magazine[66] and subsequently in the book *Pixação: São Paulo Signature*. *Pixação* has emerged from the slum areas of Brazil and represents the most authentic and energized method of marking since the birth of graffiti. Its autonomy and distinction from any tradition stemming from New York is asserted on the basis that its emergence can be traced to the favelas and its style to typefaces from 1980s heavy metal record sleeves. This practice of marking is intrinsically bound to the architectural surfaces upon which it is found. It is distinct from the New York tradition insofar as it is buildings, rather than trains, that are the primary canvas. Much like Cost and Revs, it is the limits of the available space that define the strokes of the *pixadores*, and the use of rollers to make their mark.

The physical act of climbing is very much a tradition within *pixação*, the very top of any building is the most esteemed position for a name to rest. Writers work together to climb and cover an entire building, often standing on one another's shoulders to ensure that the character fills the requisite space. This is a direct and express relation between body, space and architecture that is more explicit than any other form of urban marking (see Figure 5.20).[67] The extent of coverage in São Paulo should not be underestimated, the fabric is overwhelmed by the simple letterforms, words predominantly in Portugese, and assuming new manual forms of Runic and Fraktur scripts.[68] The calligraphic language of *pixação* is classifiable because of the unity within the letterforms and the practitioners. It is a distinct community, of individual actors; the *pixadores* are united in their battle against the city. It is a cohesive visual language that systematically engages with the grids of the city's façades, 'an empirical design method, subtended by a grid logic, an awareness of optimum space utilisation applicable to the entire city backdrop'.[69] Chastenet discusses the comprehension of the architectural façade as a blank sheet of paper and likens the orthogonal modernist building to an administrative form, a perceptive analogy given the regulated mode of urban production. This perceived reduction of architecture to a skin is emblematic of the actual process, described in Chapter 2, where architectural production is limited to that of sign within an image economy. It is also symptomatic of the type of urban space that develops without distinctive characteristics between its component parts; further evidence of the 'urban' overtaking the 'city'; the continuous neutral mediocrity of capitally driven processes occupying block after block, a predatory colonization of space. It is this condition of seemingly undemocratic territorial occupancy and a polarized social economy that drives the *pixadores* in pursuit of their own piece of city, but also to reclaim the entire city and to continue to do so until some form of, indeterminate,

Figure 5.20 Films stills from Pixo to show the acrobatic teamwork of the *Pixadores* at work, 2009

Source: © João Weiner and Roberto Oliveira, 2009.

'change' is brought about. It is revolutionary and political, but is a battle reserved to the material of the city and not attached to a revolutionary movement with a specific manifesto. It is an aggressive practice, yet paradoxically passive act, that is not to say violence does not occur, police and citizens alike have been known to physically attack writers, if caught.

Again though, it is not the socio-political context of an unequal society that is of concern here, it is the manner in which the practitioners view and engage with the urban environment. Groups of *pixadores*, when together in a social context, will work with a sheet of paper, folded into equal divisions and subdivisions in the manner of a gridded façade and collectively fill the sheet with letters, covering the entire surface. Whilst not a proposal of intent, in the way many graffiti 'blackbook' sketches are, the act mirrors the manner in which an architectural façade is examined when the target of a group hit. The distribution of space, on paper and on buildings (see Figure 5.21) demonstrates an egalitarian hierarchy, so

Figure 5.21 Building, São Paulo
Source: © Marco Gomez, 2009.

consistent and fair, that its structure calls into question its anarchic character. These unifying characteristics, of the letterforms and of their scalar relationships, have two direct effects concerning the perception of the urban environment: read as a whole, abstracted vision, unconcerned with letters, the marks assume ornamental properties, the serifs and glyphs taking on the appearance of wrought iron work. This ornamentality is in stark contrast to the bland façades of São Paulo's urban agglomeration and its presence actually begins to populate and define the visual image of the city. A building emblazoned with *pixação* can be perceived as a monument,[70] thus upsetting the indistinct order of urban space with the 'forces of exception'.[71] That an illegal practice of making marks can actually transform not only the material of the city, but its perception and identity should be viewed as a phenomenal state of emergence, a non-hierarchical, peer-to-peer, mode of exchange and production has managed to overpower, or more accurately, undermine, the state and its infrastructure. The gap, left by an absence of material discourse, has been exploited and filled by any means. The components of the urban have been reclaimed by the 'people' and, whilst unsanitary to many, the organic structure of the favelas has invaded 'Metropolis'.

Where the *pixadores* have deconstructed the geometry of the façade with their letters, Eltono, in his recent work, has begun a three-dimensional dialogue between his motif and urban space. More and more commissioned work is providing the opportunity for large-scale markings on pieces of urban infrastructure. Where once his motif delicately negotiated niches and textured surfaces, in São Paulo he was invited to paint a concrete ventilation shaft, no doubt cleaned of *pixação* prior to his arrival (see Figure 5.22)! The contextual nature of the work is obvious, from the published photograph of a glimpse of an existing painted building caught from the bus, to the formal application of the lines and forms that make the intervention. As a solo artist, rather than a group, Eltono carries out similar operations to the *pixadores* in his exploration of space. His motif is expanded and mutated to wrap and define the structure, its parts and its limits, one can anticipate a formal translation of this piece wherein the object mass of the ventilation shaft is 'removed' and the motif enters into a new formal dialogue with itself as a re-presented version of the original.

It is possible to draw all manner of observations concerning the urban environment through the examination of artists who practice in the street. Often their work reveals more about the processes of urbanization than studies of the same. The proximities between commercial branding and the repetitive icon of the artists are apparent and the authenticity of the purportedly legitimate logos is called into question by the considered production and situation of the illegal. The nature of space and form is repeatedly explored from the sophisticated evolution of handstyles in the tradition of tagging, to the dissolution of style in 1990s New York and onward to the post-graffiti landscape of Europe. Context is of paramount concern in each act, no matter how aggressive, dismissive or planned. The mapping of this activity either by protagonist or spectator reveals latent patterns within the planned geometric space of the city and the negotiative patterns of its infrastructure; this specific practice is considered in more detail in the proceeding chapter. *Pixação*

184

Figure 5.22 Eltono, *Rojo Out*, São Paulo, 2009
Source: © Eltono, 2009.

has been seen to deal with classical architectural orders of proportion and to be explicitly representative of social hierarchy and territorialization. The continued evolution of post-graffiti practice into formal three-dimensional intervention is discussed alongside contemporary intervention art in Chapter 6.

Endnotes

1   Eltono (2010), Written interview conducted by the authors by e-mail. 25 March 2010.
2   See Brook, R. and Dunn, N. (2009), 'The Control of Space: Mediating Fear in the Urban Condition', *Isolative Urbanism: An Ecology of Fear* (Manchester: bauprint) pp. 7–14.
3   Appleyard, D. and Lynch, K. (1964), *The View from the Road* (Cambridge, MA: The MIT Press).
4   Douglas, M. (1970), *Natural Symbols. Explorations in Cosmology* (London: Barrie and Jenkins) pp. 77–92.

5   Interview with Jerome Sans (1998), *Daniel Buren on the Subject of ...* (Paris: Flammarion). Reprinted in: *Intervention II, Works in-situ* [Cat.] (Oxford: Modern Art Oxford, Nov. 2006–Jan. 2007).

6   Doherty, C. (2007), *Daniel Buren: Engaging Specificities* in *Daniel Buren* [Cat.] (London: Lisson Gallery, 18 May–23 June 2007) pp. 3–4.

7   Notes by Martin Bromirski from a lecture *Daniel Buren: In Response*, Tuesday, 10 May 2005 at The Guggenheim, New York, to accompany his exhibition *The Eye of the Storm*. Available from: http://anaba.blogspot.com/2008_03_01_archive.html [accessed 8 February 2010].

8   Huyghe, P. (2002), Conversation with Daniel Buren in *Daniel Buren* [Cat.] (London: Lisson Gallery, 18 May–23 June 2007), first published in *Parkett*, no. 66/2002.

9   Ibid.

10   Massey, D. (1993), 'Power Geometry and a Progressive Sense of Place', in: Bird, J., Curtis, B., Putnam, T. and Tickner, L. *Mapping the Futures* (London: Routledge).

11   Reference to the 1970 exposition retrieved from images of card from Barbara Reise archive held in the Tate Collection. Available from: www.tate.org.uk/archivejourneys/ reisehtml/scene.htm [accessed 10 February 2010].

12   Boutoux, T. [ed.] (2003), *Hans Ulrich Obrist Interviews, Volume I* (Milan: Fondazione Pitti Immagine Discovery) pp. 128–140.

13   Robert Smithson and his contribution to the Land Art movement and subsequent impact on spatial discourse will be discussed in Chapter 6.

14   Abarca, J. (2008), *What's Graffiti? What's Postgraffiti? Julio 204 and Daniel Buren in the Spring of 1968*. Available from: http://urbanario.es [accessed 14 April 2010].

15   Interview with Jerome Sans (1998), *Daniel Buren on the Subject of ...* (Paris: Flammarion). Reprinted in: *Intervention II, Works in-situ* [Cat.] (Oxford: Modern Art Oxford, Nov. 2006–Jan. 2007).

16   *The Eye of the Storm. Works in-situ by Daniel Buren* [Cat.] (New York: Guggenheim, 25 March–8 June 2005).

17   Rorimer, A. (2003), 'Daniel Buren. From Painting to Architecture' in: *Parkett* #66/2003.

18   Literally 'wild postering'. Referring, in the first instance, to Buren's work in Paris with green and white striped printed posters.

19   Eltono (2008), available from: www.eltono.com [accessed 15 April 2010].

20   Invader (2001), *FAQ*, available from: www.space-invaders.com [accessed 15 April 2010].

21   Term used to describe and deface legal works on the street by those committed to the proliferation of illegal graffiti and the preservation of a non-commercial ethos. Famously daubed by *10Foot* over *BestEver* work at the Art Lounge, London. See: www. nerdbanite.com/2009/03/banksy-and-art-fags-attacked [accessed 29 November 2009].

22   Castleman, C. (1982), *Getting Up. Subway Graffiti in New York* (Cambridge, MA: The MIT Press).

23   Martinez, H. (1975), *A Brief Background of Graffiti* from *United Graffiti Artists* [Cat.] (New York: Artists Space, 9–27 September 1975) pp. 3–7. As early as 1975, Hugo Martinez had stated, 'Only a youth with a sense of vocation can put in the necessary amount of work'.

24   Powers, S. (Espo) (2004), 'These Definitions Are Mine', in: *Ill Communication II* [Cat.] (Manchester: Urbis).

25   Abarca, J. (2008), *Eltono*. Biography. Available from: http://urbanario.es/archives/294 [accessed 29 December 2009].

26   Eltono (2010), Written interview conducted by the authors by e-mail. 25 March 2010.

27   Abarca, J. (2008), *Eltono*. Biography. Available from: http://urbanario.es/archives/294 [accessed 29 December 2009]. In a Baudrillardian order read 'sign' for 'icon'.

28   Eltono (2010), Written interview conducted by the authors by e-mail. 25 March 2010.

29   In conversation with the artist. Madrid, September 2009.

30   Abarca, J. (2008), *Postgraffiti*. Available from: http://urbanario.es/en/i3 [accessed 18 April 2010].

31   Ibid.

32   Eltono (2010), Written interview conducted by the authors by e-mail. 25 March 2010.

33   Ibid.

34   Guillermo (2009), *Eltono y Nuria de nuevo en Madrid*. Available from: www.escritoenlapared.com/2009/10/eltono-y-nuria-de-nuevo-en-madrid.html [accessed 15 April 2010].

35   Eltono (2010), Written interview conducted by the authors by e-mail. 25 March 2010.

36   Powers, S. (2009), Written interview conducted by the authors by e-mail. 15 December 2009.

37   Powers, S. (1999), *The Art of Getting Over. Graffiti at the Millennium* (New York: St. Martin's Press) p. 42.

38   Powers, S. (1998), *ESPO*. Available from: www.graffiti.org/espo/speech.html [accessed 12 May 2008].

39   Powers, S. (2003), 'Community Service', in: McGinness, R. (2005), *Sponsorship. The Fine Art of Corporate Sponsorship. The Corporate Sponsorship of Fine Art* (Corte Madera, CA: Gingko Press). Originally published in 2003 by Anthem Books and Obey Giant INC. on the occasion of the exhibition *Ryan McGinness: Sponsorship* at BLK/MRKY Gallery, Los Angeles.

40   The 'buff' is a term used to refer to any form of graffiti removal and is derived from the buffers of the machines that are used to clean subway trains.

41   Cooper, M. and Chalfant, H. (1984), *Subway Art* (London: Thames and Hudson) p. 94.

42   *Stylewars* (1983), Directed by Tony Silver and Henry Chalfant (New York: PBS) [Film: 16mm].

43   Forsyth, F. (2009), *Crack & Shine* (London: FFF).

44   *The Tube: Series 2* (2004), 'Underground Crime' [Thursday 19 August 2004] Produced by Mosaic Films for Carlton Television.

45   Powers, S. (1999), *The Art of Getting Over. Graffiti at the Millennium* (New York: St. Martin's Press) p. 58.

46   Costello, C. (2006), *KR* (New York: Also Known As – 12oz Prophet).

47   Cooper and Chalfant (2004) p. 38.

48   The term 'rules', whilst rigorously played out by ill-informed generations of writers as they adopt graffiti, is somewhat contradictory to the original actions across early hip-hop culture, which was concerned with being fresh, new and experimental.

49   Query from the authors directed to Steve Powers as to whether or not Revs would be willing to meet, if they were to travel to New York, met with the answer, 'Revs is probably a no'.

50   Powers, S. (1999), *The Art of Getting Over. Graffiti at the Millennium* (New York: St. Martin's Press) p. 95.

51   A comment by a Flickr user [*anastassiades*] concerning her discovery of a piece she suspects is Revs' refers to its location as 'a site which seems deliberately chosen for its obscurity (as far as I know, no one ever goes to this place but crackheads, people having sex, and me)'. Thread title: *'could someone explain "d-rock" and "d-rock lives?" please ...'*. Available from: www.flickr.com/groups/revs/discuss/72157622739586587 [accessed 12 January 2010].

52   Solis, J. (2007), *New York Underground: The Anatomy of a City* (London: Routledge) p. 89.

53   Powers, S. (1999), *The Art of Getting Over. Graffiti at the Millennium* (New York: St. Martin's Press) p. 95.

54   Predominantly via online social forums, such as Flickr.

55   (1996) 'Cost and Revs', in: *Juxtapoz Magazine*, Issue #6, p. 62.

56   O'Brien, G. (1994), *Cream of Wheat Paste: Cost and Revs – Graffiti Artists – Interview* (Art Forum, March 1994). Quote from Cost.

57   Ibid. Quote from Revs.

58   Ibid. Quote from Revs.

60   Ibid.

61   That isn't to say that other artists were not using the same or similar tactics during the period in which Revs and Cost developed theirs.

62   Rivera, J. (2008), *Vandal Squad* (New York: Powerhouse Books) p. 120.

63   Forsyth, F. (2009), *Crack & Shine* (London: FFF) p. 148.

64   Cooper, M. and Chalfant, H. (1984), *Subway Art* (London: Thames and Hudson).

65   Slang for 'argument'.

66   Chastanet, F. (2005), 'Pichacao', *Eye*, 56, pp. 40–49.

67   Chastenet, F. (2007), *Pixação: São Paulo Signature* (Toulouse: Xgpress) p. 243. Chastenet writes at length about this relationship under the title *Signature, Body and Architecture*. The practice described as a '"giant ductus", vastly exceeding the limits of the hand and wrist, here calling upon the entire body in its relationship with space'. p. 240.

68   Chastenet (2007) covers the subject of the typographic content of *pixação* in great detail, charting its origins, history and development.

69   Chastenet (2007) p. 243.

70   Ibid. p. 242.

71   Ibid. p. 235.

6

Object

If we accept the conditions, described in the introductory chapters, of architecture, more specifically, the architectural product of a capitalist system, as having been reduced to the role of object, as a sign, within the image economy and that context, in this order, is reduced to the mediation of policy, then it must also be understood that the predominant production of buildings is no longer reflective of, or discursive with, the complex networks of urbanity. These networks themselves are impenetrable infrastructural edifices that have ceded to the status of 'black box' in our imaginations.[1] In the way in which Chapter 5 can reveal latent narratives about signs and branding in a contemporary urban situation, this chapter also serves to reveal a narrative, about the order and negotiation of space in the urban condition and how a critical understanding of the evolution of art in the environment can be translated to a discourse concerning the production of architecture. In this sense we limit the discourse to physical artifacts, permanent or temporary, that are placed outside of the gallery. Whilst the connections between legitimized or illegal practice are little explored with regard to the tension between their constructed realities, we shall discuss and measure 'objects' produced by a range of artists and practitioners by using the same criteria which do not necessarily differentiate between the modes of practice; what does this practice or product mean when one considers 'the city' and 'architecture'? Objects are physical interventions that may generate or activate the potential, or latent meaning, of a place. A deliberately placed object is loaded with meaning as it establishes both physical and cultural relationships with its context. It can influence the way in which a particular location is perceived, it can frame a view of something else, it can form a focal point or even a landmark. Objects may form reference points for the users and visitors of the city to orientate themselves.

The objects to which we will refer in this chapter are thus more complex in their composition than the 'architecture' with which they engage or choose to represent. Typically, this complexity is manifest in one of two ways: the object as part of a greater network, or the object as an interactive re-ordering of space. Meyer makes the distinction between the types of sites that these interventions utilize, using the terms 'literal site' and 'functional site'.[2] The first, an actual location, physical place, and the second, a 'process, an operation occurring between two sites, a mapping', an allegorical site.[3] These two terms may also be used to categorize the physical (dis)location of the works explored in this chapter. Kwon considers Meyer's functional site as 'a fragmentary sequence of events and actions *through* spaces, that is, a nomadic narrative whose path is articulated by the passage of the artist',[4] but is limited in her translation of this to a practice context as she relies on commodified and commissioned works in her exploration of site and place.

As will be made evident here, the practices of specific urban artists, outside of the art establishment, and architects who practice intervention, align more distinctly with these two theoretical projections of the discourse that art should promote with space. Projects will be presented here that encompass elements of each of the above systems and these will be proposed as able to sustain a multi-dimensional discourse with the city.

The process of objectification within the materiality of a concrete world is not latent; it is a global daily event. Marcuse[5] and subsequently Sartre[6] both held the belief that objectification lies at the basis of what we may define as a distinctive human experience, the mediation of human need through objects. The authors of *The Meaning of Things* remark that 'Man is not only *homo sapiens* or *homo ludens*, he is also *homo faber*, the maker and user of objects'.[7] What then is the nature of the object in a hypermodern and hyper-regulated society?

> *Objects are not the locus of the satisfaction of needs, but of a symbolic labour, of a 'production' in both senses of the term: pro-ducers – they are fabricated, but they are also produced as a proof. They are the locus of consecration of an effort, of an uninterrupted performance, of a stress for tangible proof of social value.*[8]

Here, Baudrillard identifies the 'object' as important in our recognition of self and of environment, that it is socially constructive, but he also acknowledges the restructured relationships in subject-object dialectics and the analytical fragmentation of function, which have transformed the traditional articulation of the object to assume the role of sign.

> *The object only appears when the problem of its finality of meaning, of its status as message and as sign (of its mode of signification, of communication and of sign exchange) begins to be posed beyond its status as product and as commodity.*[9]

The object will adhere strictly to the definition of sign; it is programmed as a signifier, and adopts the secondary function of the objectifiable signified as its primary role. Within this construct, the repeated mutable forms of certain artists act as signs of the greater system and as signs of intervention, in parallel to their discourse with site. Kwon forms a convincing argument for the dissolution of 'site' in modern art practice and the implicit paradox between popular 'site specific' works and their (re)production. The notion of site as a physical place is acknowledged as an inevitable mental association, yet the paralleled forces of networked globalization and digital space are seen to increasingly contradict a fixed idea of site and the momentum of the text gravitates towards a chronological evaporation of site into the realm of ideas and hyperspace. This position draws on Kwon's architectural education and places, without tension, the dissolution of site within the diminishing and fragmentary order of the city. She uses Frampton's *Critical Regionalism* concept to explain the desire or 'hidden attractor' in the term *site-specificity* and artists' attempts to establish 'authenticity of meaning, memory, histories, and identities as a *differential function* of places'. This practice is criticized for the limits it imposes on a particular place in the assumption that it carries only a historic identity, thus denying identities and histories that may be emergent. Perversely, the conclusion of the essay can be seen to frame the practice of artists who work, in or with, urban space, without actually proposing that this type of art satisfies the defined schematic. We are not witness to the anticipated dissolution of site, but the fragmentation of site, and a shift from the specific, to the generic. One of the final statements suggests that 'site-specific art practice might mean finding a terrain between mobilization and specificity – to be *out* of place with punctuality and precision' and that this may invert the ominous desensitized and generic urban experience.

However, the generic is not consistently destructive or diluting; the ubiquitous *Golden Arch* of McDonald's is often criticized for its intrusive global presence as a signifier of the destructive forces of capitalism, but the differences between the franchised restaurants all over the world are amplified by this conception of immutability; the nouveaux-classical version on the Champs Élysées, the Chinatown styled interior in downtown Manhattan, mock Tudor versions across

Figure 6.1 McDonald's, Southall, London
Source: Author's own, 2006.

the south of England, these differences are as valid an urban reading as that which concerns itself with the nuances of brick detailing of Georgian London (see Figure 6.1). As generic devices they are simultaneously globally homogeneous and locally specific, if not local in origin. Whether this is a success of the franchise, as having the capacity to mediate the imposed rules and demands of planning conditions and heritage landscapes, or an example of insidious malleability in pursuit of overwhelming appropriation, it is important here as this symbolic model of global accretion is mirrored in the post-pop production of certain branches of art and architecture. Of course, Hirshorn and Izenour in *White Towers* recognized this phenomenon prior to the birth of McDonald's.[10] Whether commercial or otherwise, the role of 'object' and 'site' (place) are articulated as essential navigational devices, as we read and order the world according to our own sensations and experience. These are neither specific nor generic, despite the perpetual application of suggestive memes designed to influence cognitive navigation. Maps of the city are personal constructs, formed from layers of associative memories and networked mental compositions of which 'object' and 'site' are small, but critical, components. When asked about urban navigation, the artist Truth reveals, 'Sometimes I don't remember the name of the street, but I know what graffiti pieces are there, the colour of the wall, or even what the condition of the pavement or the lawn is'.[11] This statement exhibits, perhaps, an anticipated response, that of 'graffiti', which is the tradition within which the artist exists, but goes further to suggest a personally nuanced perspective concerning the colours and condition of the surfaces of the city. Eltono is more direct: 'I navigate the city using the graffiti. I imagine that an architect uses buildings to remember his way in the city, I use graffiti. I don't do it on purpose, it came that way naturally after twenty years painting in the street.'[12]

Art Practice

Whilst it must be acknowledged that graffiti and arts emerging from graffiti do not exist within a lineage that can be seen to have any association with, or emergence from, an art history construct, there are elements or actions within a post-graffiti context that have resonance and a relevant association with earlier practices in Western art. This is not necessarily a series of positively correlated relationships, some paralleled operations are antithetical and, thus, also of importance. The intent here is not necessarily to propose art in the urban environment as part of a Western tradition, thus validating its presence and meaning, but to demonstrate how essential components of these pieces have their histories in works of the twentieth century that sought to dissemble convention and to propose new dialogues within art and with space, regulation and politics. Key to the contemporary works discussed in this chapter are the found object or readymade, the operation of chance, the displacement of the object and the record of process. Much of the work is recorded using photography and in many senses the photographic image and its representation is as much a part of the work and may act as intervention itself. The role of the photo in each piece described will be made explicit, but a wider exploration of the photograph as intervention has been deliberately avoided as its traditional proximal relationship with architecture is such that it deserves its own investigation. Certainly, if this chapter were concerned with the role of the object in art, rather than that of the art object in the city, then the photograph and its impact would warrant a more serious critical dissection. Without dwelling on this issue it is of note that several modes of practice and re-presentation may be categorized as useful in the context of this inquiry; the banal, the staged, photo-journalism and montage, all have their own extensive associations with architecture and the twentieth century.

Some of the later works analysed here make use of the found or scavenged object, this has been seen to be representative of the city in innumerable readings.[13] The practice of recovering material from the environment, and its reconfiguration at a new site, in contemporary art has its history in the *objets trouvés* of the early years of the twentieth century and, later, the *site/non-site* dialectic established by Robert Smithson. There is a distinction between objets trouvés and readymade that ought to be stated here; the latter implies the singular acquisition and presentation of the article without reconfiguration, the former is without such rigid tenet and may be assembled according to any precept that the artist chooses. Kurt Schwitters is known to have shifted his conceptual position during the 25 years spent building and adapting his renowned *Merzbau*, as his philosophical leanings migrated from Dada to Cubism.[14] Schwitters, though, was not concerned with the material translation of found objects as much as the composition of the elements to present a work with the capacity to absorb all of the arts into a single unifying construct, derived from the German tradition of the *Gesamtkunstwerk*. There were items of sentimental value embedded in the fabric of *Merzbau* and chambers created for his friends in the production of a socio-ideological personal 'cathedral', before Chtcheglov had even put pen to paper (see Figure 6.2).[15]

Conceptual art, in a neatly condensed position, may be seen to have made the switch from production to consumption following the advent of the readymade, pioneered by Duchamp, who shocked the world with his 1917 *Fountain* (see Figure 6.3). Lyotard describes this action: 'extremely important … is the manner in which he (the artist) has reacted to the situation capitalism has created as far as his activity goes: instead of continuing to produce unifying, reconciling forms, his activity has become a deconstructing one which is necessarily critical'.[16] This deconstruction of space, form and material in art is exhibited and is manifest in a myriad of works and practitioners and adequately explored in Kwon's and Meyer's previously cited essays, but may include acts as diverse as the documentation of illegal border crossings[17] and the purchase and parading of an automatic pistol through Mexico City.[18] In much the same way as conceptual art has been described as being concerned 'with writing' and graffiti as 'of the written',[19] the shift in post-graffiti urban practice towards production is also in opposition to the consumptive trajectory of art and, whilst referential, is distinct. Duchamp, as well as reducing art to a

Figure 6.2 Kurt Schwitters, Merzbau, 1932, installed at the Menil Collection, Houston
Source: © Cameron Blaylock, 2009.

consumptive act, also pioneered the notion of chance, so embraced by Debord, in art, with his 1914 work, *Three Standard Stoppages* (see Figure 6.4). The piece involved dropping three one-meter lengths of leather onto the floor, the path of the twisted strips is marked in thread and the thread used as a template for wooden representations of the one-meter unit.[20] Chance is embedded in the entropic nature of art in the urban environment, just as the copper roof patina shifts slowly to its mint green hue, so the paint, paper, metal and wood of intervention peels, dissolves, rusts and rots and speaks with the city. There is an explicit honesty about degradation that is lost in an increasingly sanitized and wipe-down city, formed from glass, terrazzo and steel.

Deckker suggests that contemporary architecture has become predominantly concerned with event and the relationship between object and broader context. He draws parallels between the minimal art of Judd and Serra and the production of recent architecture that blurs the boundaries between architecture and landscape. This typology avoids the production of the object building that, as discussed, is

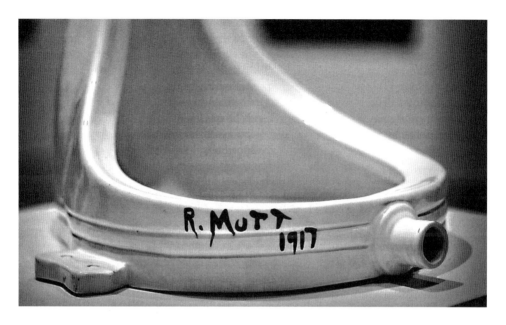

Figure 6.3 *Fountain*, **Marcel Duchamp, 1917, taken at the MoMA, San Francisco**
Source: © Gregory Schultz, 2008.

Figure 6.4 *3 stoppages étalon* **(3 Standard Stoppages), Marcel Duchamp, 1913–
1914, replica 1964**
Source: © Succession Marcel Duchamp/ADAGP, Paris and DACS, London, 2010.

reduced to a mere sign in the image economy in favour of forming 'new places in urban fabrics'.[21] In understanding this definition it is important to place it within an art history concerned with spatial practice with a series of distinct junctures that shifted the discourse concerning objects and space.

The Space and Site Situation

In the 1960s art had operated in a closed tripartite system of studio-gallery-museum. These limits that art had imposed upon itself was barely called into question as in some ways the introspective exploration of self-expression and inner space, epitomized by the hippy counter-culture, did not facilitate an open world view, it closed it down. Even the Op-Art movement, which physically stepped outside of the frame, did so within the limits of the physical space of the gallery or wall. Only at the end of the 1960s did the question of the limits of the frame come to be contested in art and theory; the space of the art of the 1970s is an open space. However, the limits of space were not the infinite future space of the 1950s; space exploration had brought to bear the realization that the monotonous

Figure 6.5 Robert Morris, *Observatory*, Flevoland, NL, 1971
Source: Author's own, 1998.

circumnavigation of the globe by the many satellites that now occupied this 'space' was as 'far' as space would exist for the immediate known present.

The open space though was not necessarily the physical space of the world around us, as it was to the Constructivists, and it is this that truly separates and distinguishes Land Art from its earlier spatial artistic context. The 'open space' of 1970s art was a mixture of political space, cultural space and historical space, the fact that much of the Land Art to which we can point and define took place in the 'natural world' or the 'landscape' is incidental to this structure. The 1970s work of art is a construction in space; many of the works of the Land Art movement may be conceived as finally breaking with the tradition prevalent since the Renaissance of the representation of space. These works seek not to represent but to enquire toward, to open-up and to ask the question. The visual perception of space was no longer the concern of the artist; this was subsumed by the physical experience of space or the intellectual conception of space. Works did not define space by delimiting it, they sought to open space by the inclusive and gestural act (see Figure 6.5).

The art and writing of Robert Smithson is most often called upon to explain this motion towards the questioning of space. It is critical to understand the shift from the confines of the gallery to an indeterminate space of a metaphysical environment, without this transition the development of ideas around site specificity would not have emerged. It is first the deconstruction of any idea of place and a sense of omnipotent entropy that detaches the object from art and art from the object. Smithson questions scale and matter and makes reference to the placelessness of the contemporary American landscape:

> By drawing a diagram, a ground plan of a house, a street plan to the location of a site, or a topographic map, one draws a 'logical two dimensional picture.' A 'logical picture' differs from a natural or realistic picture in that it rarely looks like the thing it stands for. It is a two dimensional analogy or metaphor – A is Z.

> The Non-Site (an indoor earthwork) is a three dimensional logical picture that is abstract, yet it represents an actual site in N.J. (The Pine Barrens Plains). It is by this dimensional metaphor that one site can represent another site which does not resemble it – this The Non-Site.[22]

The collection and transfer of material from mapped locations to a series of receptacles within the gallery forms the act of the work. The (re)presentation of the material and the mathematical transformation of two-dimensional to three-dimensional form, between the map and the container, performs the translation of placeless into place but without a correlation of scalar space. Smithson was conscious of the mapped relationships[23] between the work and its site and the absences promoted by the presence of material that had been displaced[24] and spoke of this relationship in a lecture at Cornell University[25] using the terms dialectic of site and non-site, he eventually published this tabulated arrangement as a footnote to the 1972 essay, *The Spiral Jetty*:

Dialectic of Site and Non-Site

	Site	Non-Site
1	Open Limits	Closed Limits
2	A series of Points	An Array of Matter
3	Outer Coordinates	Inner Coordinates
4	Subtraction	Addition
5	Indeterminate Certainty	Determinate Uncertainty
6	Scattered Information	Contained Information
7	Reflection	Mirror
8	Edge	Centre
9	Some Place (physical)	No Place (abstract)
10	Many	One

Range of Convergence
The range of convergence between Site and Nonsite consists of a course of hazards, a double path made up of signs, photographs and maps that belong to both sides of the dialectic at once. Both sides are present and absent at the same.[26]

It is this break from the confines of the gallery and its subsequent practice, not in open space but in bound space, which can be seen to elicit a formal discourse with context. Deckker uses the example of Richard Serra's *Scatter Piece* (see Figure 6.6), wherein molten lead was thrown across the floor of a warehouse, to describe the point at which 'artists began to explore the nature of an art that was contingent to its site'. This relationship is evident in the work of both Michael Heizer and Smithson, and, to a lesser extent, Donald Judd. Judd's relationship with space is not as crucially bound to its limits and his objects have less direct material association with the ground in which they are placed than the site/non-site displacements or earthworks of his contemporaries. It is, however, Judd's practice that best serves to locate this translation within the realms of architecture. The Peter Merian Haus in Basle, designed by Judd in collaboration with architect Hans Zwimpfer, is located in an interstitial site between a railway and a main road and attempts to formally negotiate the landscape in purely sculptural terms. 'There is no attempt to make the building "contextual": the serial forms of these pavilions appear remarkably like the serial forms in his work in Marfa'[27] (see Figure 6.7). Deckker concludes by suggesting that architectural 'form should create new urban spaces', reasserting his earlier position and alluding to the, subsequently reinforced, transition of building as 'component' rather than 'object'. To be considered as formal elements within a landscape composition is the privileged position of few works of architecture. That this scheme so explicitly exploits this condition is rare. When the request is made, in a conventional legal approvals context, for an image that shows projected views

Figure 6.6 Richard Serra, *Scatter Piece*, **1967**
Source: © Shunk-Kender, courtesy of the Roy Lichtenstein Foundation.

Figure 6.7 Donald Judd and Hans Zwimpfer, *Peter Merian Haus*, **Basle, 2002**
Source: Author's own, 2003.

of a new building from a distance, it is usually confrontational or oppositional rather than being a part of a positive compositional discourse. The concern usually revolves around the question 'what impact will the "new" have?' This is perhaps best exemplified by the controversy surrounding the construction of new towers in the city of London; the Gherkin and proposals by Renzo Piano and Richard Rogers have been subject to this type of scrutiny.[28]

A simple edit of Rosalind Krauss' insightful diagram, *the dialectical grid of architecture and landscape*,[29] reveals where the thematic content of these texts, driving the chapter titles and direction, lies (see Figure 6.8). Rather than examining the reductive qualities of minimal art, Krauss chose to look at the constructive realities in a positive framework, which ordered the productions as *architecture* or *landscape* or their opposites, *not-architecture*, *not-landscape*, or somewhere in-between. Deckker argues that in so doing, Krauss neglected the political and aesthetic content of these works. The aesthetics and the associated politics were not the concerns of the Land Artists, other than perhaps an anti-aesthetic, driven by process. Whilst emerging as a reaction to the economic, socio-political condition of the city and the market, the

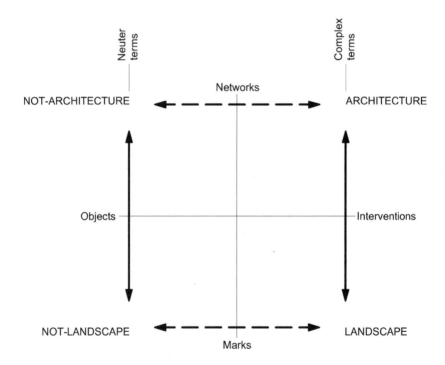

Figure 6.8 Diagram based upon Krauss' *Sculpture in the expanded field*
The diagram reveals how the classifications within these texts can be seen to be associated with architecture and urbanism and negotiate and mediate the city with the same brevity as once the classical order of a place-bound architecture could.
Source: Author's own, 2010.

subsequent development of Land Art was significantly concerned with (non)space and its limits and more concerned with the dissolution of the structures of art, than an overtly political dialogue. Deckker uses his argument to form an association between Ruscha's[30] inquiry into suburbanity and banality in the hinterland to Smithson's work in the Meadowlands of New Jersey. However, it was not banality or the everyday that was of concern to Smithson. It is argued that Smithson's fascination with New Jersey stemmed from its position as an 'out-of-date future'[31] rather than a product of capitalism.

Whilst contemporary urban art practice can be seen to embrace minimal forms and gestures which mirror qualities of the 1970s works in non-space without context, the formal impositions made by certain artists are frequently site-specific and part of a larger network, with multiple contexts. This does not make the two schools oppositional, as both seek to delimit determinate space by the implication of boundaries or open networks beyond immediate view. This type of indiscernible associative practice was perhaps pioneered by the unrestrained and unconventional Boyle Family and their development of a site-site dialectic, which involved casting and the transposition of the environment within a mapping practice and an intense examination of the everyday.

The Boyle Family are artists Mark Boyle and Joan Hills and their children Sebastian and Georgia. They have shared practice under the guise since the children were old enough to participate.[32] The Boyle Family are concerned with removing expression from their art and making a true representation of the 'world'. Their greatest art is 'reality'. They are interested in taking an uncontrolled sample of how the world is. Their work includes flats and apartments that are turned into found object compositions. Their street casting process is a map-based activity with a tradition in art. Elliot forms an account of the early years and formation of the Boyle Family myth and provides an insight into the 'earth sections', with which this text is primarily concerned. In his first public statement in 1965, Mark Boyle alluded to the fact that he wished to include everything in a single work and that reality itself was the ultimate object. In a extruded linguistic version of this ideal, and drawing from his own court experience, Boyle convened a happening in Edinburgh wherein one of the participants, playing the role of witness and requested to tell 'the whole truth', was directed to recount everything he could remember. This resonates in Revs' ambivalent attitude towards the 'meaning' of his subway monologues[33] and the express, but simple, desire to capture it all, whether life, the stories of life or the fabric of life. Contemporary to Debord, the Boyle Family used Situationist style tactics to call to question ideas of consumption and spectacle, in one work, by placing an audience in shop window and opening the curtains to reveal the viewers as the viewed.[34]

The Boyle Family do not make maps, but the map is intrinsic to their continuous process of identification, record and reproduction of the real world in 'earth sections' (see Figure 6.9). These objects, normally square relief 'sculptures', re-presentations as opposed to representation, of the real world, emerged from a process of recombining *objets trouvés* and detritus in earlier projects. The manner of site selection was, importantly, left to chance; in their first forays, the Boyles

Figure 6.9 Boyle Family, *The Barcelona Site, World Series*, construction, London, 1 June–12 July 2009
Source: Author's own, 2009.

used a found surround from a television screen and, in the manner of the biologist launching his quadrat, threw the surround to frame the ground upon which it came to rest.[35] The reasons for the transition to the six-foot square as the dimension of these works are not clear, but the method of site selection remained one driven by chance. In *London Series* (1967–1968) and *World Series* (1969–) guests to their apartment were invited, with full sight and blindfolded respectively, to throw a dart at a map to determine the location of a survey (see Figure 6.10).

The dimensions of the work are occasionally challenged by context, either natural conditions, weather driven or by means of transportation, size of vehicle available in any given location, but rarely wilfully renegotiated due to dissatisfaction with the result of the selection. This is paramount as understanding their work as a survey, as an attempt to remove consciousness from the act, in these terms the pieces of earth sections with origin in the city can be perceived as a material and textural record of urbanization, more accurately, of human intervention over the last 40 years. Again, mirroring the practice of Revs,[36] the Boyle Family work without authorization in the street, using props and costumes to deceive onlookers as to their legitimacy, not least aided by Mark Boyle's manufactured business card

Figure 6.10 Boyle Family, *The Barcelona Site, World Series*, **map, London, 1 June–12 July 2009**
Source: Author's own, 2009.

which identifies him as the Director of the fictional Institute for Contemporary Archaeology. This practice is motivated by the asserted need to avoid bureaucracy as it has the potential to dilute the integrity of the work.[37]

This archaeological approach assumes phenomenological characteristics when one considers, not simply the scientific allocation of the sample set but, the peripheral acts that take place in parallel with the production of their fossilized artifacts. Elliot cites an interview with Mark Boyle where it is stated that other data would be collected, including mapping movement around the location, recording sounds and film, taking samples of air, earth and insect and plant life. This inquiry into one extraordinarily specific location is particularly related to the act of site investigation or site analysis, embedded in the production of Western architecture. The contradistinction between the two lies in the intrinsic aim of the act; in architecture the aim is determinately the production of an addition or intervention, in the earth sections the intent is exclusively to 'Hold it in the shape it was on site. Fix it. Make it permanent'.[38] In this schism is revealed the failure of the practice in architecture, the subjective imposition of a perceived product and the justifiable ideological means to realize, pervert the course of inquiry to one which is designed to suit ends, not to truly record what is *there*. Thus, architecture's real denial of phenomenology, by its very practice, subverts and destroys itself as a valid mode of exploration or expression. Even the most rigorous study of a location in an architectural process cannot guarantee a non-discriminatory reading of place.

The work of the Boyle Family is not limited to the works described here, a divergent range of practice, invariably related to the examination and re-ordering of the real, includes the reprocessing of social indices, like the Yellow Pages, into new categories that reflect their view of 'society as a multi-cellular organism'.[39] They used new taxonomies to define the nervous, digestive and reproductive components of the city and visited randomly selected sites that fell into this categorization. Secret sound and film recordings were made in a café, a graveyard and a hair salon, and re-presented in an interior space using actors, with expressionless white face masks, miming as the recordings were played and the films projected. The factor of chance is critical to the transposition of these practices into architectural investigation; it is only by embracing chance, by embarking on experiments and inquiry without certainty as to the outcome, by allowing the 'data' to speak for itself, that the urban will actually be revealed. A wholesale rejection of choice, however, is unrealistic, if not impossible; the eradication of decision from these processes of selection, record and re-presentation in pursuit of 'the truth' is an infinite structure. Clear and determinate methodology though, is unquestionably of value; this includes the design of chance.

When considering object, the city and art in the context of an architectural discourse, it is unusual not to see mention of Gordon Matta-Clark, most obviously for his deconstruction of buildings. These acts and products are often considered as artifacts on their own right and literally translated as gestural 'voids'. It is the idea of Matta-Clark's *Anarchitecture* that is of concern here and the objects, or non-objects, contained within the posthumously recovered and presented work *Reality Projects: Fake Estates*, and its relationship with space. The term *Anarchitecture* is credited to Matta-Clark, but is thought to have emerged from group discussions,[40] and was partially informed by the challenging of conventions and enforced edicts of the architectural establishment. One such manifestation was the deliberate rephrasing of key modernist assertions; *Form Fallows Function, A machine not for living, Nothing Works*, were all suggestions for inclusion in a 1974 exhibition.[41] Attlee suggests, 'If this wordplay means anything it implies that a rigid adherence to certain ideas of form will restrict an object or a building's usefulness. An opposite approach might be to allow an object's appearance to suggest spontaneous new uses, in the way that the carriage of a wrecked train suddenly becomes a bridge in the photograph included in the *Anarchitecture* show'.[42] This statement may be read, within a contemporary urban discourse, as allowing for contingency and Matta-Clark seen to pre-empt the thematic content of contemporary discourse surrounding urbanism, that of emergence.

Matta-Clark had studied architecture, but is known to have been cynical about the capacity of architecture to improve humanity.[43] His frustration lay with those he saw as profiteers and the systems that allowed such inequitable financial exchange. In *Reality Projects: Fake Estates*, Matta-Clark purchased 15 sites, or plots, that were remnants of land deals, the carving up of larger sites or slicing through sites with pieces of municipal infrastructure. These were usually pieces of land that would be considered useless in development terms, but clearly the process of their creation fascinated Matta-Clark. The City of New York auctioned them for approximately $35.00 each. Matta-Clark only had the opportunity to document the sites through assembly of the title deeds and a physical and photographic survey, before moving on to alternative projects. This is said to be symptomatic of the man who lived out his art, acting as quickly as he was thinking and sometimes thinking and acting before he had concluded his thoughts! The work was uncovered by Matta-Clark's wife after his death and caused something of a stir amongst those who had already selectively categorized and packaged the artist as 'the one who cuts holes in buildings'.

The physical components of *Reality Projects: Fake Estates* consist of a documentary photograph, the title deed and the architectural block plan for each site (see Figure 6.11). These three edifices define the site according to their own particular rules and 'fail to coincide completely with the plots'.[44] This particular fact serves to emphasize the urban condition as a layered system of regulation with indefinite boundaries, despite the continual physical delineation of space; it is possible to locate interstitial space within the interstice. This idea could be argued to have been apparent to Matta-Clark, who left exhibition instructions to 'put them together however you want',[45] leaving curatorial chance to define the relationships or otherwise of the works, the sites and the space between. Walker suggests that the acceptance of the first posthumous arrangement of the exhibition as the now definitive and petrified version has paradoxically bound the work within the system it so successfully criticized.[46] Matta-Clark designed chance within the piece and the market removed it.

Walker draws references from Bataille and Lefebvre when describing the production and product of the spaces associated with the 'lots' bought by Matta-Clark; Lefebvre's abstract space at the intersection of regulatory and economic systems and the 'waste' space of Bataille's 'homogeneous society',[47] respectively. He continues with a series of statements that are significant here with respect to the direct relationship between art practice and the practice of architecture. The characteristics of the work can be said to reveal the 'mechanics of partition that define the market'[48] and to demonstrate the legislative nuances that produce useless space by virtue of the process of drawing. This isn't the definition of space by the cyclical development of the city, but one made by the very system that tries to establish order.

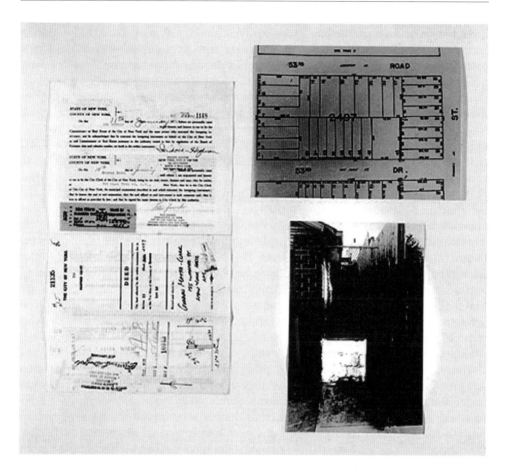

Figure 6.11 *Reality Properties: Fake Estates*, **Little Alley Block 2497, Lot 42, 1974 (posthumous assembly, 1992)**

Photographic collage, property deed, site map, and photograph, framed photographic collage: 10 x 87 3/16 x 1 3/8 inches (25.4 x 221.5 x 3.5 cm); framed photograph and documents: 20 5/8 x 22 5/16 x 1 3/8 inches (52.4 x 56.7 x 3.5 cm). Solomon R. Guggenheim Museum, New York, Purchased with funds contributed by the International Director's Council and Executive Committee Members: Edythe Broad, Elaine Terner Cooper, Linda Fischbach, Ronnie Heyman, J. Tomilson Hill, Dakis Joannou, Cindy Johnson, Barbara Lane, Linda Macklowe, Brian McIver, Peter Norton, Willem Peppler, Alain-Dominique Perrin, Rachel Rudin, David Teiger, Ginny Williams, Elliot K. Wolk 98.5228.

Source: © 2010 Estate of Gordon Matta-Clark/Artists Rights Society (ARS), New York, DACS London.

This particular project supersedes its component objects and the network of which they were born and is more than an intervention in space, it does not fall neatly within Krauss' 'expanded field', as most practice and product here does, in some senses it warrants a diagram of its own that makes explicit a relationship between law, planning and art; the context of this piece is urban. The work challenges the notion of the grid as organizing device, indeed almost celebrates its ambivalence, it usurps the architectural ideal of the grid as a rationalization of space and presents its irrationality upon its confluence with policy. Walker essentially states this as 'becoming involved with the city as oeuvre by revealing the contingency and overdetermination of its spaces';[49] urban space as the unregulated and the hyper-regulated.

Object Object, Abject Object

There is a contrast between the apparent shift in contemporary art from object to interaction, at a time when other art practice, informed by graffiti tradition, has begun to produce interactive objects. Is this art without the shackles of convention or tradition able to say more about the urban condition than that which is gallery bound? De Certeau speculates on the participatory nature of the pedestrian in the definition of space: 'A space exists when one takes into consideration vectors of direction, velocity and time variables. Thus space is composed of the intersections of mobile elements. It is in a sense actuated by the intersections of mobile elements.'[50] This notion of interference as descriptive of space and of active within it is also proposed by Suderberg, who defines installation as 'to fabricate interior and exterior environments, to alter surfaces until they envelope the viewer, to construct "all over" compositions utilizing natural and man made objects, and to reallocate and disorder space'.[51] This contemporary definition does not take Schwitters' position, as one which sought an introverted order, albeit a non-orthogonal projection, rather, it is concerned with making manifest the schisms in space and celebratory in the dislocation of space and sensation. Jan de Cock's *Denkmal* series can be viewed as within this schema, and additionally to have negotiated ideas of time, site and record, furthermore, to have straddled the realms of production and consumption in a brand relationship with Commes des Garçons, much in the manner of KR and KRINK.[52] This multi-faceted and networked approach is exemplar of the type of daily condition into which we have designed ourselves and best exemplified by an examination of de Cock's 2004 solo exhibition in Cologne.

The show was in two phases, the first was a minimal installation that was composed of a shelf and a series of small photographs showing architectural features and details of other cultural institutions. The shelf held 100 copies of de Cock's encyclopedic photo-data publication *Denkmal*, which serves as an insight into his work and influence and is ordered and constructed in much the same way as his interlocking timber constructions themselves. In the second phase, the small photographs were removed and replaced with large format lightbox mounted prints of his installation, *Denkmal 9*, in the library of Ghent University (see Figure 6.12). The library piece was concurrent with the Cologne exhibition and thus the images were simultaneously acting as a monument whilst sustaining a networked relationship between the two live works. The gallery, the publication, the photographs, the

Figure 6.12 *Denkmal 9, Henry Van de Velde Universiteitsbibliotheek, Rozier 9, Gent, 2004*
Source: © Atelier Jan De Cock.

library, the two installations and the public were interdependent and intrinsic in the conception of the entire work. The role of the exhibited photographs as, at once, a record, a networked object and an advert for the de Cock brand serves to illustrate the complex associative spatial context of a contemporary society, without being overtly explicit about networked environments. The *Denkmal* installations are usually temporary and their construction and demolition may also be seen as 'of the city', their initial form, their traces and memory imply a fractured, yet regulated, association between rules, demands and context.

The blurring between art and urbanism can be seen much more explicitly when viewed from the architect's position. Architecture, by virtue of the way in which it is taught and criticized, elicits meaning and reason from every gesture and any formal gesture can be framed as an inquiry into space. The type of objects that architects produce as installations are, invariably, bound within a wider discourse about urbanism and its forces. Maurer United develop work that explores the extreme fragmentation of contemporary culture and the city.[53]

Figure 6.13 *Streetcourt*, **Maurer United Architects, 2005**
Source: © Maurer United.

Their non-hierarchical, multi-layered approach addresses the intersection of architecture and other design disciplines in conjunction with the crossovers between architecture and youth culture. They have worked with graffiti artists and skateboarders to make inclusive urban spaces and in one project, built twice, have appropriated the term 'street' and made entire cast landscapes that mimic the street and its kerbed edges, but place obstacles in the space conventionally reserved for cars (see Figure 6.13). These 'streets' are deployed as singular elements in a parkland setting and designed primarily, though not exclusively, for skating sports, they are inclusive sculptural gestures that call to mind Michael Heizer's aesthetic. By permitting access to all onto this defined apron, but prioritizing the, often marginalized, skateboarder and also by creating a board-biased amplified version of the conventional streetscape, Maurer United are gently testing the boundaries and limits imposed physically and socially within the city. Their early project, *Urban Tetris* (2001), was conceived as a series of objects that would come together to deliver an entire message, but disperse to advertise and engage the public. Twenty-five pieces of primary coloured sculpture based on the computer game aesthetic were located around Amsterdam to celebrate 100 years of housing law and over four days migrated to come together, in the Westerpark area, to create a pavilion and forum for discussion about the future of social housing in the city (see Figure 6.14).

Figure 6.14 *Urban Tetris*, Maurer United Architects, 2001
Source: © Maurer United.

Figure 6.15 Momo, *$10,000 Bucket*, 2009
A modified bicycle with a fibreglass container to carry wheat paste and designed to the dimensions of a re-engineered roller that can support and paste a poster in one motion.
Source: © Momo, 2009.

Momo is an artist who, until recently, was resident in New York. He practices principally outside and has a history in conventional graffiti. Momo's *Tag Manhattan* project has been discussed and promoted extensively in the online environment, but only within an art history context, and with reference to the sublime. Here it is of interest because of its direct relationship to the urban morphology of New York. The work is a two-mile long line of paint of approximately 10–15mm in width that traverses the gridded street pattern of Manhattan and when transcribed as a route on a map spells 'Momo'. It took two nights to apply and two months to document, most readily consumed as an Internet video. It may be accepted that the work's existential presence in the imagined, as opposed to its partial existence in the present, is one version of the sublime,[54] displeasing in its physical legibility as a whole, pleasing as one assembles a vision of the whole in the mind. Whilst essentially a 'mark', the piece can be considered of sufficient scale and legibility to assume 'object' properties, despite its indiscernible total presence. Momo himself compares the work in scale to Smithson's *Spiral Jetty* and Heizer's *Double Negative* and Turrell's *Roden Crater*![55] Inspired by George Bliss' purple footprints all over Manhattan, Momo built his own bicycle with paint dispenser and customized actuator to drip paint at an appropriate rate for the speed of travel,[56] he has continued to modify bicycles for his own needs and that of his art (see Figure 6.15). The line did spark interest at the time, before Momo had the opportunity to record and publish the work, people had spotted the line and read its deliberate intent, though were unsure as to what its purpose was.[57]

Momo has also worked with Eltono in the creation of kinetic sculptures from scavenged material. Known as *PLAF*, and situated in the water around Manhattan, the sculptures adopt a vaguely official feel by virtue of their direct relationship with the water as they rise and fall in the form of a tidal barometer (see Figure 6.16). This notion is further reinforced by the luminous colours, deliberately applied,[58] as if to warn of the objects' presence and importance. It is vital to Momo that these works are made from scavenged material and in (re)placing the reconfigured timber into the river the cyclical nature of the city as well as its constant but erratic rhythms are acknowledged in a disruptive act with regulatory aesthetics. These processes of collection and reflection provide vital discourse about the nature of place as much as they can form allusions to destructive consumptive behaviours. It is possible to call to mind the emergent urban forms of the shantytowns or slums, that occupy the edges of many developing world cities, in particular works by Eltono and Nuria and also in pieces by critically acclaimed artist, Tadashi Kawamata. Indeed the artists both ascribed the word 'favelas' to certain works; a collaboration between Eltono and Nuria in Berlin in 2006 (see Figure 6.17) and a series by Kawamata between 1991 and 1994 (see Figure 6.18) share the term. The objects created by Kawamata are distinctly versions of shacks, they carry the typical elements of four walls and a roof in an ad hoc assemblage of cardboard, timber and corrugated metals and apertures are apparent in the typically ramshackle façades. Kawamata's objects are overtly politically charged in their relationship with issues of homelessness, but are also consistent with works made since the 1970s that involve the temporary ordering of fractured components in a discourse with space, demarcation and ownership.[59] Eltono and Nuria's work, whilst materially derived from scavenged objects that mimic the aesthetic of shantytowns, assume a wave-like form that is more akin to algorithmic design than emergent cumulative constructions of informal urban development.

These works also have an aesthetic quality that is similar to that of Outsider Art, another form of expression that exhibits bottom-up, emergent characteristics.

Figure 6.16 Momo + Eltono, *PLAF*, New York, 2008
Source: Author's own, 2009.

Figure 6.17 Eltono + Nuria, *Eigenkunstruktion*, Berlin, 2006: A 'walkthrough favela'
Source: © Eltono, 2006.

The term has been adopted by the art establishment to provide a genre with which to label and commodify products which, ostensibly, have no relation to a Western artistic tradition. The phrase *L'Art Brut* (raw art) was used by Jean Dubuffet in 1945 and *Outsider Art* by Roger Cardinal in 1972 to describe art that belongs to no movement.[60] Unsurprisingly, some of the most celebrated examples are from

Figure 6.18 Tadashi Kawamata, installation, Paris, 2008
Source: © Randy Reddig, 2008.

Figure 6.19 Truth, Manchester, 2009
Source: Author's own, 2009.

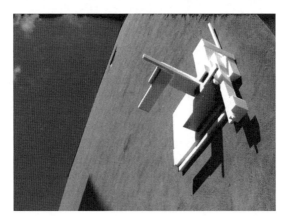

Figure 6.20 Truth, various
Source: © Truth, 2007–2009. Edyta Jezierska, courtesy of Czarna Gallery.

deprived areas of the developing world. Ned Chand's Rock Garden in Chandigarh has received much attention, not least of all for its unregulated, organic presence in the ordered matrix of Corbusier's city. Krystian Czaplicki, known as Truth, exhibits organic tendencies in his work that distinguish his work from that of the artist who uses a repeat motif. For Truth, the idea of site specificity is paramount, though the resultant form essentially an emotive response rather than one governed by rules. 'I don't have a catalogue of responses to a given space because I think that developing such a catalogue would be quite boring. That would be more like designing, while I'm more into intuitive creating. Sometimes I don't even know why I mutate an object, I just have to do it, and that's a fascinating and indescribable part of what I do.'[61] He too acknowledges the processes of decay in the city and in his work, particularly when working in and around his home, 'The value of "time" was more important at the beginning when I used more ephemeral materials. I used to work close to my home, so I could come back and check what was going on with my works anytime I wanted'.[62] With the passage of time Truth's medium has become more permanent, concrete and steel, but the biological response to the city persists. The deliberate dispersed compositions of Truth's objects in Manchester resemble fungal spores, clinging to the damp masonry of gable end walls and Victorian railway viaducts (see Figure 6.19). This approach is mirrored in other pieces, which whilst assuming geometric forms are calculably intended to appear as parasitic, growing from, but also feeding from, their environment, be it a shed, tiled alcove or featureless concrete wall (see Figure 6.20).

Object Invasion (the Networked Object)

Space Invader was one of first people to make marks on the city and place them in a more permanent manner. A description of Space Invader and his practice could have fallen within several chapters in this book, a Parisian, operating across the globe either self-directed or commissioned, he is responsible for the application of mosaic works in the urban environment, using tiles and cement, based on the graphics of the 1980s computer video game from where his moniker originates (see Figure 6.21). His works could be described as 'marks' or 'networks', and this serves to illustrate the overlaps and proximities within these practices and their products. Invader maps his 'Invasions' of cities; the re-presentation of the cities themselves speaks of an individual reading through a very particular lens, the maps do not consistently identify the same urban elements as prominent or descriptive from city to city.

Manchester (see Figure 6.22) is framed as its river, canals and railways being the formative features of the city, the principal roads are defined, but visually recede in favour of the other infrastructural elements, this is consistent with its industrial development which fundamentally relies on the east–west spine of railway and canal and, prior to that, the course of the River Irwell. Los Angeles (see Figure 6.23) is, as one would anticipate, defined by its principal highways and vast in its area

Figure 6.21 Space Invader, Soho, London, 2004
Source: Author's own, 2004.

of mapping and invasion, characteristic and a result of a response to the sprawling metropolis. The New York map is a pixelated version of Manhattan with the subway routes shown (see Figure 6.24). Tokyo is described as composed of districts within a grid and a series of cores that are amplified in scale; this is clearly representative of its poly-nucleic structure (see Figure 6.25). The gridded and digitized aesthetic of this map is perhaps an allusion to the technological basis of Japan's economy as well as a confluence with Invader's own pixelated identity. Vienna is represented as a series of concentric polygonal lines that communicate the historic form of the bastions and ramparts of the walled city and the subsequent development of ring roads that adhere to this pattern during the twentieth century (see Figure 6.26). In this way Invader, before he has superimposed his icons onto the maps, has somehow distilled the essence of a city, in the convention of an urbanist, establishing the components of a field of study or operation. The map is an integral part of Invader's process and at some point will be the only product that remains of the work, though the visual record through photography both by Invader himself and his followers will exist as a record. In much the same way as the mutable sign of Eltono and the work of many traditional graffiti artists previously, Invader is complicit in an exchange with the urban participant; by utilizing such explicitly 'game' based icons and by the self-ascription of points for the scale, difficulty and complexity of each placement Invader

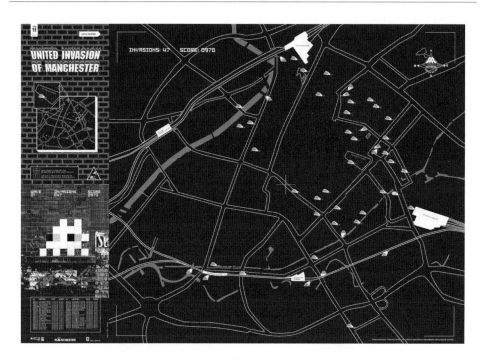

Figure 6.22 Space Invader, *Invasion of Manchester,* **2004**
Source: © Space Invader.

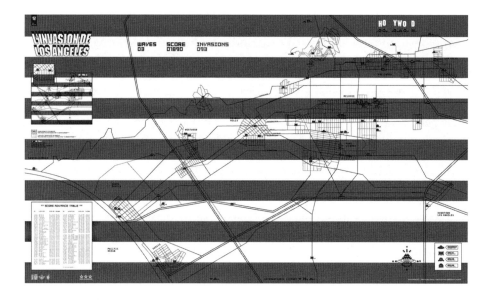

Figure 6.23 Space Invader, *Invasion of Los Angeles,* **2003**
Source: © Space Invader.

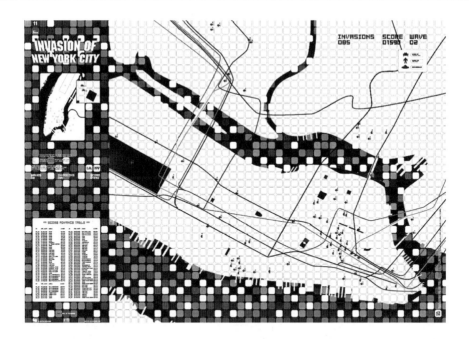

Figure 6.24 Space Invader, *Invasion of New York*, **2000/2003**
Source: © Space Invader.

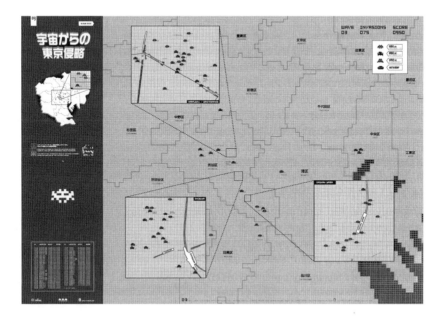

Figure 6.25 Space Invader, *Invasion of Tokyo*, **2002**
Source: © Space Invader.

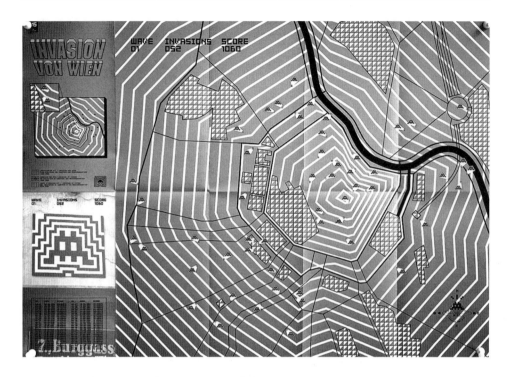

Figure 6.26 Space Invader, *Invasion of Vienna*, 2006
Source: © Space Invader.

accepts and designs his interaction with an unknown spectator. This relationship can reveal hitherto unimagined urban networks in the cognitive experience of the observer and the visual manner in which Invader marks these relationships within his maps also seems to imply such. The mosaics can be seen to map particular urban conditions and types of interstitial and infrastructural space; this is visible in the maps of Manchester, Tokyo and LA in particular.

In Montpellier (1999), rather than allowing the city to speak to him, Invader has imposed his own image on the city (see Figure 6.27). When connected together as in a dot-to-dot puzzle, the placements as viewed from above and presented on the map form the outline of one of Invader's characters. Whilst never a complete object in its own right, the map reveals a true invasion, insofar as the attack was premeditated and would not be determined by the ground level inspection of the city, as is Invader's usual practice. Each specific location would have to be individually assessed for a precise placement that would configure to the overall aim, wall, kerb or column, each site must yield a potential position for a mosaic.

By invading space, the works map various cities around the world and make visible a seam of disuse in any urban context, yet the placement is of importance, each mosaic piece is usually well balanced in its composition with existing elements. Despite its relative longevity the only permanent reference to his work

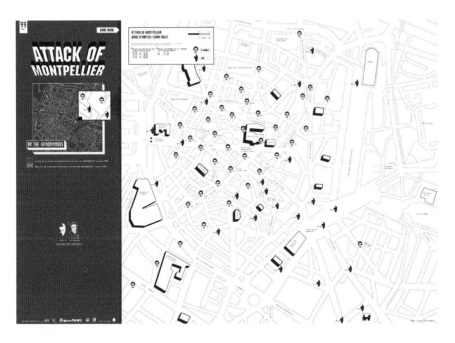

Figure 6.27 Space Invader, *Invasion of Montpellier,* **1999**
Source: © Space Invader.

are the maps he produces to locate his work. In each case the maps can describe a particular type of marginal or interstitial space in the city, be it an alcove or pediment, corner or capita. The approach that Invader takes to the city is one that calculably measures space and aspect and responds with site-specific intervention. The variables that determine scale and form are typical of the illegal artist; visibility (of piece and of artist when installing), risk (of apprehension or injury), camouflage (contextual blending consistent with city branding), amongst others. These objects communicate more about the processes of urbanization than the state of the city. The presence of the interstice is not the product, but the by-product. The custom built objects are abject negotiations between 'things', programme and space in the city. These humanist interventions best typify a contemporary architecture that is 'of the city'. They are micro-solutions that negate the neutrality of the grid and promote the material reality of the street. Non-designed, they are shrunken versions of the already minute types explored by Atelier Bow Wow in *Pet Architecture*.[63] These networked object projects, either as art or research, also call to question ideas concerning ownership, demarcation, the collision of policy and reality. The exposition of the interstice or residual space is important in these works, revealing the interstice as an object in its own right, no longer simply existing as a by-product, as in Koolhaas' *Junkspace* or Auge's *Non Place*. The ungoverned space is the new battleground of the city, prominent by its absence in a landscape of finite delineation.

Object Urbanism

This investigation of 'object', its meaning, application and role within a discourse concerning space, highlights the fractured and dissolved spatial sequences of the city and illustrates architecture's retreat, enforced or otherwise, from the capacity to define or engage with the city, as its historical precedents once did. The separate parallel development of commercial and illegal art can be seen to be convergent in the later works of post-graffiti artists who work within an exploded space, political space, infrastructural space and niche. The production of Invader, Momo and Truth, amongst others, can be seen to restate the role of the object in art within practice that acknowledges the role of governance upon urban form. These lessons in the dissolution of space and the latent regulatory landscape, that defines our urban environment, serve to demonstrate the polarization of architectural extremes and characterize the current condition; the unregulated and the hyper-regulated. The transition from architecture as mediator with the city to architecture as mediator with the urban has already occurred. As the order of space, light and form has ceded from the production of architecture it is possible to describe a situation wherein the projects that successfully negotiate infrastructure and the urban condition can be seen to exemplify this shift. OMA's entry into the competition for Parc de la Villette, Foreign Office Architect's Yokohama Port Terminal and Zaha Hadid's Phaeno Science Centre, function successfully within the image-sign-object dialectic but also transcend notions of the city by engaging with infrastructural urbanism. These building types and projects may come to represent the new dynamic of urbanism in the context of architectural production.

Atelier Bow Wow's *Made in Tokyo* alludes specifically to this condition, using a taxonomy of 'un-designed' hybrid buildings to reveal more about the nature of Tokyo as a city of flux, where no building is greater than 50 years old (see Figure 6.28). In Tokyo, as with Los Angeles and Las Vegas before it, urbanists can locate a specific characteristic of city, which provides an amplified version of a generic condition, in this instance, temporality. The numerous examples of low-tech hybrids that combine infrastructure and public space are evidence of this transition from materially bound 'city' production to network bound 'urbanism'. These buildings that negotiate their spatial limits in the pursuit of functionality do so in the manner of an intervention, their form is an explicit dialogue between programme and available spatial envelope. The clash of programmes is attributable to the sheer density of Tokyo. This contrasting functional disposition is not alien to Western cities and indeed is an emergent version of earlier seemingly disparate impositions that calculably deny the demands of a legible city and emerge as demanded. The Downtown Athletic Club as discussed by Koolhaas[64] may be seen as an early, but bounded, iteration of this condition, but no longer is the programme resident within the 'frame' of a building, but within the frame of residual spatial limits imposed by an urban order.

The architecture that operates as an object using similar devices to those described and criticized in this chapter should be seen, as Atelier Bow Wow

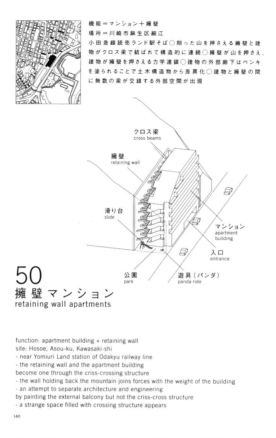

機能＝マンション＋擁壁
場所＝川崎市麻生区細江
小田急線読売ランド駅そば○削った山を押さえる擁壁と建
物がクロス梁で結ばれて構造的に連続○擁壁が山を押さえ、
建物が擁壁を押さえる力学連鎖○建物の外部廊下はペンキ
を塗られることで土木構造物から差異化○建物と擁壁の間
に無数の梁が交錯する外部空間が出現

クロス梁
cross beams

擁壁
retaining wall

滑り台
slide

マンション
apartment
building

入口
entrance

公園
park

遊具（パンダ）
panda ride

50
擁壁マンション
retaining wall apartments

function: apartment building + retaining wall
site: Hosoe, Asou-ku, Kawasaki-shi
- near Yomiuri Land station of Odakyu railway line
- the retaining wall and the apartment building
become one through the criss-crossing structure
- the wall holding back the mountain joins forces with the weight of the building
- an attempt to separate architecture and engineering
by painting the external balcony but not the criss-cross structure
- a strange space filled with crossing structure appears

140

Figure 6.28 Atelier Bow Wow, image from *Made in Tokyo*, 1998–2001
Source: © Atelier Bow Wow.

suggest, as more typical of an accelerated, kaleidoscopic, networked urbanism that any conventional orders of architecture bound by contract to the regulated mode of production that typifies UK construction. It is perhaps these occupancies and their low-tech, modifiable state that are emergent more than designed and necessarily practical over technological, that are more aligned to the visions of the Situationists and the projects of Cedric Price, Yona Friedman and Archigram and provide the possibility for a flexible, adaptable city. It would be ironic if a utility-driven, emergent model usurped the technocratic pursuit of modernity.

These two types of architecture at either end of the economic scale can be seen as objects in their own right that operate within a scheme that has its ideological foundations in the practice of the arts and their evolved dialogue with space and infrastructure. They are not exclusively opposed in financial terms, but also in regulatory and technological characteristics; the hyper-regulated landscape or building that adopts landscape characteristics and becomes urban is so governed that it is 'of the urban', embedded within the network and a part of its infrastructure.

223

Figure 6.29 Superstudio, *Continuous Monument*, 1969
Source: © MoMA.

The unregulated building or object that occupies interstitial space reveals the recession of architecture from the 'city', as it is these parasites that proffer material, space and form to the street, in a manner denied by the capitalist processes of production that create the homogeneous placeless buildings that are predominant and occupy the middle ground.

In many respects, although principally discussed as an ironic gesture,[65] Superstudio's *Continuous Monument* presupposes the architecture of the city as a single edifice, presumably, though not explicitly, intrinsically bound with its infrastructure. In contrast to the two building typologies defined here, the 'hyper' and the 'un' regulated, the Continuous Monument sought to reconcile urbanity with

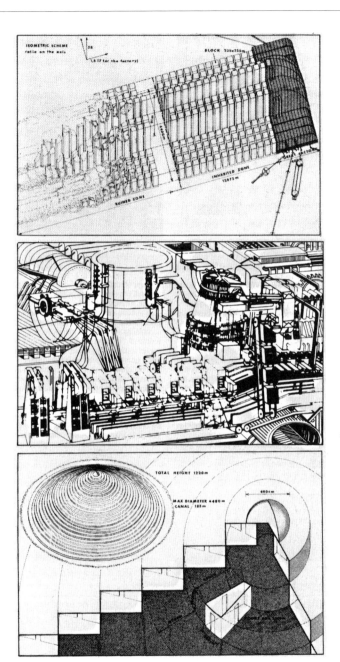

Figure 6.30 Superstudio, *Twelve Cautionary Tales for Christmas,* **1971**
From the top: Continuous production conveyor belt city, The 'Ville-machine habitee', Conical terraced city.
Source: © Standard Catalogue Co.

chance, the grid designed to provide the backdrop to an egalitarian society, rather than a signifier of totality (see Figure 6.29). That this scheme may be cited here, as an idealized and convergent model of the emergent, but distinct characteristics of urbanism, is coincidental, but fortuitous. The subsequent development of *Twelve Cautionary Tales for Christmas*, that defined thematically driven technocratic utopias, was loaded with descriptions of machine driven highly-regulated environments that obfuscated humanity and provided antithetical visions to that of the *Continuous Monument* (see Figure 6.30). Appearing in the December 1971 edition of AD, the piece concluded with a lifestyle magazine style affix to ascertain your 'character' on the basis of how many of the 'utopias' you approved of. The text cheekily chastises the sanctimonious reader who rejects them all, believing themselves to have seen through the irony, stating, 'So you feel satisfied, well you shouldn't. Because you have not caught on: you haven't understood that the descriptions represent cities now'.[66] The passage closes with a sentence, concerning the resolve of the reader as accepting their 'truth', that references their earlier work and its possibility for 'freedom'; 'you can prepare the foundations for the new city of White Walls'.

Endnotes

1   Graham, S. [ed.] (2010), *Disrupted Cities. When Infrastructure Fails* (Oxford and New York: Routledge) p. 6. Steve Hinchcliffe's definition from 'Technology Power and Space – The Means and Ends of Geographies of Technology', *Environment and Planning D; Society and Space*, 14 (1996) p. 665.

2   Meyer, J. (2000), 'The Functional Site; or, The Transformation of Site Specificity', in Suderberg, E. [ed.] *Space, Site, Intervention. Situating Installation Art* (Minneapolis: University of Minnesota Press) p. 24.

3   Meyer cites the phrase *'allegorical site'* as first used by Craig Owen when describing Smithson's polymathic investigations in 'Earthworks', an essay from Owen, C. (1992), *Beyond Recognition: Representation, Power and Culture* (Berkeley: University of California Press) pp. 40–51.

4   Kwon, M. (1997), 'One Place After Another', in Suderberg, E. [ed.] (2000), *Space, Site, Intervention. Situating Installation Art* (Minneapolis: University of Minnesota Press) p. 46. First published in *October 80* (Spring 1997) pp. 85–110.

5   Marcuse, H. (1932), 'The Foundation of Historical Materialism' written in German as *Neue Quellen zur Grundlegung des Historischen Materialismus*. In: Marcuse, H. (1972) *Studies in Critical Philosophy*. Translated by B. Reid (Boston: Beacon Press).

6   Sartre, J.-P. (1930), 'The Critique of Dialectical Reason', written in French as *Critique de la raison dialectique*. In: Sheridan Smith, A. [trans.] (1976), *The Critique of Dialectical Reason* (London: NLB).

7   Czikszentmihalyi, M. and Rochberg-Halton, E. (1981), *The Meaning of Things: Domestic Symbols and the Self* (New York: Cambridge University Press) p. 1.

8   Baudrillard, J. (1981), *For a Critique of the Political Economy of the Sign* (New York: Telos Press) p. 32.

9   Ibid. p. 185.

10   *White Towers* (1979) was an insightful study concerning a chain of burger restaurants in America, by Paul Hirshorn and Steven Izenour, who had previously collaborated with Venturi on *Learning From Las Vegas*. See Chapter 2 in this volume for further description and discussion.

11   Czaplicki, Krystian A.K.A. *Truth* (2010), Interview conducted by the authors by e-mail. 17 January 2010.

12   Eltono (2010), Interview conducted by the authors by e-mail. 25 March 2010.

13   There is a burgeoning trend that really began with the 1973 oil crisis concerning the re-use and reconfiguration of material. Perhaps unfairly and negatively labelled as a hippy endeavour, it is only with the growth in interest in emergent urbanism that salvage and make-do-and-mend has become a serious concern of critics. Artists have also picked up the mantle and Swoon's raft projects in particular speak of the waste of society and the collective need to act. See www.swimmingcities.org.

14   Bakotin, V. (1999), *Kurt Schwitters. Merzbau in Hannover.* Part of a project to remodel the Merzbau using 3D computational techniques by Zvonimir Bakotin which was unfortunately a static product, when the potential for algorithmic growth and parametric input was just around the technological corner and would have perhaps more closely mirrored Schwitter's original intent. Available from: www.merzbau.org/Schwitters.html [accessed 10 February 2010].

15   Chtcheglov, I. (1953), *Formulary For A New Urbanism.* In this report Chtcheglov makes reference to an ever shifting architecture and that 'Everyone will live in their own personal "Cathedral"'; Schwitters effectively built his own version. Chtcheglov wrote *Formulary* under the pseudonym Gilles Ivain in 1953 and circulated it as a report to members of the SI. It was not published until June 1958 in the first edition of the journal *Internationale Situationniste*. The text was appended to in its first full publication and translations to English are from a number of sources.

16   Lyotard, J.-F. (1973), *Dérives à Partir de Marx et Freud* (Paris: Union Générale d'Editions). The English translation appears as 'Adrift', in: Lyotard, J.-F. (1984), *Driftworks* (ed. Roger McKeon) (New York: Semiotext(e)) p. 13.

17   Müller, C.P. (1993), *Illegal Border Crossings* (Austrian contribution to the Venice Biennial). See Meyer and Kwon's essays in *Space Site Intervention* for further discussion. Kwon makes reference to the prerequisite presence of the artist in the work, the author as object.

18   Alÿs, F. (2000), *Re-enactments* (Mexico City). See Medina, C., Ferguson, R. and Fisher, J. (2007), *Francis Alÿs* (London: Phaidon) pp. 42–43.

19   Lykkeberg, T. (2008), 'Graffiti and Street Art', in: *Still On and Non the Wiser* [Cat.] (Von der Heydt Museum, Wuppertal: Publikat). The authors read these statements as convenient in the use of their vocabulary, but actually to suggest that the very term 'conceptual' implies a formal set of considered values and aims that may be written in respect of a piece of work, in contrast to the production of a piece of graffiti which has only latterly come to be conceptualized. See Chapter 5, this volume, for a more contextualized assessment of this relationship.

20 The Museum of Modern Art (1999), *MoMA Highlights* (New York: The Museum of Modern Art, revised edition 2004) p. 91. Available from: www.moma.org/collection/browse_results.php?object_id=78990 [accessed 9 January 2010].

21 Deckker, T. (2000), 'Land Art: City Architecture', *Issues in Architecture Art & Design*, 6(1) (London: University of East London).

22 Smithson, R. (1968), 'A Provisional Theory of Non-Sites' from *Unpublished Writings*, in: Flam, J. [ed.] (1996) *Robert Smithson: The Collected Writings*, 2nd edn (Berkeley: University of California Press) p. 364.

23 Robert Smithson and Dennis Wheeler in conversation, Flam (1996) p. 212.

24 Kaye, N. (2000), *Site-Specific Art: Performance, Place and Documentation* (London: Routledge) p. 94.

25 Flam (1996) p. 178.

26 Smithson, R. (1968), 'A Provisional Theory of Non-Sites' from *Unpublished Writings*, in: Flam (1996) p. 364.

27 Deckker (2000) p. 48.

28 See Glancey, J., 'Trust Me', an interview with Renzo Piano published in the *Guardian*, 29 March 2002. Available from: www.guardian.co.uk/society/2002/mar/29/urbandesign.arts [accessed March 2010]. The controversial 'Shard', expected to be complete by summer 2012, is discussed with an overwhelmingly negative bias on Glancey's part, who asks 'might the tower be a selfish building, a mighty machine for making money with little or no concern for the rest of the city? Might it impose too great a load on London's creaking transport infrastructure (system is too ordered a word). Do we need another air-conditioned totem pole raised in homage to London's god, Mammon? And how can we be sure that the integrity of its design might not be compromised as costs rise? Might the tower end up as a hubristic folly rather than a real contribution to the economy and culture of the city?'.

29 Krauss, R. (1979), 'Sculpture in the Expanded Field', *The Originality of the Avant-Garde and other Modernist Myths* (Cambridge, MA and London: The MIT Press, 1985). This seminal essay, originally published in *October*, 8, spring 1979, describes the abstraction of sculpture from an object based condition to one which encompassed displacements, walks, installations amongst a vast array of practice and criticizes the ascription of fake art history constructs, designed to legitimize the 'new' art of the Minimalists and Land Artists.

30 Ed Ruscha made his name as a photographer documenting the everyday banality of the American urban landscape. His most renowned studies were published as books and include *Twentysix Gasoline Stations* (Los Angeles: National Excelsior Press, 1963) and *Every Building on Sunset Strip* (Los Angeles: Edward Ruscha, 1966).

31 Hobbs, R. (1983), *Robert Smithson: A Retrospective View* [Cat.] (New York: The Herbert F. Johnson Museum of Art, Cornell University) p. 14.

32 Elliot, P. (2003), *Boyle Family* (Edinburgh: National Galleries of Scotland) p. 9.

33 Rivera, J. (2008), *Vandal Squad* (New York: Powerhouse Books) p. 120. See Chapter 5 in this volume and Revs' own essay in (2004) *Autograf. New York City's Graffiti Writers* (Berlin: Die Gestalten Verlag) for various accounts of his need and demand to act in the city.

34 Elliot (2003) p. 47.

35   The *Norland Road Studies* are one such example of this process being invoked. Elliot (2003) p. 12.

36   Rivera (2008) p. 120.

37   Elliot (2003) p. 18.

38   Elliot (2003) p. 15. Mayer, H. [ed.] (1970), *Journey to the Centre of the Earth: Mark Boyle's Atlas and Manual* [cat.] (Watford: Watford School of Art) unpaginated.

39   Requiem for an Unknown Citizen (1971) Elliot (2003) p. 18.

40   Attlee, J. (2007), *Towards Anarchitecture: Gordon Matta-Clark And Le Corbusier*. Available from: www.tate.org.uk/research/tateresearch/tatepapers/07spring/attlee.htm [accessed 10 March 2010]. Attlee proposes *Anarchitecture* as an elusive term that was used in several contexts by Matta-Clark and was also the name of a group exhibition in New York in 1974. A parody of Modernism was one of the tactics employed as anarchitecture within the exhibition, but Attlee also suggests that '*Anarchitecture*, with its use of found photographs and the aphoristic statements Matta-Clark recorded in his notebooks, is on some level both an echo of and a riposte to Corbusier's polemic'.

41   Ibid.

42   Ibid.

43   Attlee cites an interview with Matta-Clark where he states 'Matta-Clark once told an interviewer that, far from addressing humanity's problems, most architects were not "solving anything except how to make a living"'. Originally quoted in Wall, D. (1976), 'Gordon Matta-Clark's Building Dissections', *Artsmagazine*, March 1976, pp. 74–79, reproduced in *Gordon Matta-Clark* [Cat.] Internationaal Cultureel Centrum, Antwerp, 1977.

44   Walker, S. (2004), 'Gordon Matta-Clark: Drawing on Architecture', *Grey Room*, 18, Winter 2004, p. 114.

45   Ibid. p. 114. Walker cites an interview with Jane Crawford in which she recounts Carol Gooden's confirmation of an early version of the work at 112 Greene Street NYC, before all of the plots were acquired. There is no documentary evidence of how the work was arranged at this point.

46   Ibid. p. 116.

47   Ibid. p. 112. Bataille, G. (1933), 'On the Notion of Expenditure', in: Leslie Jr., D.M. [eds] (1980), *Visions of Excess: Selected Writings, 1927–1939*. Translated by A. Stoekl and C.R. Lovitt (Minneapolis: University of Minnesota Press) p. 116.

48   Ibid. p. 113.

49   Ibid. p. 115.

50   De Certeau, M. (1984), *The Practice Of Everyday Life* (Berkeley: University of California Press) p. 117.

51   Suderburg, E. (2000), 'Introduction: On Installation and Site Specificity', in: Suderburg, E. [ed.] *Space Site Intervention. Situating Installation Art* (Minneapolis: University of Minnesota Press) p. 6. This collection of texts thoroughly explores the ideas related to site and site-specific works as well as installation art and includes important essays by James Meyer and Miwon Kwon that are also referenced here.

52   See Chapter 5 for further description of KR and the parallels between his illegal and commercial activity. Jan de Cock has prepared shopfront constructions in London and

Tokyo for Commes des Garçons in the same aesthetic and material language as his *Denkmal* art installations.

53 Maurer United: www.maurerunited.com.

54 Kant, I. (1790), *Critique of Judgment*. Translated by J.H. Bernard (London: Macmillan and Co. Limited, 1914). Kant investigates the sublime, stating, 'We call that sublime which is absolutely great'. He distinguishes between the 'remarkable differences' of the Beautiful and the Sublime, noting that beauty 'is connected with the form of the object', having 'boundaries', while the sublime 'is to be found in a formless object', represented by a 'boundlessness'. In this sense, Momo's *Tag Manhattan* project may be read as sublime.

55 Press-pack online at Momo's website. Available from: http://momoshowpalace. com/+PressKit.htm [accessed 10 March 2010].

56 Momo essentially uncovered George Bliss as the creator, after Adam Purple, to whom they were often credited, wrote to inform him. It was this letter that revealed Bliss too as a bicycle designer. Available from: http://momoshowpalace.com/+PressKit.htm [accessed 17 January 2010].

57 *Tompkins Line*, Tuesday, 14 November 2006, 'A line of paint dribbled around the east and north sides of Tompkins Park Art, not accident, I think. Walking around in the East Village today, I saw this orange line on First Avenue as well'. Available from: http:// gammablog.com/2006/11/14/tompkins-line [accessed 9 February 2010].

58 Conversation with the artist whilst viewing part of the work, New York, East River, September 2009.

59 Morrissey, S. (1997), 'Making Structures out of Salvage' (exhibition review), *Architects' Journal*, 206(7), p. 53. This article describes installation work by Tadashi Kawamata at the Serpentine Gallery, London, and a parallel exhibition at Annely Juda that makes use of the doors retrieved from the renovation of the Serpentine. Morrissey does not dissect the meaning associated with the transposition of material that is inherently limiting in its composition and bound with the idea of threshold or boundary (doors).

60 *What is Outsider Art?* Available from: www.tate.org.uk/britain/exhibitions/outsiderart [accessed 8 February 2010].

61 Czaplicki, Krystian A.K.A. *Truth* (2010), Interview conducted by the authors by e-mail. 17 January 2010.

62 Ibid.

63 Atelier Bow Wow (2002), *Pet Architecture* (Japan: World Photo Press). A study of the small ad hoc kiosk developments of Tokyo that occupy marginal and niche sites where one would consider it unfeasible for many building types to exist.

64 Koolhaas, R. (1978), 'Definitive Instability: The Downtown Athletic Club', in: *Delirious New York* (New York: The Monacelli Press, 1994 edition) pp. 152–159.

65 Lang, P. and Menking, W. (2003), *Superstudio: Life without Objects* (Milan: Skira) discuss the criticism of Frampton and Jencks concerning Superstudio and specifically the *Continuous Monument*. Jencks is described as being unable to see past the irony to make any critical reading.

66 Superstudio (1971), 'Twelve Cautionary Tales for Christmas', *Architectural Design*, XLII, pp. 737–742.

7

Conclusion

The chapters in this book have provided a series of dialogues on the role of different 'maps' to enable us to explain a range of revelatory tools which expose unseen or latent spatial conditions and characteristics alongside urban narratives. These maps vis-à-vis (re)interpretations in and of the city, illustrate specific essences and nuances of space and place whether experiential or thematic. Furthermore, whilst the initial taxonomy of such entities afforded greater clarity in their description and values, the interrelationship and cross-fertilization is explicit in the context of the urban critique offered here, acknowledging the increasing complexity of cities in physical, social and cultural terms. The thematic lenses through which we examine architecture serve to reveal more about the contemporary city than the analysis of architecture itself and whilst built examples can be proffered as illustrations of the exposed conditions, it is the very nature of these as examples that serves to demonstrate the production of architecture as inherently reactive, whereas once it may be have been considered as proactive.

Through the course of these texts we have tried to present some of the key thematic drivers within architectural discourse as intrinsically bound with culture and society. This is not a new proposition, but one that posits architecture in a weakened position concerning its dialectic with the city. The negativity apportioned to such discourse has prevented the development of a responsive architecture that is accepting of its diminished role in the orders of space, form and light, and has the capacity to engage with economics, policy and commerce as part of an informed discourse. The introductory chapters seek to reveal reasoning for an examination of this sort and demonstrate the retreat of architecture from any humanist discourse and its prevalence as an output, or even servant, of production and consumption. To accept this commercial global vernacular and its liberation from physical context, to embrace the international systems of finance, product and circulation, and to allow these to become a part of the analytical canon is critical in the production of architecture that is to engage with the city, that is no longer simply composed of the materials harvested within its 'walls'. The city has been shown to be experientially composed of networks and niches for its inhabitants and to be traversed along paths that are at once predetermined by circumstance and unexpectedly altered by chance. The shape of the city and its spaces that can be defined as truly public has been revealed and a dissolved sense of place determined.

Space and place are equally bound by networks; physical and ethereal, we *are* connected, and whilst the joints are not actually 'plugged-in', the city is definitely 'walking'. Again it is possible to adopt the terminology of the utopian visionaries of the 1960s to describe the city and whilst Archigram erred towards a mechanical vision of the new city, their overriding notions of the compressed, connected and kaleidoscopic city can be seen to have arrived. Where 'form' did cede to 'image', digital networks can be seen to augment the city and to be as image laden as the urban landscape. What is different is the ordering of the sign in these two environments within the 'networked-sign' schematic. The networked sign is proven as more virulent, thus successful in the real world, than the sign or signifier that exists in isolation, with the weight of the term firmly attached to the image, logo or sign. In the digital world it is the networked aspect of this term that is of more value than the sign. The socially driven notions of freedom within the city walls and of adaptive architecture born to serve have, however, evaporated, overwhelmed by the forces of production and consumerism that, paradoxically, drove us technologically forward into collective paranoia and individualism. Surveillance is the logical outcome of a society with unlimited capacity to record. Will the software tailored to improve a company's service to its customer eventually end up delivering a predestined path for the acquisition of knowledge? May we only encounter the things that we are told should interest us?[1] Could bespoke achieve an underground status of clandestine exchanges? These are questions typical of a mass media-driven position that is fearful of technology and the control it is accused of wresting from the hands of humanity.

Whilst often viewed as a punitive expression of the contemporary urban landscape, surveillance technologies may have the capacity to feedback and facilitate greater adaptability within the built environment. The input, translation and output of the data generated through these systems requires further delineation and investigation to afford responsive behaviour on behalf of the urban fabric, whilst increasing the usefulness of such information streams for social, cultural and, perhaps even, economic benefits for those connected to the cityscape; physically or remotely. The ongoing developments of computer and media technologies may ultimately serve us with the potential to augment, (re)define and (re)map our experience of cities as we are able to engage with the 'software' of it; i.e. the dynamic, temporal and contingent elements rather than the current position which favours an autocratic view of the fixed objects and systems of built, physical 'hardware'. With the increasing prevalence of handheld devices, such as highly advanced or 'smart' mobile phones and PDAs, the nature in which we engage with urban space is perhaps witnessing the most significant transformation since the development of the automobile. This is the experiential shift in the shape of the city and like the motorcar before it will only incrementally and subtly migrate us from familiar physical conditions.

The later chapters here revel in the role of the interstice or the residual space of the city as of value when trying to interpret processes of urbanization. The negative space that is the very product of our progressive society and its infrastructure finds itself as the only physical niche available for expression and this type of intervention can be seen to be reflective of and challenging to the orders of society and space. Reactionary, parasitic, mutable and networked are all characteristics of actions that inhabit the interstice and of the built manifestations of global brands and idioms that form our cities by consumption; the parallels are as evident as the paradox. The acts of collective demarcation of space, by groups like the *pixadores*, and the cooperative environment that fosters such acts are at their most powerful when assumed as without explanation by the conventions of society. Whilst borne of many motivations, the collaborative and communicative spirit of these most desperate of urban adventurers is evidence of the power of cooperation and the capacity of local organization to greater effect. It is potentially the relinquishing of power, more specifically data, to the masses that holds the greatest opportunity for a revision of the structure of the city. The models that have been demonstrated as architecture, the hyper-regulated and the un-regulated, exhibit characteristics of a networked environment, namely the overarching and the emergent.

Architecture has become increasingly marginalized and distanced from its role as an aid to humanity and society in the last 20 years by responding primarily to the demands of the market. It may therefore be useful to shift our attention to the public role of the architect by (re)defining 'value' in the built environment.[2] If we are to assign ourselves to a redistribution of the design process that may build upon a platform of local needs via global networks, then the indeterminacy of interdependent economic, political and cultural systems should be embraced, rather than ignored, to enable suitably elastic design strategies to respond to the dynamic conditions of urban landscapes. The potential to develop an adaptive system to address the multi-scalar characteristics of cities may offer the urban, whether local, national or global, to emerge as a hybrid of topological and topographical relationships thereby providing a more comprehensive integration between digital networks and the physical urban landscape.

There is the potential for an emergent city in the rapid expansion of open source environments and the possibility for resolving the tension between the real and virtual worlds. Open source access to the datascapes of organizing bodies and regulators provides the opportunity for a bottom-up emergent model of urbanism that is politically bound to its inhabitants and would therefore facilitate various levels of self-organization. If all subjects had unlimited access to the data by which urban policy is determined then there is considerable room afforded for the introduction of radical re-readings of the political demands of locally nuanced populations. A technocratic view would allude to algorithmic design as having the potential to create unique and specific environments and a manufacturing culture of things as having the capacity for production: the object, the sculpture in the expanded field, in the hands of the consumer and the environment, a gallery. Architectural practice may need to undergo substantial transformations if this approach is to be developed in the future and thus echo the view proposed by Gordon Pask: 'The role of the architect here, I think, is not so much to design a building or city as to catalyse them: to act that they may evolve.'[3]

The development of integrated design and practice, enabled by the burgeoning innovations in digital technologies, has led to new paradigms for architecture both in terms of its design and manufacture. Collective intelligence underscores the transaction of knowledge and data sharing in systems such as Building Information Management (BIM) and fosters collaborative relationships between numerous disciplines from the beginning of the design process. Coupled with the ever-increasing demands of the market, even more pertinent in the current global economic downturn, the elements of our urban landscape are required to be faster and cheaper to design and construct whilst conforming to higher standards of building regulations and environmental targets. This framework is also open to the question as to whether it is economics or technology that drives production. Is the collaborative environment open to abuse as a standardized, mechanized system or open to use and development as a shared platform, carrying all the positive associations of cooperation?

Perhaps of most interest here is the performative nature that is inherent to these new modes of design and production. Technological advances afford the opportunity to work in a multi-disciplinary and collaborative manner that, far from the traditional focus on the individual architect, has led to an open source platform across which different experts may contribute and engage throughout the design process. The critical landscape is different to the one in which the ideals of modernism gave way to the mechanics of production. The significance of this shift is becoming increasingly apparent and has repercussions not only upon the practice of architecture itself but also on the way in which it is perceived and connected to broader societal frameworks, for example, Actor-Network Theory,[4] new business models of integrated design and fabrication,[5] etc. This alteration in the frameworks of the production of architecture is mirrored in the tools by which architecture is developed and the software that continues to evolve apace.

The move in computational architecture to urbanism, as algorithmic design is seen to have the capacity to process seemingly impenetrable networks, is seductive. However, many of the developments in the related fields are currently speculative, applying game theory or exploring formal expression through iterative processes that, intentionally or otherwise, produce the differentiated and associative designs of what Patrik Schumacher defines as 'Parametricism'.[6] Frequently innovative and visually arresting, it remains to be seen whether this approach to the design of architecture and urbanism will evolve to contain significant content in the future. An interesting parallel development is the growth of inquiry into coding and generative processes that focuses directly on these methodologies and their limitations over the resulting 'architectures'.[7] Until generative manufacture or materials are achieved/realized, the convergence of nano-technology and algorithmic processes is useless. Although there has been work developed which investigates the organization and behaviour of material in relation to performance driven algorithmic systems, such research is still in its infancy.[8] One of the primary issues is that we currently lack the 'extreme integration'[9] that Tom Wiscombe calls for, to develop the potential for technology and infrastructure to be woven into architectural form. The advancement of such responsive and inter-articulated design approaches may be more reliant on biocomputational technologies and programmers and require considerable transformation in creative practice beyond the blurred territories shared between disciplines that presently exist. We shall see. This continues to support the reason for the mapping of cities using the types of instruments discussed throughout this book since it is actually through refracting 'the urban' through the lenses of other practices that we are able to further our understanding of it rather than additional cogitation.

The constant modelling of existing systems does not necessarily make future predictions a certainty.[10] Perhaps one of the main stumbling blocks here is the attention lavished on 'form' rather than 'systems' which has to date resulted in a preoccupation with objects rather than infrastructure. The role of infrastructure, particularly with regard to transportation, is often viewed as the primary area of investment for governing bodies in the development of cities around the globe. With the increasing urbanization of the physical landscape, infrastructural development is perhaps the key defining feature of this landscape with the attendant capacity to integrate, or negate, territories and stimulate social, economic and cultural activity. Originally coined by the Japanese architect Fumihiko Maki in 1964, the term 'megastructure' was defined as a vast frame in which the many functions of a city could be incorporated. Subsequently popularized by Reyner Banham through his book of the same name in 1976, the term has evolved to describe repetitive systems that enable a high degree of variation to occur, and recur, as a response to programmatic and contextual requirements. Perhaps, therefore, the transformation of the public realm is not one of erosion but of (re)distribution of its spatial and social properties. Rather than referencing the former exemplars of architectural history, this new domain may be found as being intrinsic to infrastructure, i.e. we have moved from the piazza to the platform as a collective place. This appears to be borne out by the provision of meeting spaces, food courts and shopping arcades for people who may not even be using the transportation network. Considered in this way, the commodification of public space by privatized organizations may actually be seen to have reignited urban space rather than be the 'Junkspace'[11] it is often perceived as. This naturally returns us to notions of identity in the city and, therefore, navigation and mapping.

Have we written our own future? Will we not rest until 'New Babylon' is built? In their rejection of the modern city, the utopian visions of the Lettrist International and the Situationist International presupposed the hypermodern condition of reactive urbanism. Fundamental to the development of our understanding of cities is that the new urban landscape is compellingly different to the urban space that preceded it. In 1900, the largest cities belonged to the major world powers but, as of 2007, seven of the eight remaining cities in the worldwide top 10 were located in the global south. In a Western context, new and extensive forms of urban dispersal would have to occur to produce the mega-cities presupposed in the 1960s but elsewhere across the globe these formations are already under development. At this juncture, therefore, the city of the future is much more likely to resemble Lagos than London.

The poly-nucleic city is a symptom of the speed of growth and the speed of the city, thus not necessarily belonging to a linear progression within city form, more a symptom of an accelerated urbanism, speed.[12] Thus for the shape of our cities to change a new dynamic or paradigm would have to shift and supersede the primary force of capitalism. It may also be argued that the demand for growth has been curtailed, many post-industrial European and American cities can be seen to be shrinking.[13] Perhaps the shape of our cities is already undergoing a gentle dispersal that is linked to science, technology and infrastructure as the devices of globalization as opposed to economics. In a discourse that has primarily concerned laissez-faire economics and the free-market as the significant organizing force with regard our global structures, it is easy to forget the role of technology in the facilitation and delivery of these conditions. If then infrastructure itself has moved from a linear model to a networked model then how long will it be until our urban environments assume the same shift? The ideas of a reactive city may ultimately be revealed as static; indeed we may all build our personal cathedral, but it needn't follow us to adapt to our whim, our whims can come to us. This is at once the capsularization,[14] the dispersal and the mutation of the city and a condition that is upon us now despite its apparent futurist conception. We are at once both isolated and connected. The experiential city as one of leaps and niches is not exclusive to a part of society; it *is* society. Public space, ceremonial space and civic space as the contexts in which we gather are no longer spaces of freedom, but spaces of control, that limit the type of occupant by their rules and thus inhibit exposure to alternative social groups and systems of belief and order. Our niches may be seemingly rich and our leaps appear expansive but they are regular and actually diminished of the chance encounter or event that has been shown to enrich experience and bring character to our environment.

There are, presented here, two opposing positions concerning the future of architectural production and the city. One assumes the shift from top-down governance to an emergent and reactive model, the other perceives the continued isolation by network and systems and a growth in levels of control, which is in fact an amplification of current social constructs. The two do not, however, remain mutually exclusive and it may be the network that facilitates the hive mind.

In the current climate, architecture is a closed loop system, produced through codified exchanges and translated through a matrix of processes into a series of variables that quickly become fixed. Kazys Varnelis suggests that 'networked ecologies embody the dominant form of organization today, the network, but these networks can be telematic, physical or even social'.[15] He identifies One Wilshire, a communications hub in downtown Los Angeles, as the architectural expression of the ethereal global network. 'One Wilshire's form doesn't matter what matters is how it's been re-programmed.'[16] Such outlook may be appropriate for certain elements of the urban landscape but it belies the significant opportunities of these networks as temporal infrastructures of contemporary cityscapes that contain and evolve latent information and diversity of exchanges that are valuable to society. The mapping and visualization, therefore, of this data to produce interactive instruments through which we can expose and articulate specific locales in relation to a global continuum may provide greater creative transparency, collaboration and decentralization. In the context of architecture as having a diminished role in production of the city, the importance of transforming the design process that underpins our cities and understanding the creative practices that may greater inform us of their nature, should not be underestimated, and is a recurrent theme of this book. The 'maps' explored here, whether embedded within the narrative of a film, part of a brand or network, or attached to a series of marks or objects, serve to remind the architect that there exists a wealth of latent conditions and expositions beyond the conventions of their inquiry into site, space and place. This collection of writings, whilst explorative of a breadth of associative practice, is intended to expose the critical value of the recording and (re)presentation of data and the opportunities presented to architecture and urban design in engaging with the systems of our society. Architects are strategists and whilst the production of buildings may have ostensibly been reduced to a process of mediation, the production of reflective and reactive urban models that begin to account for the demands of a city in flux is at hand and undetermined in its extent.

Endnotes

1   The author has two Amazon accounts (.com and .co.uk), each of these has different information concerning his interests and purchases. The .com account carries far less information, yet regularly offers interesting purchases that are never produced by the .co.uk search algorithms.

2   There are an increasing number of academics, practitioners and organizations examining these notions as illustrated in: Bouman, O. (2009), *Architecture of Consequence: Dutch Designs on the Future* (Rotterdam: NAi Publishers).

3   Frazer, J.H. (1995), *An Evolutionary Architecture* (London: AA Publications) p. 7.

4   For example see Latour, B. and Yaneva, A. (2008), 'Give me a Gun and I will Make All Buildings Move: An ANT's View of Architecture', in: Geiser, R. [ed.] *Explorations in Architecture: Teaching, Design, Research* (Basel: Birkhäuser) pp. 80–89.

5   The emergence of digital design and fabrication loop systems in which a design practice develops buildings and components from concept to assembly via development and manufacturing is becoming more commonplace and facilitating an interesting transformation in the way designers may work. This shift has also been paralleled by the growing number of architectural practices with increased specialisms and associated research teams engaged with exploring the edges and crossovers of the discipline with other fields including but not limited to: geography, engineering, product design, and computer sciences.

6   Schumacher, P. (2009), 'Parametricism: A New Global Style for Architecture and Urban Design', in: Leach, N. [ed.] *Digital Cities*, Architectural Design (London: John Wiley and Sons) pp. 14–23.

7   There is an ever-expanding number of researchers and blogs experimenting with the possibilities for, and implications of, algorithms in relation to architecture, for example, Nick Pisca and Roland Snooks. For further information see their respective websites: www.nickpisca.com/0001d.htm and www.kokkugia.com.

8   Oxman, N. (2007), 'Digital Craft: Fabrication Based Design in the Age of Digital Production', Workshop Proceedings for *Ubicomp 2007: International Conference on Ubiquitous Computing*, Innsbruck, 16–19 September 2007.

9   Wiscombe, T. (2010), 'Extreme Integration', in: Colleti, Marjan [ed.] *Exuberance*, Architectural Design (London: John Wiley & Sons) pp. 78–87.

10   Leach, N. (2009), 'The Limits of Urban Simulation: An Interview with Manuel DeLanda', *Digital Cities*, Architectural Design (London: John Wiley & Sons) pp. 50–55.

11   As defined by Rem Koolhaas (2000), 'Junk-space', *Acrhplus*, 149.

12   Virilio, P. (1986), *Speed and Politics: An Essay on Dromology*. Translated by Mark Polizzotti (New York: Semiotext(e)).

13   www.shrinkingcities.com and www.shrinkingcities.org are two research networks in Europe and the United States that have been considering the impact of shrinkage since 2002 [accessed 31 May 2010].

14   See de Cauter, L. (2005), *The Capsular Civilization. On the City in the Age of Fear* (Rotterdam: NAi Publishers).

15   Varnelis, K. (2008), 'Introduction', *Infrastructural City: Networked Ecologies in Los Angeles* (New York: Actar) p. 15.

16   Ibid. p. 129.

Bibliography

Abel, R. [ed.] (1988), *French Film Theory and Criticism: A History/Anthology 1907–1939*, Vol. 1 (Princeton: Princeton University Press).

Abrams, J. and Hall, P. [eds] (2006), *Else/where: Mapping New Cartographies of Networks and Territories* (Minneapolis: University of Minnesota Design Institute).

Abruzzo, E. and Solomon, J.D. (2008), *Dimension* (New York: 306090, Inc.).

Alberti, L.B. (1443–1452), *De re aedificatoria. On the Art of Building in Ten Books*. Translated by Joseph Rykwert, Neil Leach and Robert Tavernor (Cambridge, MA: The MIT Press, 1988).

Allen, S. and Agrest, D. (2000), *Practice: Architecture, Technique and Representation* (Amsterdam: G+B Arts International).

AlSayyad, N. (2006), *Cinematic Urbanism: A History of the Modern from Reel to Real* (Abingdon: Routledge).

Andreotti, L. and Costa, X. [eds] (1996), *Situationists. Art, Politics, Urbanism* (Barcelona: Actar).

Appleyard, D. and Lynch, K. (1964), *The View from the Road* (Cambridge, MA: The MIT Press).

Aranda, B. and Lasch, C. (2006), *Tooling*, Pamphlet Architecture; 27. (New York: Princeton Architectural Press).

Atelier Bow Wow (2002), *Pet Architecture* (Japan: World Photo Press).

Augé, M. (1995), *Non-Places: Introduction to an Anthropology of Supermodernity*. Translated by John Howe (London: Verso).

Aumont, J. (1997), *The Image*. Translated by Claire Pajackowska (London: British Film Institute).

Aurigi, A. and De Cindio, F. [eds] (2008), *Augmented Urban Spaces: Articulating the Physical and Electronic City* (Aldershot: Ashgate).

Banham, R. (1971), *Los Angeles: The Architecture of Four Ecologies* (London: Allen Lane).

Banham, R. (1976), *Megastructure: Urban Futures of the Recent Past* (London: Thames and Hudson).

Barber, S. (2002), *Projected Cities* (London: Reaktion Books).

Batty, M. (2005), *Cities and Complexity* (Cambridge, MA: The MIT Press).

Baudelaire, C. (1978), *The Painter of Modern Life and Other Essays* (New York: Garland).

Baudrillard, J. (1981), *For a Critique of the Political Economy of the Sign* (New York: Telos Press).

Bayer, H. (1967), *Herbert Bayer* (New York: Reinhold Publishing Corporation).

Benjamin, W. (1973), *Charles Baudelaire: A Lyric Poet in the Era of High Capitalism*. Translated by Harry Zohn (London: New Left Books).

Benjamin, W. (1985), *One-Way Street and Other Writings*. Translated by Edmund Jephcott and Kingsley Shorter (London: Verso).

Benjamin, W. (1999), *The Arcades Project*. Translated by Howard Eiland and Kevin McLaughlin (Cambridge, MA: The Belknap Press).

Bhagat, A. and Mogel, L. [eds] (2008), *An Atlas of Radical Cartography* (Los Angeles: Journal of Aesthetics and Protest).

Bird, J., Curtis, B, Putnam, T. and Tickner, L. (1993), *Mapping the Futures: Local Cultures, Global Change* (London: Routledge).

Blake, P. (1960), *The Master Builders* (New York: Knopf).

Blake, P. (1963), *God's Own Junkyard: The Planned Deterioration of America's Landscape* (New York: Holt).

Blandford, S. (2007), *Film, Drama and the Break-up of Britain* (Bristol: Intellect Ltd).

Bouman, O. (2009), *Architecture of Consequence: Dutch Designs on the Future* (Rotterdam: NAi Publishers).

Boutoux, T. [ed.] (2003), *Hans Ulrich Obrist Interviews, Volume I* (Milan: Fondazione Pitti Immagine Discovery).

Boyer, M.C. (1996), *Cyber Cities: Visual Perception in the Age of Electronic Communication* (New York: Princeton Architectural Press).

Brinckerhoff Jackson, J. (1994), *A Sense of Time, a Sense of Place* (New Haven: Yale University Press).

Brook, R. and Dunn, N. (2009), *Isolative Urbanism: An Ecology of Control* (Manchester: bauprint).

Brooker, P. (2002), *Modernity and Metropolis: Writing, Film, and Urban Formations* (New York: Palgrave).

Bruno, G. (2002), *Atlas of Emotion: Journeys in Art, Architecture, and Film* (London: Verso).

Bulmer, M. (1984), *The Chicago School of Sociology: Institutionalization, Diversity, and the Rise of Sociological Research* (Chicago: University of Chicago Press).

Bunschoten, R. and Binet, H. (2001), *Urban Flotsam: Stirring the City* (Rotterdam: 010 Publishers).

Burckhardt, J. (1860), *The Civilisation of the Renaissance in Italy*. Translated by S.G.C. Middlemore (New York: Harper & Row, 1958).

Burgin, V. (1996), *In/Different Spaces. Place and Memory in Visual Culture* (Berkeley: University of California Press).

Burke, A. and Tierney, T. [eds] (2007), *Network Practices* (New York: Princeton Architectural Press).

Calvino, I. (1974), *Invisible Cities*. Translated by William Weaver (London: Secker and Warburg).

Careri, F. (2002), *Walkscapes: Walking as an Aesthetic Practice*, Land&scape Series (Barcelona: Gustavo Gili).

Carney, R. and Quart, L. (2000), *The Films of Mike Leigh: Embracing the World* (Cambridge: Cambridge University Press).

Castells, M. (2000), *The Rise of the Network Society*, 2nd edn (Oxford: Blackwell Publishing).

Castells, M. [ed.] (2004), *The Network Society: A Cross-Cultural Perspective* (Cheltenham: Edward Elgar).

Castleman, C. (1982), *Getting Up: Subway Graffiti in New York* (Cambridge, MA: The MIT Press).

Chastenet, F. (2007), *Pixação: São Paulo Signature* (Toulouse: Xgpress).

Clarke, D.B. [ed.] (1997), *The Cinematic City* (London: Routledge).

Cooper, M. (2008), *Tag Town* (Arsta, Sweden: Dokument Forlag + Distribution).

Cooper, M. and Chalfant, H. (1984), *Subway Art* (London: Thames and Hudson).

Corby, T. [ed.] (2006), *Network Art: Practices and Positions* (Oxford: Routledge).

Corner, J. [ed.] (1999), *Recovering Landscape: Essays in Contemporary Landscape Architecture* (New York: Princeton Architectural Press).

Cosgrove, D. [ed.] (1999), *Mappings* (London: Reaktion).

Costello, C. (2006), *KR* (New York: Also Known As – 12oz Prophet).

Cousins, J. (1986), *British Rail Design* (Copenhagen: Danish Design Council).

Czikszentmihalyi, M. and Rochberg-Halton, E. (1981), *The Meaning of Things: Domestic Symbols and the Self* (New York: Cambridge University Press).

Daniel, N. [ed.] (2006), *Broken Screen: Expanding the Image, Breaking the Narrative: 26 Conversations with Doug Aitken* (New York: Distributed Art Publishers).

Davis, M. (1998), *The Ecology of Fear* (New York: Metropolitan Books).

Debord, G. (1998), *Comments on the Society of the Spectacle*. Translated by Malcolm Imrie (London: Verso).

De Cauter, L. (2005), *The Capsular Civilization. On the City in the Age of Fear* (Rotterdam: NAi Publishers).

De Certeau, M. (1984), *The Practice of Everyday Life* (Berkeley: University of California Press).

De Landa, M. (1997), *A Thousand Years of Nonlinear History*, Swerve Editions (New York: Zone Books).

De Quincey, T. (1821), *Confessions of an English Opium Eater* (New York: Dover Publications Inc., 1995).

Diller, E. and Scofidio, R. (1994), *Flesh: Architectural Probes* (New York: Princeton Architectural Press).

Douglas, M. (1970), *Natural Symbols. Explorations in Cosmology* (London: Barrie and Jenkins).

Edensor, T. (2005), *Industrial Ruins: Space, Aesthetic and Materiality* (Oxford and New York: Berg).

Elliot, P. (2003), *Boyle Family* (Edinburgh: National Galleries of Scotland).

Elliott, B. and Purdy, A. (1997), *Peter Greenaway: Architecture and Allegory* (Chichester: Academy Editions).

Flam, J. [ed.] (1996), *Robert Smithson: The Collected Writings*, 2nd edn (Berkeley: University of California Press).

Forsyth, F. (2009), *Crack & Shine* (London: FFF).

Frazer, J.H. (1995), *An Evolutionary Architecture* (London: AA Publications).

Fuller, G. (1995), *Naked and Other Screenplays* (London: Faber and Faber).

Gane, M. (trans.) (1993), *Symbolic Exchange and Death* (London: Sage).

Geiser, R. [ed.] (2008), *Explorations in Architecture: Teaching, Design, Research* (Basel: Birkhäuser).

Ghent Urban Studies Team (1999), *The Urban Condition: Space, Community, and Self in the Contemporary Metropolis* (Rotterdam: 010 Publishers).

Goldman, R. and Papson, S. (1996), *Sign Wars: The Cluttered Landscape of Advertising* (New York: The Guilford Press).

Goldman, R. and Papson, S. (1998), *Nike Culture: The Sign of the Swoosh* (London: Sage Publications).

Graham, S. [ed.] (2010), *Disrupted Cities. When Infrastructure Fails* (Oxford and New York: Routledge).

Graham, S. and Marvin, S. (1996), *Telecommunications and the City: Electronic Spaces, Urban Places* (London: Routledge).

Graham, S. and Marvin, S. (2001), *Splintering Urbanism: Networked Infrastructures, Technological Mobilities and the Urban Condition* (Oxford: Routledge).

Halberstan, D. (2000), *Playing for Keeps* (London: Yellow Jersey).

Hall, P. (1988), *Cities of Tomorrow: An Intellectual History of Urban Planning and Design in the Twentieth Century* (Oxford: Basil Blackwell).

Harvey, D. (1990), *The Condition of Postmodernity* (Oxford: Blackwell).

Healy, P. and Bruyns, G. [eds] (2006), *De-/signing the Urban: Techno-genesis and the Urban Image* (Rotterdam: 010 Publishers).

Highmore, B. (2005), *Cityscapes: Cultural Readings in the Material and Symbolic City* (Basingstoke: Palgrave Macmillan).

Hillier, B. (1996), *Space is the Machine: A Configurational History of Architecture* (Cambridge: Cambridge University Press).

Hirshorn, P. and Izenour, S. (1979), *White Towers* (Cambridge, MA: The MIT Press).

Huysmans, J.-K. (1884), *À Rebours*. Translated by R. Baldick as *Against Nature* (London: Penguin Classics, 1956, revised edn).

Ibelings, H. (1998), *Supermodernism. Architecture in the Age of Globalization* (Rotterdam: NAi Publishers).

Incerti, G., Ricchi, D. and Simpson, D. (2007), *Diller + Scofidio (+ Renfro): The Ciliary Function* (Milan: Skira Editore S.p.A).

Ingold, T. (2000), *The Perception of the Environment: Essays on Livelihood, Dwelling and Skill* (Aldershot: Routledge).

Ingold, T. and Vergunst, J.L. [eds] (2008), *Ways of Walking: Ethnography and Practice on Foot* (London: Ashgate).

Jackson, J.B. (1994), *A Sense of Time, a Sense of Place* (New Haven: Yale University Press).

Jacobs, J. (1961), *The Death and Life of Great American Cities* (New York: Random House).

Kant, I. (1790), *Critique of Judgment*. Translated by J.H. Bernard (London: Macmillan and Co. Limited, 1914).

Kaye, N. (2000), *Site-Specific Art: Performance, Place and Documentation* (London: Routledge).

Kitchin, R., Perkins, C. and Dodge, M. [eds] (2009), *Rethinking Maps: New Frontiers in Cartographic Theory* (Oxford: Routledge).

Klein, N. (2000), *No Logo* (London: Flamingo).

Klingmann, A. (2007), *Brandscapes: Architecture in the Experience Economy* (Cambridge, MA: The MIT Press).

Knabb, K. (2006), *Situationist International Anthology*. Revised and expanded edn (Berkeley: Bureau of Public Secrets).

Koolhaas, R. (1978), *Delirious New York: A Retroactive Manifesto for Manhattan* (New York: The Monacelli Press).

Kuroda, J. and Kaijima, M. (2001) *Made in Tokyo* (Tokyo: Kajima Institute Publishing).

Lang, P. and Menking, W. (2003), *Superstudio: Life without Objects* (Milan: Skira).

Laplace, P. and Tabuteau, É. [eds] *Cities on the Margin; On the Margin of Cities* (Besançon Cedex: Presses Universitaires Franc-Comtoises).

Latour, B. (1993), *We Have Never Been Modern*. Translated by Catherine Porter (New York: Harvester Wheatsheaf).

Laxton, P. [ed.] (2001), *The New Nature of Maps: Essays in the History of Cartography* (Baltimore and London: Johns Hopkins University Press).

Leach, N. [ed.] (1997), *Rethinking Architecture: A Reader in Cultural Theory* (London: Routledge).

Lefebvre, H. (1991), *The Production of Space*. Translated by Donald Nicholson-Smith (Oxford: Blackwell).

Lerup, L. (2000), *After the City* (Cambridge, MA: The MIT Press).

Leslie Jr., D.M. [ed.] (1980), *Visions of Excess: Selected Writings, 1927–1939*. Translated by A. Stoekl and C.R. Lovitt (Minneapolis: University of Minnesota Press).

Lootsma, B. (2000), *Superdutch* (London: Thames and Hudson).

Lynch, K. (1960), *The Image of the City* (Cambridge, MA: The MIT Press).

Lynch, K. (1981), *A Theory of Good City Form* (Cambridge, MA: The MIT Press).

Lyotard, J.-F. (1984), *Driftworks* (New York: Semiotext(e)).

Macdonald, N. (2001), *The Graffiti Subculture: Youth, Masculinity, and Identity in London and New York* (Basingstoke: Palgrave).

McDonough, T. [ed.] (2009), *The Situationists and the City* (London: Verso).

McGinness, R. (2005), *Sponsorship. The Fine Art of Corporate Sponsorship. The Corporate Sponsorship of Fine Art* (Corte Madera, CA: Gingko Press).

McLuhan, M. and Fiore, Q. (1996), *The Medium is the Massage: An Inventory of Effects* (San Francisco: Hardwired).

McLuhan, M. and Powers, R.B. (1989), *The Global Village: Transformations in World Life and Media in the 21st Century* (New York: Oxford University Press).

Manaugh, G. (2009), *The Bldg Blog Book: Architectural Conjecture, Urban Speculation, Landscape Futures* (San Francisco: Chronicle Books).

Marcus, A. and Neumann, D. [eds] (2007), *Visualizing the City* (Abingdon: Routledge).

Marcus, G. (1989), *Lipstick Traces: A Secret History of the Twentieth Century* (London: Secker and Warburg).

Marcuse, H. (1972), *Studies in Critical Philosophy*. Translated by B. Reid (Boston: Beacon Press).

Marling, G. and Zerlang, M. [eds] (2007), *Fun City* (Copenhagen: Arkitektens Forlag/The Danish Architectural Press).

Martin, R. and Baxi, K. (2007), *Multi-National City: Architectural Itineraries* (Barcelona: Actar).

Mathews, S. (2007), *From Agit-prop to Free Space: The Architecture of Cedric Price* (London: Black Dog).

Mau, B. (2000), *Lifestyle* (New York: Phaidon).

Medina, C., Ferguson, R. and Fisher, J. (2007) *Francis Alÿs* (London: Phaidon).

Meyerowitz, J. (1985), *No Sense of Place: The Impact of Electronic Media on Social Behaviour* (Oxford: Oxford University Press).

Mitchell, W.J. (1995), *City of Bits: Space, Place and the Infobahn* (Cambridge, MA: The MIT Press).

Mitchell, W.J. (1999), *e-topia: 'Urban Life, Jim – but not as we know it'* (Cambridge, MA: The MIT Press).

Movshovitz, H. [ed.] (2000), *Mike Leigh: Interviews* (Jackson: University Press of Mississippi).

MVRDV (1998), *FARMAX: Excursions on Density* (Rotterdam: 010 Publishers).

MVRDV (1999), *Metacity/Datatown* (Rotterdam: 010 Publishers).

MVRDV (2005), *KM3: Excursions on Capacities* (Barcelona: Actar).

Nadeau, M. (1965), *The History of Surrealism* (London: Macmillan).

Neumann, D. [ed.] (1996), *Film Architecture: Set Designs from Metropolis to Blade Runner* (Munich: Prestel-Verlag).

Nock, S.L. (1993), *The Costs of Privacy: Surveillance and Reputation in America* (New York: Aldine De Gruyter).

OMA/AMO and Koolhaas, R. (2001), *Projects for Prada Part 1* (Milan: Fondazione Prada Edizioni).

Oosterhuis, K. (2002), *Architecture Goes Wild* (Rotterdam: 010 Publishers).

Owen, C. (1992), *Beyond Recognition: Representation, Power and Culture* (Berkeley: University of California Press).

Pallasmaa, J. (2001), *The Architecture of Image: Existential Space in Cinema* (Helsinki: Rakennustieto).

Papadakis, A.C. [ed.] (1988), *Deconstruction in Architecture* (London: Architectural Design Profile, Wiley Academy).

Paul, C., Vesna, V. and Lovejoy, M. [eds] (2010), *Context Providers: Conditions of Meaning in Media Arts* (Bristol: Intellect).

Perec, G. (1999), *Species of Spaces and Other Pieces* (London: Penguin Books Ltd).

Plant, S. (1992), *The Most Radical Gesture: The Situationist International in a Postmodern Age* (London: Routledge).

Polanyi, K. (1957), *The Great Transformation* (Boston: Beacon Press).

Pope, A. (1996), *Ladders*, Architecture at Rice; 34. (New York: Princeton Architectural Press).

Powers, S. (1999), *The Art of Getting Over: Graffiti at the Millennium* (New York: St. Martin's Press).

Rattenbury, K. [ed.] (2002), *This is Not Architecture* (London: Routledge).

Rivera, J. (2008), *Vandal Squad* (New York: Powerhouse Books).

Rowe, C. and Koetter, F. (1978), *Collage City* (Cambridge, MA: The MIT Press).

Ruscha, E. (1963), *Twentysix Gasoline Stations* (Los Angeles: National Excelsior Press).

Ruscha, E. (1966), *Every Building on Sunset Strip* (Los Angeles: Edward Ruscha).

Sadler, S. (1998), *The Situationist City* (Cambridge, MA: The MIT Press).

Sakamoto, T. and Ferré, A. [eds] (2008), *From Control to Design: Parametric/Algorithmic Architecture* (Barcelona: Actar-D).

Sartre, J.-P. (1930), *The Critique of Dialectical Reason*. Translated by A. Sheridan Smith (London: NLB, 1976).

Sassen, S. (1991), *The Global City: New York, London, Tokyo* (Princeton: Princeton University Press).

Sassen, S. [ed.] (2002), *Global Networks, Linked Cities* (London: Routledge).

Schöffer, N. (1978), *Perturbation et Chronocratie* (Paris: Editions Denoël-Gonthier, Grand Format Mediation).

Schwarzer, M. (2004), *Zoomscape: Architecture in Motion and Media* (New York: Princeton Architectural Press).

Sennett, R. (1990), *The Conscience of the Eye: The Design and Social Life of Cities* (New York: Knopf).

Sennett, R. (1996), *Flesh and Stone: The Body and the City in Western Civilization* (London: Faber and Faber).

Shane, D.G. (2005), *Recombinant Urbanism: Conceptual Modeling in Architecture, Urban Design, and City Theory* (Chichester: John Wiley & Sons Ltd).

Shannon, K. and Smets, M. (2010), *The Landscape of Contemporary Infrastructure* (Rotterdam: NAi Publishers).

Shiel, M. and Fitzmaurice, T. (2003), *Screening the City* (London: Verso).

Silver, M. and Balmori, D. [eds] (2003), *Mapping in the Age of Digital Media: The Yale Symposium* (Chichester: John Wiley and Sons Ltd).

Simmel, G. (1903), 'The Metropolis and Mental Life', in: Wolf, K.H. (1950), *The Sociology of Georg Simmel* (New York: The Free Press).

Solis, J. (2007), *New York Underground: The Anatomy of a City* (London: Routledge).

Solnit, R. (2000), *Wanderlust: A History of Walking* (London: Penguin Books).

Sowers, R. (1990), *Rethinking the Forms of Visual Expression* (Berkeley: University of California Press).

Speaks, M. (2002), *Doug Aitken A-Z Book (Fractals)* (Philadelphia; Zürich; Ostfildern-Ruit: The Fabric Workshop and Museum; Kunsthalle Zürich; Hatje Cantz).

Spuybroek, L. (2004), *NOX: Machining Architecture* (London: Thames and Hudson).

Suderberg, E. [ed.] (2000), *Space, Site, Intervention. Situating Installation Art* (Minneapolis: University of Minnesota Press).

Thompson, N. [ed.] (2008), *Experimental Geography: Radical Approaches to Landscape, Cartography, and Urbanism* (New York: Independent Curators International and Melville House).

Tonkiss, F. (2005), *Space, the City and Social Theory* (Cambridge: Polity Press).

Toy, M. [ed.] (1994), *Architecture and Film*, Architectural Design; 112. (London: Academy Group).

Trigg, D. (2006), *The Aesthetics of Decay: Nothingness, Nostalgia and the Absence of Reason* (Oxford: Peter Lang).

Tschumi, B. (1996), *Architecture and Disjunction* (Cambridge, MA: The MIT Press).

Varnelis, K. (2008), *Infrastructural City: Networked Ecologies in Los Angeles* (New York: Actar).

Varnelis, K. [ed.] (2008), *Networked Publics* (Cambridge, MA: The MIT Press).

Venturi, R. (1996), *Iconography and Electronics upon a Generic Architecture: A View from the Drafting Room* (Cambridge, MA: The MIT Press).

Venturi, R., Scott-Brown, D. and Izenour, S. (1972), *Learning from Las Vegas: The Forgotten Symbolism of Architectural Form* (Cambridge, MA: The MIT Press).

Virilio, P. (1986), *Speed and Politics: An Essay on Dromology*. Translated by Mark Polizzotti (New York: Semiotext(e)).

Virilio, P. (1991), *Lost Dimension*. Translated by Daniel Moshenberg (New York: Semiotext(e)).

Vitt, A. [ed.] (1998), *Architektur und Grafik* (Baden: Lars Müller Publishers).

von Borries, F. (2004), *Who's Afraid of Nike Town? Nike Urbanism and the Branding of Tomorrow* (Rotterdam: Episode Publishers).

Watson, G. (2004), *The Cinema of Mike Leigh: A Sense of the Real* (London: Wallflower Press).

Webber, A. and Wilson, E. [eds] (2008), *Cities in Transition: The Moving Image and the Modern Metropolis* (London: Wallflower Press).

Whitehead, T. (2007), *Mike Leigh* (Manchester: Manchester University Press).

Wilford, J.N. (2002), *The Mapmakers: The Story of the Great Pioneers in Cartography – From Antiquity to the Space Age*. Revised edn (London: Pimlico).

Williamson, J. (1978), *Decoding Advertisements* (London: Marion Boyars).

Witten, A. and White, M. (2001), *Dondi White: Style Master General, The Life of Graffiti Artist Dondi White* (New York: Regan Books).

Wood, D. (1992), *The Power of Maps* (New York: Guilford Press).

Zukin, S. (1991), *Landscapes of Power: From Detroit to Disneyworld* (Berkeley: University of California Press).

Index